# Broken Lunch

## Simon Dewhurst

First published on Amazon Kindle in 2016

This book has been lodged with the five legal deposit libraries and the British Library in accordance with the Legal Deposit Libraries Act 2003 (UK) and the Copyright and Related Rights Act, 2000 (Ireland).

This edition of *Broken Lunch* is available in the UK
ISBN-13: 978-1-5272-0720-2

Printed in the UK by Lightning Source UK Ltd,  Milton Keynes

## ABOUT THE AUTHOR

Simon Dewhurst has led an eclectic life doing many different jobs.

He began writing aged ten when he had a short story published in the Catholic Times. 'Broken Lunch' is his first full length book. His other works include 'Secrets of Better Skiing', and many internet articles on subjects as diverse as 'arthritic remedies' and 'crane proximity sensors.'

He is 70 and lives near Liverpool in the UK, where he writes and goes rock climbing.

What readers on Amazon and Goodreads say:

*'Broken Lunch is hands down one of the ... funniest and most interesting memoirs that I've read in a long time!'*

*'Fun, real, honest, fast-paced, and well-written, Broken Lunch was an unexpected delight for me ... Happy I discovered this author as he has real talent. Hope he keeps at it!'*

*'Witty, hilarious and insightful – a must read book ... He leads the reader through hysterical adventure after hysterical adventure ... Once started I had great difficulty stopping to eat and drink, I just had to read on.'*

*'Make sure you read this book!! A brilliant glimpse into a way of life now forgotten – a little bit of social history and a hilarious read.'*

*'I haven't laughed out loud reading a book since the Tom Sharpe novels in the 70's. A very enjoyable and easy read.'*

*'What a hilarious book! I laughed and cried so much!!'*

# CONTENTS

# PROLOGUE – STORM IN HOLYHEAD

I was born a long time ago with a silver spoon in my mouth, but by the time I was thirty I'd just about swallowed it. This is how it all started, rather too seriously for my way of thinking.

George sat back and read through the letter he had just written:

'Beechwood, Lymm

24th June 1864

Dear Sam,

I hope I find you and Rachel and the children all well. We are all well up here, and as I look out of the window I can see Lizzie wandering around the garden looking no doubt for more roses to put on the dining room table. Thank you for your letter and your advice – thanks to you we are weathering the storm and still have half the mills running. It cannot go on for much longer. We all feel that Lincoln will come off best in the end and lift the blockade.

Can you come fishing in Ireland for a few days in August? I have a cousin, James Martin, who takes a beat on the Blackwater River at Ballyduff and has asked me if I would like to bring a friend. We can have three or four days fishing and discuss what we are to do after this damned war. It is not important that you are no fisherman, only that you can enjoy the fresh Irish air for a few days and some very good fresh food too, and all away from the dreadful air in London! It is bad enough in Manchester! The dates are from August 5th to the 14th.  Please let me know and I can send you the details – we have much to discuss!'

Satisfied, he signed it and put the letter into an envelope addressed and stamped it, and walked to the post box.

Samuel Lewis had replied that he would be delighted to come. Sam had changed his name from Louis Samuel some years back. His parents had come over from Russia in the early 1800s and raised their three children in London's East End in the rag trade. His father, who was christened Shpolyansky, had changed his name to Samuel. He was a tailor but young Louis was what we call today a sharp cookie, and had got a job aged sixteen as a runner to a broker on the London Stock Exchange. By now aged forty he was advising private clients how to invest their money. He was small and wiry with red hair and a red bushy beard and looked more Scottish than Jewish, but he could add and divide and subtract and hold figures in his head better than anyone George had ever met.

They had met two months later and spent the night of the 4th August in the Railway Hotel, Holyhead, 'which had hot & cold shower baths and was fitted with a style of elegance in every way fit for the highest grade of

2

people in Society,' as the advertising said. They then took the four hour mid-morning steam packet, the RMS Connaught, to Kingstown[1] – the port for Dublin. George did not enjoy crossing the Irish Sea, even though it was quite calm. The mere thought of going on the sea made him queasy but Sam was immune and made fun of him. It was a little late in the season for good salmon fishing and the water was low but they had a relaxing time in Ballyduff with James Martin.

Twenty years before George had set up a yarn spinning company with his brother, Richard, after serving a long apprenticeship with Swainson's Mill near Preston. Now aged fifty six, he should be slowing down, but the American Civil War, which had begun four years before, had changed all that. The two brothers had done well and by the time the war started in 1860 they had four mills in Manchester and George lived in a large house with plenty of land in Lymm, Cheshire. George had five grown children by this time, but his wife, Harriet, had died in 1859. Within a year he had met and married Elizabeth Dundas, from Edinburgh, who was twenty three years younger.

In 1861 Abraham Lincoln and the Union decided that one way to quicken the end of the war was to blockade all the southern ports so that raw cotton could not be exported, primarily out of New Orleans, thereby cutting off the main source of income to the Confederate south. George was paying a heavy price for the raw cotton to keep his workers partially employed.

It seems ambivalent that the Manchester burghers had supported the blockade of the Confederate ports. In the UK public feeling against slavery ran high and had been doing so for the past ninety years. Trading in slaves was

---

[1] Now known as Dun Laoghaire (dun-leery).

abolished in 1833 in the UK, and it now seemed possible that the same would happen in North America.[2]

For George and Samuel the return journey was not as pleasant as the outward voyage, as the wind had got up when they arrived back at Kingstown on Sunday, August 14th. A summer storm had stirred the Irish Sea into a fury and combined with a strong north-south tide, it looked as though the noon packet back to Holyhead would be cancelled. George was hoping so. Little did he realize at the time how this storm was going to change his life. Persuaded by Samuel, who said he had to be back in London by Tuesday at the latest, they climbed aboard the RMS Connaught again for the return journey. They both suffered this time and George in particular was very sick. The gale coming up from the south worsened as the ship tossed and turned, and it took nearly six hours before they made the breakwater and the relative calm of Holyhead harbour.

Because of the storm they decided instead to spend another night in the Royal Hotel and catch the first morning train. After a few hours recovering in their rooms, they were sitting in the glass fronted lounge looking out over the harbour as the rain and wind rattled the windows. From the comfort of their wicker arm chairs with large whiskies in their hands, they watched as ships of all shapes and sizes were driven into the shelter of the harbour. At one point they saw a large three masted clipper, with most of its sails reefed and carrying just two or three forward of the bow mast, dropping anchor. A tender with a double pair of oars was lowered into the water and rowed towards the quayside.

---

[2] In 1865 the Thirteenth Amendment was ratified, which finally abolished slavery in the United States. In Canada, a British colony, slavery was abolished in 1793.

The two of them went into dinner at seven o'clock. There were other diners dotted around the room and the waiters and waitresses bustled among the tables. George looked up from their table and saw a very large man, standing in the dining room doorway. His dark hair was long to his shoulders and swept back and his face was burnt brown and well weathered. George assumed he must be off the cutter in the bay. The man paused for a moment, then made his way to a table close to theirs.

'Good evening, gentlemen. Forgive me for sitting next to you, but you look as though you can tell me all the news. Jonas Baring. I'm off the cutter you see in the bay.' And this was said with a confident easy smile and a slight burr in his accent, which George recognized from previous encounters with ships' captains in Manchester as either West Country or American. They introduced themselves too. The waiter came over and George ordered a bottle of good burgundy.

'You're welcome to share with us,' he says to Jonas Baring 'Now tell us, where have you come from in such a magnificent looking ship?'

'Well,' and again with a smile, 'We've just had the best run across from New Orleans. We left sixteen days ago. We're headed for Liverpool and should be there tomorrow. We were the first ship out for three years. I wanted to be the first away so we left only half loaded – with cotton!' He was now grinning, almost laughing. 'The blockade is over!'

Before George could exclaim Sam said 'The blockade?' Now this was strange coming from Sam as he knew all about the blockade and they had been talking about it on holiday, but George remained silent. The waiter arrived with the wine and poured it out.

'And some for Mr Baring too,' says George. 'Thank you kindly. Yes, the civil war is over, gentlemen!'

5

'Well I never. Good lord. Well I'll be dammed! At last!'

By the time dinner was over the three had drunk two more bottles and by nine o'clock Baring thanked the others and excused himself, saying that he needed to get his men out of the pub next door and back to the ship so they could get going first thing in the morning.

The moment he had gone, the two got talking. They agreed immediately that this news was dynamite, especially where the stock market was concerned. Sam was exceptionally shrewd when it came to the markets and George had relied on his advice for the past three years to help him through the bad times.

Because there was so little cotton during the war, the price had rocketed to five times its pre-war value. But now, with raw cotton about to pour back into Liverpool and Manchester, the price would drop like a stone, and Sam saw an opportunity.

'I'd go short[3] for as much as possible on this, and I think you should too. This is a chance we won't get again,' Sam said. 'It's worth risking everything we can.' He was actually getting very excited. 'We haven't got much time. I won't wait until the morning. I'm going to catch the eleven o'clock train now if it's running. I'll need

---

[3] Selling short. Simply put, an investor borrows shares from someone else and sells them on for their current price. He can wait for a time before he is expected to give the shares back, but by then the price has dropped. When he has to pay them back he can then buy identical shares but they are now at a lower price, so he can pocket the difference. It can be an extremely risky strategy when employed speculatively.

On the commodities market the cost of Middling Orleans, a standard medium quality cotton always in demand, had gone up from 6½d in 1861 to 2s 6½d in 1864. But now, with raw cotton about to pour back into Liverpool and Manchester, the price would drop like a stone, especially on the futures market.

all day tomorrow to do this, and just hope our Mr Baring won't be in Liverpool until the evening.'

'That is if he hasn't telegraphed Liverpool already', said George.

'He won't have done yet. It's Sunday, remember – the office is closed.'

'Of course. Perhaps he will have asked someone to send a message. Someone here will surely let the news out first thing and the markets will know too.'

'Well, I'll find out tomorrow. Let's just hope there's no one here who's that interested. Do we agree to share the risks and the rewards equally on this?'

'Sam, I'm prepared to stake everything I've got with you on this too – here's to success,' said George and they raised their glasses. Sam then got up, and they said their goodbyes, and off he went to get his baggage and leave for the night train to London. The train was running so he changed his ticket and climbed aboard.

George sat for a little longer nursing a glass of brandy. He had taken risks all his life. Making impulsive decisions on the moment was in his genes, but it had done him well. If he had never taken any risks he would still be working in Swainson's Mill sweeping up after everyone had gone home. He found he was excited at what could happen in the next day or two.

Samuel Lewis sat back on his well stuffed seat in first class running through his mind what was to be done in the morning. The train rattled on through the night. He hardly slept and after taking a hansom cab straight to his office in Leadenhall Street at half seven on the Monday morning, he set about making medium size trades with many different brokers. As the day went on he increased the size of his trades and there seemed to be little or no change in the prices he negotiated. There was no news about the blockade being lifted and prices held steady all day until after the close of business when the news that Jonas Baring had carried across the ocean came through on the telegraph from Liverpool; on the Tuesday the price of cotton futures began to fall.

As the contracts completed, the profits mounted and George Charnley Dewhurst, my great-great grandfather, trousered a half share of £420,000, which equates to £36million today. Among other things he bought an estate from his father-in-law, Aberuchill Castle, up in Perthshire Scotland. It stayed in the family for over a hundred years, and was sold in 2009 to a Russian oligarch for £7 million. With Elizabeth, he retired there, and left the running of the business to his two sons, George and John. He died there, aged eighty six, on St Valentine's Day 1894, hoping perhaps that he had secured a family fortune for generations to come. It had been a good move of his to buy a place in Scotland. He no longer had to take the ferry across the unpredictable Irish Sea when he wanted to go fishing.

# 1 – EARLY LEARNING

I can only imagine the scene as I had not yet arrived in this icy world and was personally quite warm at the time. My father, Tony, and mother, Noel, had only been married a polite month when she announced she was pregnant. I suspect my mother would have considered her pregnancy a bit of an inconvenience. My father on the other hand would have been immensely proud of his imminent parental status. They had married in St James' Spanish Place on a wet morning on the last day of April 1946. I've no idea why they went all the way from Cheshire, where they lived, to London to get married, but St James' was undoubtedly a very grand Catholic church in Mayfair, an area of London that had escaped the bombing five years before.

Aged 47 he was still living with his mother and his sister, my Aunt Bettsan. My grandfather, whom we never knew had died in 1945 and it was probably a good thing that my grandmother, whom we never met either, could be with her family in the same house. One morning while they were all three having breakfast, no doubt being waited on by a reduced staff of flunkeys owing to an unfortunate drop in cotton prices after the war, my father spoke from behind The Times he was reading,

'I say, guess what? Noel Winterbottom's got engaged!'

'Goodness me, who to?' says his mother.

'Me,' my father replied and that was the start of something new. With twenty years between them, they stayed together for the next thirty three years.

My father was quite compliant when it came to marrying a Catholic. He had to agree that the children would be brought up in the Catholic faith by my mother and her consorts. No artificial contraception would ever be allowed. Instead couples were to practise the rhythm method; this had nothing to do with music or dancing. It referred to the intricate timetable applied to menstruation. I had imagined that my father wound up an old gramophone before attempting coitus and that I was conceived to the stirring chords of Land of Hope and Glory. This was not the case. Rather, with strict reference to the timetable, the rhythm method suggested that a family could be carefully planned without man made paraphernalia such as condoms – in those days known as rubber johnnies which were forbidden. In fact they were so forbidden as to constitute a mortal sin if used in the fashion recommended by the manufacturers. I'm going off on a red herring here but we need to pass the time while my father drives my mother the thirty miles very slowly through the snow to the hospital…

Committing a mortal sin meant you would go to Hell when you died, unless of course you confessed to a priest and were genuinely sorry for what you did. He would then tell you to say five hail marys and five our fathers after asking you first whether you had done anything else sinful like thinking impure thoughts or doing impure deeds. Even when you admitted to these you would still get five hail marys and five our fathers regardless. These sins were called venial sins, which meant that you would only go to Purgatory if you died without confessing them. Purgatory was a place somewhere on the way to Hell but not quite as bad. It was not all fire; on the contrary it was quite dark and gloomy and very depressing, it rained a lot, and had inadequate lighting and living accommodation because there were a lot of people there. It was like the departure lounge at Corfu Airport on a wet Saturday night without the heat. There was no wailing or gnashing of teeth in Purgatory like there was in Hell. Everyone was just gloomy. It would have been a better place if there had been a fire or two so you could keep warm, but there were no trees in spite of the rain, and hence no wood. At least Hell and the departure lounge at Corfu Airport were warm.

Anyway, my father was very keen to stick to the rules as my mother was a great catch – very attractive, highly intelligent and twenty years younger than him. He was forty six. She laughed easily as did he and was addicted to Fox Hunting; in those days a mutual interest in Fox Hunting was more than a justifiable reason for getting married.

The fact that she was a Catholic didn't worry him at all. She came from a solid Lancashire family, the Winterbottoms, and only lived just across a quiet main road near Tarporley in Cheshire. Both families had made their money in cotton, or to be more precise, spinning yarn. Lancashire was a good place to do this as the climate was just right, damp and foggy and not too hot – a bit like Purgatory. Back in the 1760s a very hairy man with a bushy black beard by the name of James Hargreaves had invented the spinning jenny, a steam driven machine which saved a lot of work. This was something the Winterbottoms and the Dewhursts had always strived for and they made good use of it. It also brought in lots of money and they made good use of that too. My maternal grandfather, Ocky, was the master of survival when it came to work. He stimulated his school masters into a creative fury that persuaded one of them to produce the following: 'Winterbottom is a cheerful idiot who hasn't the good manners to conceal his contempt for work.' The Winterbottom family made book cloth and had a world wide monopoly on the stuff, and on my father's side it was great-great grandfather George who had made all that money in the 1860s after slavery was abolished.

My father eventually made it to Didsbury Hospital in spite of the freezing conditions, but it wasn't until the next morning at about ten to seven that things really got going. Inside the hospital it was warm and the atmosphere cheerful, but for my mother it was getting very painful. She always told us that she had stopped riding her horses only a week beforehand, so she would have pretended that this was just an inconvenient break in her routine.

Fortunately there were no complications and my father came and collected us the next day, March 3. Manchester had been partially flattened by Goering and his boys after they had finished with London less than five years before. Liverpool had got most of the bombs of course, but anything left after the Germans turned round had been dropped on Manchester. My father's office and warehouse were left standing but only just – thank you Goering – so he didn't have far to drive to pick us both up from the hospital. The weather on March 3 was not good. It was cold with snow flurries and more snow was forecast. It was piled up on either side of the road out of Manchester and unlike today there was little traffic. A day later on March 4 the heaviest snow of the winter began to fall and brought the country to a near standstill for the next three weeks.

The bad weather had started in mid January and now persisted until the Big Thaw on March 23. Coal couldn't be delivered to power stations because the railway lines were under fifteen foot snowdrifts, and there were countrywide power cuts. Clement Atlee and his government had to declare a State of Emergency, and the adverse weather and their handling of it nearly brought them down. In the last week of March, as the thaw began another problem caused more trouble. The ground was frozen solid and the quickly melting snow produced the most appalling floods, which affected over 100,000 homes across the country.

The bad weather, however, would have suited my father, who rather enjoyed adversity, as he cared not a jot for keeping warm. The house he was now driving back to had no such comforts as central heating, and one large lump of coal an evening was quite sufficient for heating their study. The house was called Stoke Hall, a mildly ironic name for the house as my father lit as few fires as possible. If you were cold you put more clothes on. It was a challenge in later years in our next house to wear enough layers and remain mobile. If they were too thick it became impossible to lift your arm from the plate to your mouth at meal times and I suppose that's why I still eat soup with my face a few inches from the bowl. My father always did, accompanying each spoonful with a slurping noise that kept the dogs awake; they lay together in a flatulent heap under the dining room table, farting anonymously at regular intervals, whereupon my father would stop slurping for a few seconds while he lit a match to neutralize the smell. It wasn't that the soup

13

was hot – far from it. It had lost most of its heat during the long journey from the kitchen, but my father liked to give the impression that it was just off boiling point.

In our second house, Barmere, where we moved when I was four, there was a large radiator under the front stairs, but it was seldom more than tepid. To service it was a small coke-burning boiler about a hundred yards away as the pipe work travelled. By the time the water reached the radiator it was almost cold but at least the water coursing along the start of the route had kept the back wing of the house from freezing. Unfortunately, after a couple of winters, the boiler was turned off as my father thought it a waste of money. The three of us, that's my sister and small brother, who were both born within two and a half years after me, were left to freeze in the back wing. The pipes in any part of the house could be frozen quite often during the winter; one night when I was older I went for a piss in the middle of the night. The water had frozen solid in the bowl and the cistern. When I came back the next morning the piss had frozen too. When the pipes began to thaw out the resultant bursts kept the plumbers busy for days.

The earliest film clip I can be sure of was aged three and a half, sitting in a grubby sand pit with my two and a half year old sister, Gemma, at Stoke Hall. There was a thunderstorm brewing and we were being bitten by ants and this for me was a film clip with no talking. She says she remembers me saying that it was safe in the sandpit as lightening never strikes children playing in sandpits, but I suspect that was too much knowledge too soon. Later I was in the nursery sticking a poker into a coal fire, and watching with infantile fascination as it got red hot. Cut to a few minutes later when I offered the hot end of the poker to Gemma, who took it thinking, I guess, we were going to pull a cracker. Cut to Gemma screaming, having her hand wrapped up in loose white gauze bandages. I can't remember what happened to me afterwards but it probably wasn't very pleasant. For some reason Gemma can recollect the whole incident with amazing clarity.

Later still I was in the garden at the edge of the lily pond, reaching with a stick for a piece of wood someone had stuck a nail into; it was floating just too far away and I fell into the water. Next I was screaming at full volume and banging on the front door. Somehow all my clothes had disappeared save for a woolen Chilprufe vest, which was now sagging with the weight of the water well below my knees. My mother and Mary, the cook, laughed and laughed when they opened the door, and I just screamed and screamed. I guess they were relieved that I hadn't chopped my leg off with an axe.

As far as I can remember my childhood was a happy spoilt existence, punctuated by much laughter and my own innate curiosity that only lasted for as long as it took me to pull a toy apart, find I couldn't repair it, and then throw it to the bottom of the toy box. To counter this was the continual and boring imposition of good manners (my father), religion and horses (my mother), and rough and ready discipline from Mary (the cook). She would often chase us round the kitchen table with a brush or a mop for the smallest of misdemeanors shouting 'I'll tell your father and your mother about you now then!' If she caught one of us, we would be bundled upstairs and shut in the broom cupboard for twenty minutes, where on my own learnt quite happily to contemplate and ponder the mysteries of life.

Aged five I went to school round another large table next to the doctor's surgery in Whitchurch. By this time Gemma and myself had a younger brother, Jonathan, but I remember very little of both of them; I was already displaying the traits of a solipsistic egotist. Jonathan at that time would have been two and a half and far too small for me to bully. My mother had made a conscious decision to fulfill her breeding duties as quickly as possible, and then leave us to a succession of nannies and keepers while she got on with more serious matters such as horses, painting and praying.

The large table in Whitchurch is just a one picture memory with a lot of other children sitting around it. I have no idea what we did; there were quite a few children and it was very noisy. I guess it involved plasticine and small bricks and probably quite a lot of biting and scratching and sticky fingers. A year later I was being taught by a governess, called Miss Ball, in a large green room with a huge four poster bed in Cholmondeley Castle, which was just up the road.

Miss Ball was small and round, obviously, who tried to teach us stuff I can't remember. The alphabet and counting may have come into it and some rudimentary letters and figures, but I have a feeling she was just employed as a prison warder – mornings only – to prevent us from doing anything dangerous. The 'us' was Rose Cholmondeley, Carolin Grant and myself. Rose was my first girl friend aged five and very pretty; Carolin, although the same age, was quite grown up and told me what to do and I was a little frightened of her. Miss Ball came from Malpas and was the green grocer's daughter. After a year or so she got engaged to be married to the butcher's son. About a month before the wedding she had all her teeth out; they seemed perfectly all right at the time but this was the custom. She then came back to look after us with no teeth. This was not a good idea and we became disruptive – so disruptive that one day Carolin crawled under the table we were working/fighting at, and bit me on the leg. That was the signal for an all out battle. I can't remember how it ended but Miss Ball left soon afterwards, minus her teeth, to start her married life.

Later I remember the dancing classes in the drawing room at Cholmondeley. By this time Gemma and Jonathan were old enough to join us together with Rose's sisters Margot and Caro, and Carolin's sister Zanie and a few others. I pretended to hate it but that was mainly because I was made to wear a cream frilly shirt and shiny black shoes. I wasn't allowed to dance but they let me hold up one end of the silk rainbow so that the others could trip along underneath it, pretending to be rabbits or pixies or whatever, and trying to keep in time with the piano music, which was played very loudly with some fury by an old lady with a grey bun called Mrs Bucket. The dancing class was run at great speed by Miss Loney, a dynamic and attractive woman, who delivered a continual torrent of instructions and hardly drew breath, clapping all the while. Her real name was Mrs Thistlesthwaite, but she had to concede quite early on that this wasn't going to work.

Thinking now, gosh weren't we lucky? None of us were aware then of course that we had been born into the luckiest place. I don't mean Didsbury Hospital but specifically the social order we found ourselves in. We were upper class without much cash. What we did have was rapidly running out – on both sides of the family. We were not involved directly in the slave trade (although we profited by it) or coal mines or sugar or even politics – places where all the real money had been made. Our families had been in trade – slightly frowned upon by those higher up the social ladder than us. Basically, all those in the aforementioned categories had never had to do a day's physical work at any point in their family history. They had relied instead on luck and being in the right place at the right time and whispering the right words into the right ear of the king or queen or the king's mistress or whomsoever. Most of those on the other hand who had made a packet in trade (including cotton, brewing, leather and even shipping), had at least one generation at the start who had grafted their socks off to lay the foundations for their hard earned millions, and in some cases even pass that energy gene on to their descendants.

When our generation arrived the energy had nearly run out, and all we could do was spend what was left – enjoyably. We were still full members of the club; we enjoyed all the privileges that the lifestyle niche provided but ours was a budget version without central heating.

We had an advantage over the aristocracy[4] too. We could all hammer a nail into a piece of wood and brush a horse's tail without being kicked and shovel coke into a boiler to keep the water hot. We may not have liked doing it but we could if we had to and this gave us a useful functionality that was generally missing in the higher social orders.

My mother and father managed to do all the things that their friends did, which mainly centered around killing. They shot, hunted, raced, played golf, and sometimes even travelled abroad, specifically for reruns

---

[4] An aristocrat is anyone with one of the following inherited titles, and excludes a baronet (a knight – 'Sir Peregrine Ragwort'). Family members are also aristocrats. The titles (apart from the monarch and royal family), are in order of seniority – Duke, Marquis, Earl (or Count), Viscount, Baron. A duke is addressed formally as 'Your Grace' or 'Duke' while all the other males are addressed as 'Milord' or 'Lord Ragwort'. A duke's wife is addressed as 'Your Grace' or 'Duchess', and all the others as 'Milady' or 'Lady Ragwort' … *That's quite enough – Ed*

of my father's war exploits. They entertained a lot around the dining room table where they ate what they'd shot, and although the quality of the food was generally abysmal, the ball kept rolling along in a languid fashion, fuelled by a good wine cellar.

I'm not sure whether my parents were snobs or not; if they were they were quite good at hiding it, although my father once wrote to me at school listing the guests around the dining room table. These included a duke and duchess, an earl and countess, two viscounts and viscountesses, and a baronet and his wife. On these grand and slightly frayed occasions he would employ George Clawley, who lived a few miles away, as a butler.

George, known only as Clawley, was the foreman of a team that went round repairing the roads for the Cheshire County Council during the day, but in the evening he two timed as the perfect butler, immaculate in white tie and tails and with a name to go with the job. His face looked like it had been left out in bad weather for sometime, which indeed it had. He put on the perfectly modulated voice that only good butlers can do – heard and understood, but somehow unnoticed by anyone else bar the recipient. He would stand at the end of the dining room noticing everything, and giving away nothing. I learnt a lot from him, which would prove useful in the future. My father, always parsimonious because he had to be, could get away with paying him a few quid for the evening. To get up and clear the plates himself would have been impossible, although on two nights a week when Mary, the cook, had half days off, he was quite good at doing the washing up.

# 2 – DADDY & FOXHUNTING

Both my parents were more than a little unusual, but it was my mother who bordered on eccentricity. She was a Catholic in a society where religion was seldom discussed; she also wore trousers and swore a lot. This was a paradox but perhaps it gave her something to confess to the priest – not about the trousers and its associations but rather the swearing. She rode a horse out hunting as though she was charging the Russian guns at Balaclava. Her bravery and risk taking, notwithstanding foolhardiness, gave her a certain kudos.

My father, on the other hand, did not take many risks and was generally more conventional than the rock of Gibraltar. Born two years before Queen Victoria died, he was the epitome of an Edwardian gentleman. He was brought up in a household reminiscent of a TV costume drama. He used to fold his underpants and hang them over the back of a chair at night. He wore a black bow tie every evening for dinner, except when he wore a white one to go to hunt balls etc. Whatever the weather outside and regardless of the temperature – and I make no distinction between the outside and inside temperature as they were usually the same – he would have a cold bath every morning. The only time he didn't have a cold bath was when the pipes were frozen. Everything you saw him wearing apart from vest, pants, shirt, tie and stiff collar were tailor made by Huntsman in London. His shirts came from Harborow – again in Savile Row. His shoes and boots were made by Maxwell in Jermyn Street. He would have to go to London regularly for fittings etc – never on business – and would always wear a bowler hat on the train.

Well he took it off when he sat down of course which was always in a first class compartment. It was always a taxi in London and he never went on a bus. He would often talk of 'the electric hollow tube[5]' but I don't believe he ever took it. He didn't really like staying in the big smoke overnight, but if he did it was always at the Cavalry Club, a rather gloomy porticoed building two hundred yards up Piccadilly. Back in the sixties we would sometimes go with him; it smelt of old dust and cabbages, but the food was no worse than what we generally ate at home.

Like most people who have been brought up in the country, he was slightly in awe of London but he had the greatest respect for its sartorial conventions. He never wore brown shoes or a tweed suit or a felt hat. It was always a bowler hat. He felt comfortable playing the part of a city gent but didn't much like all the cultural stuff London had to offer; it must have been agony for him to be dragged off to the ballet by my mother and some friends one time – at least for the first act. Five minutes into the second act he was fast asleep and no doubt dreaming of hunting the fox or shooting the pheasant. His culture was one of country pursuits and impeccable

---

[5] London underground

manners, reinforced by a foundation of rigid discipline and strict social rules, but, having said that he was like all of us – contradictory. Although he was unlikely to stand in front of a Rembrandt in contemplative mood for a long time or appreciate the depressing intricacies of a Bergman film (love always had to be triumphant), he did read The Times and the odd thick biography – usually about how we beat the Germans in the war. He was incisively funny, and until he got married, argued a lot about any subject under the sun. Marriage put a stop to the dialectic as my mother always made it personal, which was a pity.

Like many fathers he was full of odd expressions that I guess he had inherited from his own father. If we mobbed him as small children with something exciting we had found or seen, he would invariably say 'Well I never, did you ever, see a monkey dressed in leather!' On cold wet days when it was pouring with rain and the wind was howling around and through cracks in the dining room windows, he would walk into breakfast and shout 'Tickle your arse with a feather!' to which we would reply 'Tickle your arse with a feather??' and he would come back with 'No – I said particularly nasty weather!!'

His most annoying expression, not just because it was glib and ignorant too, and probably coined by some gentleman as his footman piled more coal on to an already roaring fire, was 'Only a beggar or a fool is cold!' What made this infuriating expression even worse was that he only said it when the temperature inside our own house was barely above freezing, and instead of chopping the tops off our boiled eggs and eating them, we would be using them as hand warmers, and struggling to prevent our teeth from chattering. The only form of heating in the dining room was a double bar electric stove with a huge shiny reflector behind it. My mother and father both sat with their backs within two feet of it, while we sat on the other side of the table where the temperature was at least ten degrees colder.

For some reason, like most of his generation, he was impervious to cold, and deaf to the pleas of his wife, who would sometimes appear at dinner dressed like Captain Scott, complete with a black balaclava. His above the waist uniform for dinner which never altered unless it was less than forty degrees or more than eighty degrees Fahrenheit in the dining room was – woolen short sleeved vest, soft white dress shirt with long sleeves and cuff links, short sleeved woolen v necked sweater, heavy duty orange corduroy smoking jacket, and to top it all off, a black single-ender bow tie. If the temperature was below forty degrees, he sometimes wore mittens, and if it was over eighty, he was prone to taking the smoking jacket off and rolling his sleeves up.

After his daily cold bath he did thirty press ups, except when he had broken something like a rib. 'Why do you have a cold bath every morning Daddy?' we would ask. 'Well, so I can go back to bed and feel rosy.' This was one of his favourite jokes, but of course it was lost on us five year olds.

Twice a day he would weigh himself on an ancient pair of rusty boxing scales and as we watched him he would ask us to guess his weight to the nearest ounce. The measurements would go into a note book, one of a number he had going back to 1932. Again, if he had broken something or was ill, this was put off. He used to get vaguely depressed if he was more than thirteen stone, and go on a strict diet like three potatoes instead of four, and only one egg at breakfast.

To all those who met him he was an amusing and affable fellow with impeccable manners.  He was no academic, but neither was he much good at changing a light bulb. His tool kit consisted of a flat bladed screw driver that you just pushed down to screw a screw in or screw it out, a pair of pliers specially designed for extracting the nails from the lids of wooden wine cases, and a hammer that wobbled loosely on its handle and was no good for anything. These three tools were kept in a large metal concertina tool box under the front stairs and I never saw him using any of them. He occasionally helped the gardener to dig the rose beds, possibly as a bolt on to his diet regime, complaining when he came back indoors that digging made him sweat 'alternate drops of ink and blood.' Thinking about it now I guess the ink came from all the letter writing he did. The blood came from the wounds inflicted by the rose bushes, which although rather sparse, still managed to snag him on his digging forays.

Both my parents' desks were in a dark and gloomy room known as the Nerve Centre. They would also sit and relax here. There were bookshelves all around the walls, by and large filled with Baileys Hunting Directories, huge leather bound editions of ancient Punches, and other tomes related to the chasing of foxes and the shooting of fowl. All the books smelt of damp as the fitted bookshelves were fixed to walls that had no damp course; many were naturally ruined, but on the whole this was no great loss to bibliophiles, who were never going to appreciate the kill rate statistics of foxes by hounds during the 1859 hunting season.

As small children, continually fussing around our parents, we spent quite a lot of time in the Nerve Centre, lying around on the floor drawing pictures and stuff. We would steal my father's yellow pencils which infuriated him; these were always lined up like soldiers next to his silver fox head letter opener. This was known as 'the

Pricker' and we would often be in some other part of the house and hear his booming voice echoing off passage walls 'Who's taken the Pricker!?' I still have it here slightly tarnished on the desk as I tap. It is solid silver and about six inches long with the head of a surly looking fox at one end tapering into a flat blunt blade. On it is engraved 'Master Cheshire Hounds 1949-54 – Happy Days from JD.'

Different times. Different ways. To him, in those different times, foxhunting was a passion, an addiction that had all the perils and excitement of dangerous sports today. I gave up hunting when I was twenty one and took up skiing instead; in similar ways you could leave the margins of relative safety at any time and put your life on the line. Skiing down a gully hardly wider than your own skis, not quite knowing what's below you produces the same amount of adrenaline as approaching a fence on a fast horse and not knowing exactly what is on the other side. I've done both. Fortunately, I gave up the hunting nearly fifty years ago; the margins for killing oneself were much narrower than skiing. I'll always remember seeing an old boy by the name of Paterson[6] being carried across the fields on a five bar gate by four stout men in breeches and red coats. He was very dead. His crumpled top hat rested on his crumpled and muddy red coat close to his crumpled neck, broken in a fall; disappointingly, we all went home early out of respect.

Seventy years ago the upper classes were in charge of the countryside. Everyone else did as they were told especially in this part of the country where they were either employed by, or tenant farmers to, local landowners. Even the vicar tugged his forelock to the fetlocks of the master's horse. Well not literally, but

---

[6] Grandfather of Owen Paterson – one time cabinet minister

fetlocks and forelocks were an integral part of rural life in those times. Resentment for galloping horsemen charging along country lanes and across rain soaked fields shouting at the local yokels to open the bloody gate, festered under many a flat, greasy, hat. There is something about people on horses, dressed in a uniform, while you are on foot, cantering past shouting mild abuse. It's an old natural hackle instinct; if each of you had a spear you would probably come off worst standing on the ground, unless of course you had been trained to kill people on galloping horses. I still find these people mildly irritating, but I can balance this with some smugness as I don't think they do it with the same sort of excitement that we got from it sixty years ago. There's too much traffic and people are too safety conscious for a start. Today the foxes have wised up – they are all on Foxbook and other social media.

As far as I could tell, my father was not affected by any psychological hang ups. He was driven by the baser instincts of tribalism – the hunt, the chase, the kill. Having been a soldier and a commander of men, he understood and respected all human beings unless they had offended him in some way. He was well aware that he'd had the good fortune to have been brought up in a happy, rich, upper class family which indulged itself in all the sports and pastimes of the day, especially those where killing animals was involved. He was also aware that there were others he met who were not nearly so fortunate.

In the days between the wars, as he grew up, hunting had never been more popular and took up five months a year between November and March. Hunt boundaries vaguely followed county lines. In those days large tracts of the English countryside were still unfettered by motorways, village sprawls and thick traffic. During the mid nineteenth century there had been a scare that the new fangled railways would put a stop to hunting but in the main it had not happened and the golden days prevailed, usually about three times a week, while the other four days were taken up by planning, exercising the horses and the hounds and talking about it. Throw in a spicy mix of hissy fitting, back biting, wife swapping and social gaffes on the hunting field, and the resulting stew was enough to keep all country folk looped in and happy for seven days – and nights – a week[7]. There were a few exceptions of course and they were generally the farmers over whose land the horses galloped, churning up good pasture land, smashing fences, and occasionally letting cattle loose.

On a good scenting day, if the hounds found a fit fox, up to two hundred people and horses would charge across the fields and jump enormous fences and gates for miles and miles, until either the fox eluded the hounds, ran to ground down an earth or was killed by them when it got too knackered or was unable to outwit them any longer. If the fox found an earth to run down and hide, it was then dug out by men with terriers and thrown to the hounds. It may have been shot first – in which case bits would be cut off and handed out as trophies. If there were any children around at the kill, they would have the bits smeared on their faces in a final act of unnecessary barbarism. I remember, aged about nine, being 'blooded.'

Primitive, sickening, thoughtless? It is now, but it wasn't at the time. Mud, rain, sleet or snow added to the fun, and there was, although I hate admitting it, often a

---

[7] Those families such as the Delameres, Broughtons, and de Traffords that didn't like hunting and shooting in the Cheshire winter moved to Kenya in the 1920s, where their scandals (including murder) as the 'Happy Valley Set' became the stuff of legend, celebrated in such books as White Mischief and notably a film of the same name.

hair on the back of the neck moment when you heard the hounds give tongue as they found a fox in the covert[8] nearby. Standing on a narrow bridle path, horses all jammed up arse to head, sweating, snorting and steaming and smelling of horsey sweat and warm mud, the fading conversation at the sound of the huntsman's horn, and above all the tension, defines the zeitgeist of real foxhunting. There were even some men among us who had fought in the First World War, and had scrambled over the top of their trenches to the sound of a hunting horn. I've no idea how they felt.

In the twenty first century hunting as we knew it as children does not exist. It is a ersatz version with no balls at all. There's a law against it which has castrated the very essence of what it was sixty years ago. Although I see hunting as a ridiculous pass time now, for some years after the Second War it was literally a way of life, and we were caught up in it. To my father it was the great game, a symphony of hierarchy, management and ritual that suited him down to the ground. After leaving Eton in 1918, he had gone to Sandhurst and been commissioned into the Royal Scots Greys as a second lieutenant, and for the last few weeks of the war was actually stationed in France, narrowly missing his time in the trenches. With the war at an end he was given the choice of carrying on in the army and hunting three days a week or going into the family cotton business and still hunting three days a week.

---

[8] 'give tongue' – bark; 'covert' – wood.

# 3 – TOOTH DECAY

My father left the army in 1923, and until the Second War started in 1939, when he was called up again, he reluctantly made the choice to go into the cotton business. He had hoped that his younger brother, Peter, might have taken the job on himself but Peter had other ideas. Known as 'Jig' he was the black sheep of the family.

Jig was a good looking fellow and very charming; he had lots of girlfriends and fell in love with a well known actress. But she was Jewish and Jig's mother didn't approve. This was strange as there was probably more Jewish blood on her side of the family than the actress's. So Jig fell out with his mother and father and left the country for Canada in 1924. His sister, my Aunt Olivia, had married an Irishman by the name of John Martin, who had bought a ranch next to the Canadian Pacific Railway line at a place called Bears Paw near Calgary.

The idea was to breed polo ponies and send them back to Ireland. Jig was really just escaping and trying to get over the heartbreak, but while he was there he met a beautiful black Bajan girl called Alma, in Calgary, who was working in the hospital as a nurse. Perhaps he'd fallen off a polo pony and broken something, but it was all very romantic and she took him down from the frozen north to the tropical heat of Barbados. They got married and shortly afterwards moved to Roseau in Dominica, where they brought up eight children. I say 'brought up' because Alma told me that Jig had a fancy lady on the other side of town who gave birth to three of his children.

There is now a diaspora of the Dewhurst family that stretches from the southern Caribbean as far north as Texas. To me this is a great story as it ran against the grain of convention, and Uncle Peter got his own back on his mother big time. He never came back from the West Indies, but his younger sister, my Aunt Bettsan, went over to Dominica a few times and stayed with him. My father visited him once in Canada and came back with a buffalo overcoat, which I still wear occasionally.

Jig bought a property up on the wild north east side of the island which included a small white sandy beach, unusual for Dominica, where all the other beaches are predominantly black lava sand. I went there once after he had died; rough concrete steps were cut in the cliff face coming down from the main house. The beach was surrounded by tall Emperor Palms, which stood firm against the warm wet wind that drove a constant stream of white rollers in from the ocean. They seemed to come all the way from England, and Uncle Peter, when he wasn't tending his small banana plantation, would sit there and look wistfully out to sea, perhaps hoping one day that he'd be able to go back. He never did and he died on Dominica in 1972. Aunt Alma, who had been born in 1902 just missed living in three centuries, and died in 2003.

In the sand I walked across a twenty foot square of

concrete that was the foundation for a shack he had rebuilt there many times. Whenever a hurricane came through, which was often, it would be washed away, and each time, with his children's help, he would re-build it.

My father, who never saw his brother again after he had left Canada, felt duty bound to keep the family enterprise going; at least he could still hunt three days a week. He didn't want to go and sit behind a desk in a gloomy warehouse office looking out over the yellow fog of Manchester but felt he must; someone in his immediate family had to do it, and although he would lose the chance to play soldiers which he loved almost as much as hunting the fox, he did at least have his hunting three days a week.

I've a vague idea of how his work life went; it must have been awful. He had no aptitude or interest for business or making money and Manchester was a smoke filled industrial city until the Clean Air Act in the mid fifties started to have any beneficial effect. The family firm, G&R Dewhurst Ltd, was set up against the arches of a railway line fifty feet above the building on one side, with a derelict bomb site on the other. The road in and out was through the gloomy black maw of one of the arches.

I can smell the place now as I write, acrid wet soot mixed with a sulphurous jaundiced fog. Once inside it was not much better – tall ceilinged offices with dark brown wooden paneling up to head height, topped with crimped glass, serving as partitions between each office. The meagre lights had to be kept on all the time and the windows were dirty enough to keep out most of the natural light. They were high enough not to be seen out of – probably a good thing in view of what was outside, but nevertheless it must have been depressing for my father, who spent most of his time there writing letters, mostly to us when we were away at school, and to all the people involved in fox-hunting. He had a secretary, Miss Gregg, a dumpy little woman, who tittered graciously at all his quips, finishing off with 'oooh Mr Tony.'

To live and work in a place like that you'd need a good sense of humour to ward off suicide. On the other hand Franz Kafka had probably visited Manchester and gone away happy as Larry because he'd found a great backdrop for a new book.

To us small children it just – was. We were always glum every time we went into Manchester, because it meant we were going to the dentist, and that was always an ordeal. In fact it was a living nightmare. We would all three sit on tubular chairs in a cavernous waiting room with our mother, who would try to make us laugh with stories that we'd heard many times before. She was lucky to get a smile out of us. Through the door into the chamber of horrors we could hear what was going to befall us. This was a time before the downside of sugar and the upside of fluoride were even considered. Sweeties were doled out as treats without a thought for decay, so we were always going to have cavities to fill with tons of mercury and other toxic substances.

The noise we could hear was the drill accompanied by grunts and moans of anguish and the occasional gruff voice of the dentist. The sound of the drill, or rather the Merlin engine which drove it, although muffled through the door, did not bode well. People would come staggering out through the door clutching their faces until it was our turn. The dentist, a lugubrious and frightening man called Mr Heap with a large brown brush moustache, stained yellow in the middle from nicotine, would welcome us all in with fake bonhomie – smearing his blood soaked hands down his white tunic.

He'd probably serviced tanks during the war. His breath stank of tobacco, and he would hold the door open, bending his head in a patronizing fashion with the hint of a smirk, just like I imagined a spider would look before it leapt on a fly. I can hear him thinking – right you little fuckers you're all mine now and you're even paying me to do it. The headache which had started shortly after I left home nearly always got worse as I walked into that room. A phantom in white, mopping up the mess on the floor from the last customer, would float silently into the shadows as we sat down and surveyed this psychopath's lair.

Dropping from the ceiling above a padded seat that rested on a pillar covered in foot levers, was an articulated drive system, looking like the tendons on a skeleton's arm, with small wheels and a thick black pulley running over them. Fixed to the end, instead of a skeleton's hand, was an object that appeared to be a large electric silver torch. This was of course the gearing mechanism that drove the various drill bits, which Mr Heap would pluck at random from a tin bucket next to him and plug into the end. We'd climb up into this armchair, lit from above by one bright light bulb, and would half sit and half lie there. Mr Heap would peer into our mouths very close with tobacco smelling breath and go 'Hum hum. Oh my, what HAVE we got here?' The next thing we'd see would be the drill bearing down; from my point of view in hindsight as I've done a bit of carpentry since, it closely resembled an inch long wood screw. At the same time Mr Heap would touch a foot to one of the pedals under the seat and the infernal machine would start up. It sounded like a badly tuned Spitfire engine at first – a few coughs and splutters and then the deep cackle of a propeller going round until it settled into a terrifying screeching and thrumming as the pulley eventually engaged with the little silver wheels. The screw drill, now only inches from our face started to go round at about seventeen revolutions a minute in a slightly asymmetrical fashion as though it was not quite centered properly. There was an acrid whiff of burning bakelite mixed in with the exhaled breath of Mr Heap.

Remember, this was over fifty years ago; there was no namby-pamby stuff like novocaine, which from a dentist's point of view nowadays takes all the fun out of inflicting gratuitous pain. Instead, Mr Heap would lean over our shoulders and apply pressure with his upper arms, pinning us into the over padded chair. Not to put too fine a point on it, we were held to the chair like mice in a trap. We could flail with our legs as much as we wanted, but he had us held fast. Of course we stayed motionless as we didn't want to appear to be cry babies and be told off by our mother. Just before the drill made contact was a bad moment *within* a bad moment; this was when the word Aaaaarrrgh!!! really meant what it expressed – an onomatopoeic gurgle that started in the back of our throats and worked its way up into a whimpering ululation, and just as quickly petered out as the drill hit the tooth, when it became virtually impossible to make any noise at all.

I marvel now at the ability of Mr Heap, who was able to dock the flailing drill with the precision of an astronaut arriving at the International Space Station. Perhaps I'm wrong in this. Maybe he just started drilling whichever tooth the drill bit hit first, but boy you knew it when he did. There was no pain as such – it was more a paralysed convulsion. If you can understand Newton's Third law of Motion, you'll be aware of what was happening. The low geared drill bit was rotating slowly in an asymmetrical fashion so it had a lot of power and when applied to something solid like a tooth, our heads tried to rotate at the same time. Of course Mr Heap had prepared for this and managed to clamp his free hand over our faces to minimize the effect; it was amazing that he still managed to operate the drill with his other hand. Something had to give, and it just happened to be small chunks of tooth flying off in all directions. There was that familiar smell of charred bone and a plume of bluish smoke, but it was the infernal noise that was worse. The screech of the pulleys, the squealing wheels, and the grinding of drill bit on bone was altogether off the scale. If you can visualize a Motorhead concert and you're two feet from the stage, and then imagine that most of this noise is coming out of your *mouth*, then that's a close approximation.

Anyway, presumably on the assumption that people can get used to anything, Mr Heap ploughed on, literally, until the drill hit a nerve. I can't even begin to describe what happened next. For the first time I've had to reach for a thesaurus, but I can't find a single word to describe it. Let's just say it was bad, very bad, very very bad – and my headache got worse. And then even Mr Heap couldn't go on, for although he was a lot stronger than us, he couldn't hold us down for ever, and his foot would ease off the pedal and the noise would start to fade. 'Why don't you have a little rinse and then we can fill her up?' he would say, standing back, pretending to admire the recipient of his handiwork with his chin to his chest and a little smile. 'Urrrggh' we would reply, and the phantom in white would appear from the shadows and help us up and hand us some pink antiseptic liquid in a glass, and we would try to gargle with it, spitting out blood and bits of bone, and would sink back down again, limp as rag dolls, as he stuffed a poisonous mixture of mercury and god knows what other toxins into the gaping cavity. Then he would dab it all off with tincture of arsenic or something and we'd slide off the over stuffed armchair and collapse back on to the tubular chairs, and then thank goodness, it was somebody else's turn.

Like all small children we recovered quickly and were taken off to Kendal Milne in the middle of Manchester's Deansgate, and treated to a slap up lunch on the top floor by our mother. She was not completely without sentiment and understood Pavlov's theory of pain and reward, and we gratefully chomped and slurped our way through overcooked beef, carrots and mashed potato and then jelly, all washed down with over sweetened Kiaora orange juice, and then later she would buy us some chocolates and the whole damned cycle of tooth decay would start all over again.

I guess my mother was quite long suffering, even to spend the short times she did with us. If things got really bad she would hand us over to whichever nanny was being employed, and because we were pretty awful as children and we hadn't learned to hide our more psychotic tendencies, the nannies came and went quite fast. It was reasonably simple to take a dangerous weapon such as a carving knife or a pair of scissors off a small child who is standing in front of you without much trouble, but you had no idea which child or how many were coming up behind with a chipolata stick or a sawn off piece of Meccano. There was a Nanny Smith I remember, who stayed longer than most, but it was Mary, the long suffering cook, who had arrived when I was about three, who soon became housekeeper and finally nanny to all of us, including my mother and father.

When my parents had married and settled at Stoke Hall, they needed someone to cook as my mother couldn't even boil an egg. I can imagine how she conducted the interviews. It would have been a short meeting. 'Can you find us something to eat and can you make sure it's warm when we eat it? Yes? You can? Wonderful. When can you start?' They employed two or three women, who were unable to achieve either of the aforesaid requirements; the last one was called Annie. I never knew Annie but every time her name was mentioned my father used to get the giggles. There was no radio in his Manchester office so one day as he left for work, he asked Annie to remember the Test Match score against the West Indies from the Oval. This was back in 1950. The only source of immediate news then was the wireless so when he got home he was desperate to know if England had won the final test.

'So Annie what was the score?'

'Well England went in and batted the Red Indians for six and one of them hit another one over the roof of the pavilion.'

Poor Annie couldn't read or write – she couldn't cook either so she had to go, but during her time Mary arrived and started as a housekeeper. She would have been about forty. We never knew her real age; she always said she was ninety nine. She lived in a tiny terraced house with no bathroom in Tarporley about ten miles away with her two sisters. They all slept in the same bed. She never learned to drive and my mother or father would take her home and bring her back on her two half days off, Thursday and Sunday. For a fortnight in August she would take her annual holiday – back home in Tarporley. Otherwise she spent the next thirty five years with us, bustling around and hardly ever stopping. She was quite small with grey hair she cut herself and lovely brown eyes. At one time she must have been good looking but as far as I know there had never been a man in her life. She was now cylindrical in body which she covered with colourful calico dresses. She made them herself on an old foot driven Singer sewing machine in the kitchen at Barmere. My father would bring rolls of this brightly patterned material back from his warehouse where it was stored for export to India to make cheap saris. She hardly ever stopped wiping, scrubbing, cleaning, stirring, shovelling. When she did stop, it would be poring over a frayed and well thumbed Mrs Beeton[9] on the large bleached kitchen table, or sitting on a chair in front of the cooking range with one of the oven doors open after drinking a teacupful of sweet cider with her lunch. She would rest her head on the silver rail and say 'I think I'll just have five minutes,' and go fast asleep for half an hour. At eleven o'clock most weekday mornings she would hold court in the kitchen over a cup of tea and packets of ginger biscuits. It was usually the groom, the gardener and anyone who was helping her clean the house. The postman would always call in too, whether he was delivering mail or not, as would PC[10] Ashford if he was passing. Once a week Mr Bickley, who delivered the groceries, and George, who delivered the meat, would swell the numbers.

When Annie left back in 1950, Mary became the cook and housekeeper. When the last nanny gave up the fight and left, she added 'nanny' to her portfolio too. She was no pushover and you never messed with her. Of course we were never clean enough and she would line us up in the bath and scrub us until we were nearly raw with some foul smelling stuff she called soap. More than likely she probably used it to clear blocked drains as well.

---

[9] The bible of Victorian household management.
[10] Police Constable

We weren't allowed into the dining room until we were about ten, and would have to sit at a small table in the corner of the kitchen, while she would stand over us making sure we ate everything.

'Think of all the starving children in China,' was her favourite saying as we filled our mouths up with her version of Shepherd's Pie, our cheeks bulging out like hamsters', wondering how we were going to swallow it without throwing up. Chinese children were the last things on our minds. Thinking about it now, I could happily have scraped mine off the plate into an envelope and posted it to China.

At the start she wasn't much of a cook and sometimes the stuff she produced was barely edible but we got used to it as we got older and she got better. My father wasn't too keen on garlic and 'all that foreign muck,' but she knew about onions which was some sort of a concession. She was best at roasting the beef George brought every week, and occasionally when my parents had dinner parties she made the most delicious Charlotte Russe[11]. She was our second mother really.

As the years went by, and with the help of the battered old copy of Mrs Beeton, she was able to produce some good food on special occasions and Christmas was one of them. At the end of the summer holidays in early September she would make the Christmas pudding and all three of us would gather round, our noses barely above the kitchen table, and standing in turn on a kitchen chair, would give the mixture a stir and make a wish. The pudding would be

---

[11] A classic Edwardian dessert similar to a trifle. Boudoir biscuits or lady fingers line a cake mould, the centre filled with a silk bavarois cream that is set with gelatine and underneath a mixture of fruit, whipped cream and fruit pureé.

cooked and allowed to mature for three months and then join all the other stuff she prepared – a huge ham and a turkey nearly as big as her, together with mince pies, brandy butter and a soggy alcohol Christmas cake encased in rock hard white icing that broke teeth and needed a chain saw to get into.

The Christmas festivities included my mother's birthday on Christmas Eve. That's why she was called Noel, and there would always be the same party including her two sisters, Myra and Sheila. Aunt Sheila had once been a nun and had no family and usually came for a week and made my father quite grumpy. Aunt Myra was married to Geoffrey Churton and we had three first cousins, Nigel, Guy and Sally and they would come too. Sometimes our grandmother would come from London and stay as well which made my father even grumpier. And then there was our father's sister, Aunt Bettsan, who lived quite close, together with anyone else hardy enough to withstand the coldest house in Cheshire.

Now for some reason that has been lost in the mist of time my father and my Uncle Geoffrey were not the greatest friends although they appeared to be perfectly civil to each other. My father, somewhat restricted by his obsession to observe good manners at all times and be polite to all, nevertheless made it quite plain that he didn't really like parties very much, not even his own, but he was prepared to endure them in the interests of social propriety.

One Christmas Eve when we were in our teens with the outside temperature well below zero and the inside temperature not much higher, we repaired to the drawing room after a boozy dinner. The dining room had a fireplace and a roaring coal fire that was only lit at Christmas, but the drawing room had a pathetic excuse for one that could only hold about four lumps of coal.

The women all wore long woolly dresses and knew the score and we congregated at one end of the room trying as best we could to get some of the thin heat from the fireplace, jockeying for the best position like Antarctic penguins in a blizzard.

Uncle Geoffrey, who was tall and thin, had taken the best spot – backside to the fire, arms folded to retain his own body heat with his legs slightly apart. One enormous lump of coal, barely alight, was smouldering in the grate. My father was nowhere to be seen, and had disappeared at the end of dinner. We were finishing off the coffee and dipping into a box of chocolates when he strode in wearing his pyjamas and dressing gown. The conversation stopped. He went straight to the fire and bent down to pick up the tongs.

'Stand aside would you please Geoffrey.'

With that he got the large lump of coal in the tongs, stood up and strode back out of the drawing room leaving a cloud of stinking tarry smoke behind him, at the same time shouting over his shoulder, 'I'm not made of money you know!'

We couldn't believe it and I ran to the door and peered round the frame. He opened the front door and dumped the coal down on the steps outside and then came back past me, put the tongs back by the fire, sighed with satisfaction and said 'Well, there we are. Happy Christmas everyone.'

As he padded out of the room with the hint of a smile on his face, he turned all the lights out.

# 4 – MUMMY & HER WARS

Meanwhile my mother had other stuff to get on with. When we were old enough, some of what she was interested in involved us too, but she left us and all the domestic chores to Mary. Her first priority was God. Her second was horses. Then a close third came her husband, then the dogs and then us. I'm not saying she didn't love us; of course she did but put quite simply, the others came first.

With God there was absolutely no compromise. God was a Roman Catholic and boy did we know it. Of course then we took stuff in at its face value. The word 'belief' did not come into it. Once again – it just was. When she was about eight in 1927 she was sent to a Catholic convent in Berkshire called Denford Park with her sisters, Myra and Sheila. Later they all went to the secondary school, Newhall in Essex, again run by nuns. They had to tie cloths with drawstrings over the tops of their baths and round their necks so that they couldn't see their naughty bits; not being able to see their naughty bits was supposed to stop them having impure thoughts. It hadn't occurred to the nuns that covering everything except their heads might have encouraged them to perform impure deeds under the cloth while affecting a nonchalant air above it.

Aunt Myra was not as devout as her two sisters, but she still went to Mass on Sundays and by her own admission played the organ badly in Tarporley Catholic Church. Aunt Sheila was even closer to God than my mother and that was saying something. She was a nun before we knew her. Nuns have to take vows of poverty, chastity and obedience. Chastity and obedience were fine, but the poverty bit was too tricky for her. She had a certain predilection for port and good food and the finer things in life and it all became a bit too much for her. In the end she became a PA to some big wig Catholic chaplain in the Royal Air Force, and we all agreed that she should have been the first female Pope if such a person were to exist.

I have been sitting looking at the computer screen for about ten minutes and not been able to write a word about my mother. My father was easy to describe. Apart from a few secrets he hid well, he was what you saw and heard, and did what you had learned to expect with little or no deviation, but my mother was altogether more complex. The simple way her friends described her was eccentric, which I translate as well away from the normal. I guess over the years we did come to expect certain patterns of behaviour, ingredients of character so diverse that still melded to produce some sort of consistency, but sometimes her reactions would have been impossible to predict.

This I can tell you: she was five foot five, very glamorous with long black wavy hair, a strong straight nose, hazel eyes and a wide smile. She was a war baby – born just after the First World War and the oldest of the three sisters. When she was twenty three, she was sitting in the back of Mickey Mosely's car on the way back from a summer party during the second war. There were two others, both girls, in the car with them. Mickey was a pilot flying Lancaster bombers out of a Lincolnshire airfield and she had just joined the WRAF, the Women's Royal Air Force. It was June 1942, four in the morning, still dark with double British summer time, but the sun was beginning to lighten the eastern sky. I can see the photo now – the small milk delivery truck empty on the side of the road with a bent wheel and a crushed rear end – with their wrecked car in the ditch on the far side, with shards of windscreen and window spiking up from the crumpled metal work. Perhaps Mickey had been on the first 1000 plane bomber raid on Cologne the month before and the stress was getting to him. Bombing the Germans was not a happy experience for any of the pilots and crew; to alleviate the pressures and stress Mickey used to have a crate of Guinness put on the plane whenever they went on a raid. One night he got the plane back safely about three o'clock in the morning, and had more to drink in the mess. He then drove back home to Cheshire. On the way he ran over a policeman going to work on his bicycle. The man was only shaken and together they slung the broken bike in the boot and Mickey took the policeman on to Northwich police station. On another night he turned for home somewhere over the Ruhr, thankful to be escaping the exploding flak all around them, and asked his navigator for a bearing. There was no reply. The navigator had taken a piece of stray shrapnel straight through his head.

The alcohol helped Mickey to forget his day job, and together with being a party animal he was more than usually pissed on that warm June night – he was paralytic. My mother, who told me this much, says she lay back and thought to herself it's quite possible I could die shortly, but at least I'll die happy, and that was the last thing she could remember – until she miraculously woke up in a hospital bed. The others in the car escaped any serious injuries, but her face was a mess and her nose was all but gone; she landed up in Sussex and a man by the name of Archie McIndoe built her a new one, with bone taken from her hip. McIndoe was a New Zealander, who was a pioneer in plastic surgery at a newly built hospital in East Grinstead. My mother was very lucky. Most of his patients were Air Force pilots and crew, burns victims who had escaped with horrific injuries from the fighters and bombers they had been flying and navigating. To my mother he was a hero of the war and so was Mickey Mosely.

This accident and my mother's attitude to it says quite a lot about her. She was an attractive woman and Mickey was a very close friend. I really have no idea how close he got to bedding her, but it was unlikely because she was far closer to God, and part of the deal with Him precluded any sex before marriage in order to get listed for Eternal Salvation. After all, adultery was included in one of the Ten Commandments. Death of course would have been just a temporary blip in the course of Eternal Life, rather like moving house or buying a new car. So she was not frightened of dying – as later escapades on horses would show. Most of us would calculate our risks most of the time, but I don't think she ever did – she got a kick out of taking uncalculated risks all the time, excepting of course adultery. Neither was she averse to pain, and the pain she experienced after the accident, especially in her hip after McIndoe took a slice out of it for her new nose, must have been pretty bad even by her own standards.

She had first sat on a horse aged three, and first fallen off one not long afterwards. As anyone who rides a horse knows, the first seven times you fall off a horse are going to hurt like hell. After that it doesn't hurt at all. Of course this is bunkum like all the other stuff we were told as children to persuade us that pain had its rewards. It was a tenet of the Catholic faith after all; Jesus Christ died a horrible death for us, nailed to a piece of wood, so the least you can do is experience some of the pain He went through – yourself. She didn't say that in so many words of course when we were small, but I know she thought it. As young children there was no way to understand it, but as we grew older she tried to drum it into us – redemption through suffering. It has its practical uses in the secular world too – souffrir pour etre belle. You must suffer to be beautiful.

Am I describing a blinkered, single minded, unintelligent, humourless zealot, who has dedicated her life to her God? Partly, yes. She was a zealot, and certainly dedicated, and she was absolutely sure that the Catholics were the top dogs compared to other Christian denominations. However, she was outgoing and vivacious, highly intelligent but chose not to show it among her friends, and could laugh fit to burst discussing practically any subject under the sun. She could tell a funny story well and although some of her jokes were quite filthy, others even made us, her children, laugh. I often wonder, if she had been born at the same time as us, and been schooled in a more secular environment, whether she would have escaped the refined brainwashing she was exposed to during her own school years in the twenties. It might seem strange that she wasn't because the twenties were liberating times for those who were rich enough to indulge in what they had to offer, but in reality my grandmother, an obedient Catholic herself, saw that she was sent to the best Roman Catholic boarding schools that money could buy.

If she had been a man, my mother would have been a Jesuit priest. Outwardly worldly, loquacious, charming, a man of the people no less, she would have sailed to South America with the conquistadores and given her life for the glory of God. She would have ridden a mule well. I say the Jesuits because Ignatius Loyola, who founded the Order of Jesus back in 1540 had a maxim that he had borrowed from even earlier times 'Give me the child before he is seven and I will give you the man.' In other words it's a piece of cake to brainwash a human being until he reaches the age of reason. After that it's a bit more difficult, so grab 'em early. Whether he is as thick as a plank or a budding Einstein matters not. Everyone is susceptible.

It doesn't matter whether you are intelligent or stupid. Your capacity for being brainwashed and indoctrinated is the same. I find it difficult to reconcile intelligence with the belief system I was brought up with, and drummed into me at an early age. For my part, however much I say I am now an atheist, however hard I have tried to shake off this indoctrination, there still remains this picture in my head from way back, before the age of seven, of an omnipotent God, an old man with a beard, sitting on a cloud. Behind him is a bloke in a white robe with large feathery wings playing a harp. Jesus Christ and the Holy Ghost are nowhere to be seen, but they are there somewhere – perhaps in a back room playing poker over a sandwich and a bottle of beer. The three in one bit, the Trinity – an abstract concept – was far too difficult to take in and therefore doesn't exist in my head. But I just can't shake out this picture of God; I do my best and when I'm with other people and two drinks up I have to shout 'If there is a god may he strike me dead within the next ten seconds!' There is always a stunned silence. Like my mother, like me, most of the people I'm with have been brainwashed too.

Tribal instincts still govern us, however hard we try to change ourselves. I've said my mother was 'single-minded', which to me is a word that defines something strong and good. However, tap that word into a thesaurus looking for synonyms and in about four clicks up comes 'barbarous'. Was my mother good or evil when she contributed to the IRA coffers in the late sixties, by sending money to a Catholic nuns' support group in southern Ireland, because she believed that her fellow Catholics were being socially and politically persecuted in Northern Ireland? I haven't mentioned her yet, but was my friend Roma, whom I shared a flat with briefly in London during the sixties, good or evil, when she returned in 1972 to her Catholic family, which lived off the Falls Road in Belfast, to fight for 'The Cause'?[12]

There was a word I mentioned some pages back – miraculously. Of course I used it metaphorically, but for my mother recovering in her hospital bed after the car crash with the morphine to help her, she must have come to the conclusion that she had been saved to do God's Will. It was a miracle that she had survived.

We three children became the recipients of her religious zeal. She didn't bother with her friends or relations or even my father. She took that maxim used by Ignatius Loyola to heart. Like Mr Heap, the dentist, she'd got us. We were her children but we were also God's children, and it really was her duty to see that we stayed that way. At about the same time as the visit to the dentist, she had left me at her friend's house where I played with her friend's son, and we did the sort of stuff that nine year olds do, like killing wasps and kicking

---

[12] This was shortly after 'Bloody Sunday' on 30 January 1972 when 26 civilians were killed by British soldiers during a demonstration.

stones around. For lunch we had sausages and mashed potato, and junket which I hated. The trouble was, and this is why I remember it so well, it was Friday. If you are a Catholic the one thing you never do is eat meat on Friday. If you do it's most likely you will go to hell. Perhaps, as it's such an important place I should say Hell with a capital H. That evening I told her for some reason that I'd eaten sausages and mash and junket and she went ape shit. Because I'd eaten sausages I was bound for Hell and Eternal Damnation and there was nothing I could do about it … unless … unless … unless I was really really really sorry, then there could be a way out. I went to bed quite scared and crying; I then remember my mother holding me and saying it was quite all right and that if I went to confession and was still really really really sorry, I could be forgiven. I make not a word of this up. I can't remember any more of the footage. I can't even remember if I ate the sausages deliberately; I doubt it being a god fearing nine year old. As an afterthought though, I don't reckon there was much meat in the sausages – they were mostly made of sawdust, cardboard and fat.

My mother's second love was the horse and this was an activity she introduced us to even earlier than God. It was marginally better than being dragged off to Latin Mass in the local Catholic church every Sunday. My earliest memory was being thrown on the back of a donkey called Jesse aged about four and a half (me not the donkey), and being led up the road outside our house. Dragged out of bed at six o'clock in the morning it was still dark and was an introduction to fox-hunting – cub hunting it was called where the young foxes and the young hounds got used to being chased and chasing, and of course where many of the foxes got torn apart by the hounds. There was a lot of clip clopping and whinnying and yelps from the hounds. This was a main trunk road we were assembled on and no one seemed to care that there were a few early morning lorries and cars backing up. Jesse the donkey seemed to be the only one who cared about anything and that was because she wanted to get back in the field and eat thistles.

Of course this was another form of indoctrination but we were much happier to go along with it. By the time I was nine and Gemma and Jonathan seven and eight, we all had our own ponies. Jesse the donkey was passed down through each of us for a while, but she was only there to get us used to sitting on a four legged animal. Our three ponies suddenly gave us some freedom with a capital F. For a short while we didn't have to kneel down and listen to an old geezer in a long white frock incanting the Lord in a language we didn't understand. We learnt how to gallop and jump and play Cowboys and Indians. This was a time when the Lone Ranger and Tonto were all the rage. We didn't watch them on television because we didn't have one until we were ten nine and eight, but I was at a school up the road and every week there would be a half hour film and I'd come back with the latest plot – of course I was the Lone Ranger and Tonto combined, and the others would be the Baddies or the Indians.

There is a photo of Jonathan sulking and wearing a Red Indian headdress and Gemma and myself smiling smugly in cowboy gear, complete with guns, mounted on our trusty steeds. Jonathan only had the Red Indian costume so he was never allowed to be a cowboy. Our three ponies were the three stars of the show – Millington, Mickey and Peggy. Millington was Jonathan's – he was small and brown and squat with a mane that stuck straight up. He jumped anything and was a solid upstanding sort of chap. Mickey was

Gemma's and light brown with a curly coat. He was an obstinate sod and would only gallop and jump if he felt like it. His claim to fame was his rubber neck. It didn't matter how hard my sister pulled on the reins to turn either left or right; if he didn't want to go either left or right but only straight on, he would bend his head right round till he was looking at her while still moving forwards. This was quite disconcerting for Gemma and hilarious for anyone who was watching. My pony Peggy was also a bit of a wild card. She was flighty and would occasionally buck and kick if she was in a bad mood, but she was the fastest and jumped well, and spent a lot of time with her tongue hanging out.

Two or three years on we were allowed to go off on our own into the Peckforton Hills, which were a short ride away through the fields of Cholmondeley. Seven miles long they rise up from the Cheshire Plain like a tired old sea monster – not more than eight hundred feet high, sandstone humps dressed in pine and gnarled weather-beaten deciduous trees, they stand out as a landmark in the middle of the flat green fields of south Cheshire. Just known as the Hills they were everything that our imaginations needed – the wild west right outside our door. They have remained the hitching post for my imagination ever since, and whenever I need to exercise either mind or body, I head for the Hills. There is nothing special about them; they are just important. Most of my life has been spent on mountains and the Hills are a perfect substitute for training for whatever's coming next, be it skiing or just staying fit. Sixty years ago they were the perfect cowboy training area, crashing through the undergrowth, trying to ride bareback and whooping at the tops of our voices until the ponies objected and decided they'd had enough and it was time to take us home by themselves.

Back home in the stables it was not quite so much fun. It was great to jump on a pony and gallop off, but we had to take the good with the bad. There were always a lot of other horses at Barmere because my parents hunted the fox and my mother usually had what she would call a racehorse or two, but what other people would refer to as beaten up has-beens. To look after all these sturdy and not so sturdy animals would be a groom, as there was no way either my mother or father would do this themselves. They had both been brought up in houses where practically all the real work had been done by servants. At my father's family house there had been fourteen staff – outside. There were another dozen inside, attending to every whim and request.

The groom at Barmere was called Barrow. This wasn't short for wheelbarrow although that's what he had to push most of the time. In case you are unfamiliar with the digestive system of horses they generally eat and defecate continuously, apart from when they are being ridden or hanging their heads over a stable door, so you are forever barrowing hay and other stuff into their stable at the same time as you are barrowing out the dirty straw and crap. Barrow had no other name that I was ever aware of. He was an affable chap and looked a bit like Stalin, quite small with a walrus moustache and a twinkle in his eye. My mother and he got along fine and they used to drink sometimes in the saddle room, where all the horsey kit was kept.

Calling male servants by their surname was standard practice in those days and as my father had been a regular soldier he knew no other way to address his staff lower in rank than himself, except by their surname, so that was that. From today's perspective it's not only ridiculous but faintly embarrassing to write about it.

Two world wars had mortally wounded the old order,

which was staggering around like a headless chicken, knowing its days were numbered as it slowly bled its life away. Empire, class structure and general social mores were taking a right old clobbering. People in Britain were left exhausted after fighting a war which had finally been won by America and Russia. The great Empire was shrinking too. In 1947, the year I was born, India cut free and became independent, and in 1956 Britain lost the Suez Canal, which had been the strategic jewel in the Empire's crown since the 1880s. In fact we had been losing chunks of our colonial past all the way through the fifties with successful challenges from Malaysia, Kenya and Cyprus, and we had no option but to let them go. It would have been interesting to know what the chattering classes were chattering about at Cheshire dinner tables in those times, but we were too young. I suspect it was more navel gazing and regret rather than outright hostility towards the rest of the world. The fight was gone. But at least we still had Rhodesia, the Monarchy and the rest of the Commonwealth, as well as foxes to chase and pheasants to shoot.

British class hierarchy and social mores, had already started to take a severe bashing during the Second World War. Nearly three million American soldiers and airmen had invaded the UK by 1944, and they brought with them nylon stockings, Glen Miller, chewing gum and an altogether ritzier lifestyle. Although they didn't get into every corner of Britain, their influence was felt everywhere. They fraternized with British servicemen and women regardless of social class and rank, and that included marrying more than sixty thousand British girls. But it was their popular culture that had the greatest effect. They overwhelmed us with it. Nearly everyone in Britain had a wireless and could get to a cinema and a dance hall, even if they'd never met an American. In 1943 there were hardly any British bands, solo singers, or groups in the top twenty music hits. Apart from a couple, they were all Americans – Frank Sinatra, Harry James, Benny Goodman, Perry Como, Fred Astaire, Rudy Vallee, and of course Glen Miller. The list was endless but you begin to get the picture. And talking of pictures, out of the top thirty feature films showing in Britain in 1943, only five were British. Most of the others were Hollywood studio movies. In that year, even with a war on, cinema goers in Britain went to the movies nearly 1.6 billion times – that's nearly once a week for every man woman and child in the country, or to put it more simply – a lot. Until recently, apart from just after the war, that figure has never been surpassed. Every social class in the country was influenced by popular American culture, and no more so than in the armed services where people from all walks of life were thrown together. It wasn't a factor whether you worked with the Americans or not. A common denominator in the services, apart from the obvious one of fighting together, was the film you'd seen last night or the music you'd heard on the wireless or danced to in whichever mess[13] you were attached to.

But British class hierarchy, not as stultifying as it had been thirty years before, was still a tough nut to crack even for my mother, who gave the impression she was trying to do it from the inside. I'm not sure if her iconoclasm coupled with cheerful bonhomie was done for effect or because she was a true Christian socialist. Being an officer in the Air Force, she had a lot of contact with servicewomen from a different class to herself.

---

[13] These were the separate facilities and living quarters for the lowest ranks, non-commissioned officers, and officers in all three services.

However hard she tried to break down social barriers, she would never have fully succeeded, but at least she was living in a time when it was now acceptable to make the effort. But I really don't know whether it was put on or genuine.

Somerset Maugham writes in Cakes and Ale 'She introduced us to a clergyman and a lady, who got up as we were shown in. They were the Vicar of Blackstable and his wife. Lady Hodmarsh and the duchess immediately assumed the cringing affability that persons of rank assume with their inferiors in order to show them that they are not in the least conscious of any difference in station between them.'

It all gets very complicated even if you have been brought up with it. And it still exists today whether we like it or not. This is 2015 and I was recently on a conducted tour of that great house Chatsworth in Derbyshire, the home of the Dukes of Devonshire. The man taking us round said 'Oh everything's so much less formal nowadays. The staff no longer have to address the duke and duchess as 'Your Grace.' We can call them 'Duke' and 'Duchess' now!' In some ways the Bolsheviks had a point when they called everybody 'Comrade.' It was so much simpler.

So Comrade Barrow, aided by my mother, was responsible for our equestrian education, and as soon as we were physically able, we had to push the wheelbarrow full of shit, fill up the ponies' hay nets and clean them and the saddles and bridles. Barrow was a kindly soul, but my mother was tough. Once we were on the ponies she never stopped telling us how to ride them. It was all in good faith; she wanted us to be as good a rider as she was. All we wanted to do was gallop around without saddles and bridles so we wouldn't have to clean them. Then there was the Pony Club. This is still the countrywide organization for children that in our day was run like the Hitler Youth Movement. My mother was high up in the organization and was an SS Obergruppenführer First Class or something like that. During the school holidays we would have to ride to the nearest pony club meeting and be taught how to ride properly – 'TOES UP HEELS DOWN COLLECTED WHILE YOU TROT SIMON AND DON'T LOLL AROUND LIKE A SACK OF BLOODY POTATOES FOR GOD'S SAKE…!' And all this would be coming from my mother shouting as she stood there like Cecil B de Mille smacking her jodhpurs with a silver topped cane as ten or twelve of us dutifully trotted round her in a large circle bouncing erratically. Some of the other instructors were harsh too, but never as harsh as my mother. In her book there were no such words as favouritism or mummy's darling. But then, after a gruelling two hour session of ridicule and insults, we could gallop home and jump fences on our own without our mother, who always seemed to go separately and stop off on the way at a friend's house. It was discipline within a liberal framework if you see what I mean.

# 5 – SERVANTS OF GOD

Combined with all the fun of growing up was the misery of religious education. By the time we were eight nine and ten we used to go into my mother's bedroom and kneel down in front of the fireplace, minus my father who was always referred to as the 'heretic,' and we'd say prayers together. I shudder now to think of it. And of course before we went to bed we had to kneel down again, alone, and say the same prayers once more – hail Mary full of grace blessed be the fruit of thy womb... The night time ones were OK as nobody was watching and I managed to say them while I thought about what Airfix aeroplane I was going to buy tomorrow, and I could sometimes get through them in thirty seconds.

Once a week during the school holidays, and until I was thirteen, my mother would drag me off to the Catholic seminary in Malpas. I was always on my own and have no idea if the others were dragged off too. I shudder again. There was no funny stuff or anything like that, but the experience was a form of mental abuse. My mother would drop me off at the door of this large house overlooking the Welsh mountains on a nice sunny day, and a young student priest would lead me down a dark echoing passage and show me into a cheerless room. 'Would you like to sit down? Father Doo Da will be with you in a minute.' Apart from a bare wooden table and two tubular chairs, there was no other furniture. High up on the wall was a small black wooden crucifix with Christ dangling on it. He was made out of white plastic and the large nails through his hands and feet were splodged with red paint. I really didn't need reminding of any more suffering. The walls were painted green and brown. After a few minutes Father Doo Da would glide silently in wearing a long black cassock as though he was on wheels. I can't remember what his real name was – it began with a D. He was tall and thin, fortyish, with fair wavy hair and long girl like fingers, and he spoke with a soft northern accent. He would sit down uncomfortably, and I would produce this little red book, the Catechism, and hand it over to him and he would test me on the questions and answers therein. I only remember two of them which go like this:

'Who made you?'

'God made me'

'Why did God make you?'

'God made me to know him, love him, and serve him in this world, and be happy with him forever in the next …' and other such gubbins in a similar vein, and all I could think was why couldn't I be outside in the sunshine playing Cowboys and Indians on my pony, or damming up the brook with sticks? Without doubt it was an hour of hideous awfulness; there has been little in my life since those torture sessions that have been anywhere close. I don't think he was enjoying himself either. More likely my mother, who had opinions about God and horses that would have given Attila the Hun a run for his money, would never have taken 'no' or 'sorry I can't teach him' for an answer. Father Doo Da would have succumbed meekly to whatever my mother threw at him.

Every Sunday and on holy days such as the Feast of the Immaculate Conception or the Day of the Failing Kidney, we would be dragged off to church. Sometimes it was Malpas and sometimes it was Whitchurch. My brother and I would occasionally be made to dress up as altar boys in black cassocks and white surplices and have to accompany the priest as he said Mass. We would ring bells and swing incense holders at pre-rehearsed times as well as intoning at intervals in squeaky treble voices. This was infinitely more fun than being out front as it involved getting through an hour long service with a straight face without giggling, and was a good opportunity to hone my acting skills. Whereas being in the congregation was nearly as boring as Catechism tuition – stand up, sit down, kneel, sit down, pick nose, kneel, stand up, flick excavation on end of finger at Jonathan, and only the occasional hymn to break the monotony.

The priests at the Malpas seminary church changed all the time and I can't remember their names, but in Whitchurch there was an old boy called Father Calderbank. He was a tall lumbering Irishman who was quite deaf; he was an amiable fellow and would give us sweets at the end of Mass. He moved very slowly and was probably about 99. Now I know what you are thinking, but no, there was no funny stuff going on at either of these places – well at least nothing that involved us. That happened later when we went away to school.

The congregation in the Whitchurch church was usually about six including us four. We sat at the front.

There was nearly always a large woman with long blonde hair, wearing a light green buttoned-up overcoat that was grubby and slightly too small for her. She knelt behind us. Then there was a small dark haired man wearing square tortoiseshell glasses. He smelt of tobacco and sat at the back, keeping us awake and probably Father Calderbank too, with his periodic explosive coughs. With nicontine stained fingers, he would proffer a brass soup plate with a disc of red felt in the bottom to mask the sound of the few shekels we dropped into it. The church was a large red brick building on the outside and quite pleasant looking, but the inside was a miserable place. It was painted for the most part in duck egg blue and a lot of the paint was peeling off the walls and ceiling. Below a head high daydo it was painted in a yellow ochre marbling effect that was somehow rather depressing. It was cold and draughty and there were many times when there was snow on the ground outside and little powdery drifts just inside the door that never shut properly. On very cold days Father Calderbank would take Mass wearing mittens and an overcoat and black fur lined slip on shoes. Under his overcoat he would be wearing his cassock and on the outside he would be wearing the long white dress thing called an alb and on top of that a satin poncho known as a chasuble. The colour would change with the time of year. On happy days like the feast of the Immaculate Conception he would wear white and on miserable days like the Day of the Failing Kidney it would be either purple or black, and there were other colours in between. Now I know there is no such feast day as the Failing Kidney but it's a catch all name I'm using to cover all the other ones. After all it's no more ridiculous than the

Feast of the Immaculate Conception[14], which is a genuine feast day. Of course with all this gear on and being about ten stone heavier, Father Calderbank moved at the speed of a snail, even slower than he would normally, which was generally the speed of a tortoise. Added to this his memory had started to go by the time he was 109, and this resulted in a protracted Mass that would last for about three hours. In the silences while Father Calderbank fumbled through the Latin liturgy and his way round the altar, we could hear each others tummies' rumbling; this would send us into fits of giggles.

I don't know whether you're aware of it, but the white wafer that father Calderbank held up in the air – if he remembered to do it – became the *actual body* of Jesus at the moment he intoned the grave declaration 'Hoc est enim corpus meum' – 'For this is my body.' Likewise, when he raised the chalice filled with wine and intoned once more, the wine was turned into Jesus's blood. I'm not sure for how long they remained his body and blood after Father Calderbank swallowed them. At what point in the digestive process did they turn into mush, mingling with the other stuff in his small intestine? If we could add up all the times Father Calderbank and his fellow priests ate Jesus's body and drank his blood over the past two thousand years, how much would all this add up to? Did they imagine what bit of him they were eating? Even with eating just tiny morsels at what point did they actually finish him off, or are there still some bits left, or did they start all over again? Was he still Jesus when he got to Father Calderbank's large bowel?

---

[14] Mary, the mother of Jesus, was apparently born without the taint of original sin (explained elsewhere).

I'm going off track a little but I write about all this religious piffle in the 21$^{st}$ century as human beings around the world are blowing themselves and others into little bits, sawing people's heads off, and stoning to death adulterous women. They adhere to a barbaric belief system that is very similar to that which the Catholic Church invented and refined hundreds of years ago, the same Church I was brought up on and have now obviously discarded.

What strikes me as a little strange is our attitude to these sorts of things. Have we stopped thinking, or is history no longer taught in schools? These belief systems, based on instinct and superstition and fuelled by propaganda, have been around since we began to stand upright and probably for some time before that. Do we imagine for one moment that we in the west have got rid of these instincts by saying *we* are good and *they* are evil? I don't think so. Will we ever? No, we won't! We know that, unless science can somehow obliterate them from the human genome, these instincts will forever be a part of our own species' psyche.

This present, 21$^{st}$ century intifada, directed against anyone who doesn't want to join it, is all to do with belonging to and controlling a tribe. The desire to imitate and follow someone else and be part of the crowd is one manifestation of tribalism. We see it everywhere, not just in religion, and we are all a part of it whether we like or not. We see it in language, in fashion, in the creative arts. If we look hard enough we see it in the natural world around us among insects, mammals and even plants. It depends for its success on safety in numbers. This again appears in nature – locusts, starlings, sardines, Catholics, Daesh, and even the guys in the pub down the road.

My mother's religious beliefs transcended everything

else that governed our early lives. They crept into our thought processes. They affected our diets. Not only did we have to eat fish on Fridays and sacrifice our bacon and egg, we weren't even allowed to eat breakfast on the Sundays when we took Communion. When we ate God we had to do it on an empty stomach. No wonder our tummies rumbled and made us giggle.

Her religious beliefs even affected our early attempts to develop our entrepreneurial skills. There were thousands of daffodils up and down the drives at Barmere and every Spring there would be a bright yellow carpet of them gently waving in the breeze. One day during the Easter school holidays when we were seven eight and nine we waded in snapping off hundreds. We set up an old table at the top of the back drive, laid them out and sold a bunch to nearly every car that came past. We collected a massive £1.7s.6d, which in today's money would be about £90. That was good money, even divided three ways as far as we were concerned. When our mother found out she was delighted, took it off us and put the whole lot in the church collection plate at Malpas. I discovered what dumfounded felt like for the first time; now, a little far fetched I admit, I use that one episode to tell people why I have never earned any proper money.

Finally her beliefs affected our schooling. From the age of eight we were bundled off to boarding schools for two thirds of the year. Looking back now, I can feel and taste and smell the two schools I was sent to; these virtual memories are still quite horrible. The first was a taster aged seven – Hampton House, eight miles up the road. It was a rambling, faux Tudor mansion with some playing fields. I don't remember much of it but the classrooms and dining room were dark and smelt of dust and floor polish and well cooked cabbage. In my head are film snapshots of the green potatoes we had for lunch and the utility green walled changing rooms with their smell, and crying every Sunday night and Monday morning at home before I was dragged off there. This is where I learnt to read so there was an upside. During this time my parents were looking for a good Catholic boarding school for Jonathan and myself. They eventually came up with a place in Seaford, Sussex, over two hundred miles away on the south coast. Someone they didn't know very well had told them that this was the place where all the top aristocratic Catholic families in Europe sent their children. From my mother's point of view this sounded fine and they just committed themselves and us on his recommendation, without even visiting the place. If they had done, they might well have thought again. For us it was little short of Hell on Earth, and for the people who ran it, this indeed was their intention. It was called Ladycross. Years later when the school was running out of money (not a surprise), Jonathan had a letter from the school asking him to send a £100 or whatever he could afford to keep the place open. He wrote back and said he would send them a £100 if they promised to close the place down – it was that bad. Luckily for them I was never asked. I would have got a can of petrol, driven down there and burnt the place down. It was a place that should be forgotten, but I will probably remember it as I lie dying.

# 6 – DESCENT INTO HELL

There are more film clips now – standing on Crewe station aged eight wearing brown shorts and brown shoes that were too small and hurt my toes, sitting with my mother in a carriage and the smoke from the steam engine passing the window as we rattled and puffed through the countryside up[15] to London, hardly eating the lunch in my grandmother's gloomy flat in Kensington because of the apprehension, and then taking a taxi to Victoria Station, where I and a hundred glum small boys wearing identical uniforms mingled in a noisy tangle of luggage, parents and brightly smiling teachers from the school. Around us hundreds of other small boys, going to other schools in the area, added to the confusion and noise of the trains as they rumbled and whistled under the echoing dome of the station. I felt what I imagined a chicken must feel the second before a

---

[15] Until the 1970s it was fashionable, regardless of whether you lived in the north or south of the UK, to go *up* to London. Even higher than London were Oxford and Cambridge Universities which you also went *up* to even from London. You went *down* to London and Cheshire from Oxford and Cambridge and *down* to Cheshire from London.

gnarled fist breaks its neck – paralytic fear. Of course I couldn't show it as my mother kissed me goodbye and left me in the charge of the smiling teachers. For the next four years, and three times a year, I would sink slowly into this slough of gloom and despair as the new term approached. Once at Ladycross I would blub into my pillow for two or three days, as did most of the other boys, until we all got used to the routine.

Of course the smiling teachers smiled for as long as it took the trains to pull out of the station. I don't remember a teacher smiling at all at Ladycross for the next four years apart from the sports days when the parents came or didn't come to visit. Well maybe Mr Holmes smiled. He was the history teacher – the man I loathed more than anyone else. He looked rather like Reinhard Heydrich, Hitler's deputy in Czechoslovakia, with the same pointed nose and thick lips and smarmed down hair. He was tall to us but probably no more than five foot four. He always smiled just before he walloped us on the back of the head with a flat hand. Sometimes you didn't see it coming as he would creep up from behind and then – thwack!

Once a week he would test us on history dates – specifically on the kings and queens of England. By my second year in Mr Holmes's history class I was getting forty out of forty. This was the only time in my scholastic career that I consistently got full marks. Even now, without checking, I can tell you that Steven and Matilda ruled from 1135-1154, a useful snippet for a sophisticated dinner party conversation. I just didn't like being thwacked on the back of the head.

There was nothing funny about Ladycross at all; the ethos adhered to extreme Catholic dogma – the only way to Heaven was through pain, mortification and suffering, which tied in nicely with my mother's viewpoint.

Occasionally there were brief respites like going home at the end of term and messing about in the bushes at the bottom of the playing fields and even roller skating, but they only emphasized the unpleasantness and mild torture which took up the rest of the time.

At mealtimes we would have to stay silent for the first ten minutes until a bell was rung. This was torment for small boys. Even worse was the food itself, which was indescribably horrible. The only edible food I can remember was the thin sausage on a piece of greasy fried bread we had on Saturday mornings, and the sweets and chocolate we could buy in the tuck shop once a week.

At tea times there would be a process called 'Milk and Bread.' We would all line up in the corridors silently facing the wall. On the order to turn, a trolley loaded with small bottles of milk would rattle past and we would take one. Right behind it was another trolley loaded with half slices of bread smeared with margarine. Now this bread could sometimes be a week old – I kid you not – and each day would be sprayed with atomized water to stop it going rock solid. I can still smell it today and it's the smell of bread mould, mixed with the smell of a dustbin when you take the lid off. We weren't allowed to talk. Well we couldn't really talk as the bread was so revolting that all our wits were fully engaged in masticating it. One day I ventured into a back kitchen and found the bread stash piled up on the trolley. It was covered with damp tea cloths. I lifted one up and there on a slice was a dead mosquito, and on another a slick of hardened raspberry jam. At least I think that's what it was.

During the last year at Ladycross aged twelve I summoned up enough courage to complain about the food to the headmaster's wife, who appeared to have a little more humanity than any of the teachers. It was, in the short term, a very bad decision. I should have found one of the other boys to do the job. The aforementioned expedition to inspect the bread was part of my plan, but anyway shortly afterwards I was summoned to the headmaster's study. Now for venial offences, as in this case complaining about the food, a severe thrashing on each hand with a tailor made thick leather strap called The Tolly, was the norm. It was usually three whacks with The Tolly on each hand but wow did it hurt! The usual remedy was to get your friends to fill up a washbasin of cold water ready because there was no way you could do anything with your hands for hours afterwards. For more serious offences like cheating in exams or thumping Burgess major, you would be caned on the bottom; luckily I avoided this. Because I had no idea that I was to be beaten, I'd taken no precautions with the washbasin and so I was in double-pain-mode for the rest of the day. I suppose Mr Tolly invented the damn thing. Maybe he's on a list somewhere together with Dr Guillotine and Alfred P Southwick, the dentist who invented the electric chair.

An even bigger surprise though, was that within a couple of days the food suddenly got better. We had real fried eggs for breakfast and strawberries at lunch time! None of the other boys could believe it and thought they were dreaming. I was unable to put two and two together and thought it was a trick to relax us before we were all taken outside and shot, and then I'd get the blame again. But it was for real! Typically, there was a sting in the tail; at the end of term my father told me that the school bill had increased by £2000 or something similar. The whole episode was quite extraordinary when I think about it. How come I got thrashed for suggesting something that was almost immediately implemented?

The hundred and twenty boys at Ladycross were

divided into three sections. The twenty smallest boys from five to seven had their own white bungalow called Whipsnade in the grounds. Some of the youngest were day boys who lived in Seaford. But there were a few, like my brother Jonathan, just seven, who were sent there as boarders. From eight years old you landed up in The Zoo, which was the Lower School, and from ten to twelve you moved to the Upper School. I started out in The Zoo, which was a large wooden hut beyond the roller skating rink, where thirty of us would play and change for games and generally make a lot of noise. It was a light and airy place as opposed to the main building, which was dark and gloomy, where we went for other stuff like classes, eating and sleeping. From ten upwards we progressed to the Upper School, where everything went on in the main building.

The film clips are getting longer now with movement and sound, and one or two sequences have more than one scene in them. There was a grown up dining room with pictures of past headmasters on the wall and a wooden parquet floor. When the bell went for us to talk, the cacophony was sensational. It was impossible to hear yourself speak for two minutes; perhaps they had a point about the no-talk rule.

The classrooms for the Lower School upstairs had high windows you couldn't see out of, but in the Upper School's rooms downstairs, there was a view out over the playing fields to the South Downs. The rooms had fluorescent lighting, which used to give me at least one headache a week; I would be rendered useless and sometimes have to throw up and go to sleep at my desk and the Matron, called Miss Dock, a cynical little woman with a gravelly smoker's voice and a face like a frog, would accuse me of not going to the lavatory enough, and grudgingly give me half an aspirin and sometimes send me to bed. She had not one iota of sentiment and from her I learnt the expression 'cry wolf.' I didn't know what it meant, but quite frankly I couldn't give a toss. She wore an old fashioned navy blue dress and a large nun-like white hat. I suspect that she was not a real matron at all, and had probably been in charge of a group of anti aircraft gun batteries during the war. Her side-kick was called Sister Hughes, and although superior in rank, was really quite a pleasant old woman. She was tall with a slight stoop and wore a pink dress and a little white hat. She really had worked in hospitals, but maybe because she dithered a lot and sometimes couldn't remember your name, she erred on the side of humanity and sentiment, and sent you to bed after dishing out a little bit of every medicine in the dispensary. I liked Sister Hughes and was always relieved when she was on duty.

Once a week these two would supervise the routine known as 'Rhubarb and Soda.' The authorities were obsessed with our bowel movements and had developed an inflexible strategy for dealing with Constipation. The first stage was this revolting spoonful of pinky brown liquid that we queued up for. I guess at one point in its life it had been rhubarb, but I've no idea what it was by the time we drank it. It was far worse than a wallop around the head, but not quite as bad as The Tolly. There was a bucket by the wall for retching into just in case it was too much. If you did retch into it you were given another spoonful, and for some reason this usually stayed down. I've no idea if it worked or how, or if indeed it really was for Constipation, but I seldom suffered from this dire affliction. It usually went the other way as I was always in trouble and literally *scared* shitless.

The second line of attack against Constipation was

'Plus and Minus.' Every day, except Sundays, we would line up yet again and report to the on-duty teacher. He or she would have an exercise book with squared pages and against our names would write plus (+) or minus (-) depending on whether we had experienced a normal Evacuation or not. If our efforts made the lavatory bowl look like a painting by Jackson Pollock, it was a double plus (+ +), and if we had been sitting there for twenty minutes making grunting noises, it was a double minus (- -). At either end of this spectrum there were two more possible notations that are difficult to reproduce here. At one end there was double minus with a ring round it, which meant you hadn't been for a week and had a large pink circle printed on your bum cheeks. Then there was double plus with a ring round it, which meant you probably had cholera.

The authorities inspected and correlated all this information, more than likely on an abacus as computers were not yet invented, to decide whether you needed a double dose of Rhubarb and Soda. This was where we learnt to lie with justification as the last thing we wanted was a double dose of Rhubarb and Soda.

Most of the staff were awful – specimens of humanity that had drifted through the private school system after the war and been washed up as flotsam at Ladycross. Coupled with their differing peccadilloes they were also Catholic, secure or so they thought, in their invincibility as the soldiers of God. There were one or two exceptions – literally – and that was all.

Miss Barnett was in charge of The Zoo. She was Irish with reddish salt and pepper hair held in a bun. She'd never married. Her favourite weapon was a foot long ruler that she administered on the back of your hand, sharp edge down, for the slightest misdemeanor. She was gloomy and glum and disapproved of any humour in her pupils. God was always on her mind, and this must have weighed her down. We must have weighed her down too – the smell, the noise, the disruption – when all she wanted was a quiet dark room and contemplation with a prayer book, and no doubt occasional relief from the polished handle of her hair brush. She should have been a nun – a nun with a bun, but no bun in the oven. Poor woman. I feel sorry for her now.

God may have been on *her* mind, but certainly wasn't uppermost on the mind of the school priest. He spoke with an Irish lilt too, and was tall and well built, swarthy with a five o'clock shadow and the matinee idol looks of a Hollywood film star; he also had the charisma to go with it. He reminded me of Gregory Peck and he was popular among staff and boys alike. If Miss Barnett thought she was in the wrong place, from his point of view he couldn't have been in a better place. *His* main interest was small boys, and his name rather appropriately was Father Tinker. He wore a long black cassock with nothing on underneath it. My mother got very excited one sport's day when he was substituted for a father during the parents' race and his cassock flew up to reveal his hairy bare bottom as he raced away from her towards the finish line. She couldn't stop talking about it all day. Ironically as it turned out, at that moment I think she rather fancied Father Tinker.

He was responsible for our spiritual welfare and said Mass in the school chapel twice a week on Wednesdays and Sundays which we had to attend. Added to the Sunday purgatory he ran another show called Benediction, which was also compulsory and was an all singing, all Latin affair in the evening with a lot of smells and bells and organ music. His popularity with the boys relied on his bags of cherries and jelly babies. He had a garret room at the top of the main school

72

building that was only accessible via a steep staircase. Every now and again most of the eleven to thirteen year olds would be invited up to his room one at a time, especially the blond ones. He would sit us down and pull his chair up close, take our hands in his and ask us if, during the previous week we had had any 'impure thoughts' or done any 'impure deeds.'

At that stage in my development it was quite difficult *not* to have had impure thoughts. Back home in the holidays when I couldn't have been more than nine, our mother and father had gone out and it was the cook's day off, so the gardener's daughter had come in to baby sit. She was about fourteen and responsible enough, and had given us all a bath; she had put the other two to bed and was walking with me back down the passage to my room when she suddenly fainted just like that and lay on the floor. Even at that age something must have been stirring deep in my pre-pubescent loins, and hers too I guess; she was moaning quietly as I gingerly bent down and pulled up her skirt and even now can recollect she was wearing pink cotton knickers. I went no further, although my curiosity was egging me on, because her moaning was getting a little louder; she then opened her eyes and recovered remarkably quickly before putting me to bed, so yes, I sure did have impure thoughts. As for impure deeds that goes without saying, although Father Tinker's definition was probably different to mine. Practically every morning since I was minus one I'd have a stiffy and fondle it first thing in the morning whilst still abed – it felt good I suppose. I don't think I was associating it with girls at the time. That didn't come till around now – aged eleven or twelve. To be honest his question and my affirmation, repeated every time I went to see him, is the only connection I have to remind me of this early-morning occurrence. To a man we all did it, holding on to our willies – every morning. It was a security thing and no more significant than cleaning our teeth, so most of us have forgotten we did it, or didn't even notice when we did do it. But to Father Tinker it was the trigger for his excitement and a chance for my imagination to run riot, seamlessly making the connection between a stiffy and the question he asked me: 'Do you think about girls when you do it?'

'Er yes father, I suppose I do,' and of course I carried on doing it. He may have asked me if I thought about boys; I really can't remember if he did or didn't. If I did think about boys it certainly wasn't while I was playing with my willie. It was more likely to have been worrying about whether Greenwell was going to give me some of his birthday cake at tea-time or if I could get away with bashing Burgess major in the chops again. To be frank, playing with my willie and girls seemed a rather pleasant new association, and I must confess I haven't grown out of it.

Father Tinker would then offer me the bag of cherries with one hand and his other hand would be in his cassock pocket-without-a-pocket playing with his own stiffy. I'd given the right answer and my reward was a handful of wonderful juicy red cherries. What bliss for me! What bliss for Father Tinker! After eating as many cherries as I could stuff in, he dismissed me. To me, he did little else than hold my hand and masturbate with the other. I hadn't a clue what he was doing, and I never mentioned my encounters to anyone else, probably because I thought I'd lose out on the cherry ration. Nowadays, in the present frenzy of outing historic child sex abuse, he'd probably be caught in the net if he was still alive. I don't expect he is. He'd have to be over a hundred and at that age he couldn't possibly be doing it any longer.

Mr McCurnock, the PE teacher and the third of the

Irish trio, tried a different tack. He was swarthy too, but ugly, although I suspect he wanted to give the impression he was a lady's man. Built like a gorilla, he had black bushy eyebrows that met in the middle and a thick head of black hair that started just above his eyebrows and was swept back in a brilliantined slick. Occasionally this hairdo would fail and the end slicks would hang down round his face, making him look even more terrifying. He nearly always wore a brown corduroy jacket, sometimes even while taking us for PE. He was also in charge of us while we were in the wooden building called the Zoo, where we changed for PE and for games, and generally messed around in our free time. We were all frightened of Mr McCurnock. If you had done something wrong he would call you out in front of everyone else. He used two methods of torture. The first was to grab whatever hair he could hold onto just above both our ears with forefingers and thumbs, and twist the hair round and round. This was painful and used to make our eyes water. His other trick was both violent and sinister. Same as before, he would call out a first timer who had committed a wrong doing in Mr McCurnock's view, and carry on talking to the assembled crowd without appearing to notice the boy's existence. The boy standing before him for the first time would have had no idea what was coming next. Without any warning his left hand would come in at speed and smack him hard on the side of his head. A split second later his right hand would come in and do likewise – a double whammy that was short of rendering him unconscious, but enough to stun him and shock those watching. As he reeled back into the throng, no doubt with the same high pitched whistling noise I experienced, Mr McCurnock just carried on talking as if nothing had happened.

I've no idea if he got pleasure out of doing this to us; only he would have known that. I'm pretty sure that he got pleasure out of his next trick. Before we changed for games in the Zoo, he would order all thirty of us to strip naked for 'medical inspection' and get into three lines. It took me some time to work this out but he would then shout 'Back! Back!' He'd then inspect each boy by having a quick fiddle with his front bits and shout 'Next!' Of course, as we had all been squeezed up against each other some of us had willies pointing skywards, and this must have been the object of the exercise for Mr McCurnock.

Sixty years ago physical and sexual abuse was endemic in our schools, and it's sometimes difficult to make connections with the past and understand why teachers did what they did, or how we put up with it when it was done to us. Call it control, brainwashing, tribal ritual or whatever you want; aged eight and nine it was easy to instill fear into us, to make us do what we were told and not question it. I'm sure, in light of the historic abuse cases (including sexual abuse) that are emerging now, many boys really were traumatized. I never was and I don't know why not – I always tried to make a joke out of the mild torture that was meted out all the way through my school career. Perhaps I was lucky and psychologically insensitive. If something really awful had happened to me, maybe this would have been different and impossible to write about now. Three years later, when I was at Eton, I was walking with a friend past our classrooms. We were both fourteen. He said he had to go in and get a book and five minutes later he came out crying and in a hysterical state and could hardly speak. A random man from Slough, who had just wandered into the empty classroom, had grabbed hold of him and done something to him that I can't even put down here. The poor boy left the school a few days later and never came back. The man, who had a record of sex offences was arrested and sent to prison.

One day back at Ladycross in the middle of term time and about a year and a half before I left, there were rumours flying round the school. Father Tinker and Mr McCurnock had both left the day before. This was good news that Mr McCurnock was gone, but it was a pity about the cherries. Nobody knew what the reasons were, but I suspect an older boy had spilt the beans and that was that. How far these two had gone I'll never know but I expect it was more serious than what I've written here. The physical abuse alone would not have been enough. That was part of the curriculum.

There was, however, one master at Ladycross I have to thank. Bernie Fillingham taught us Maths in the sunniest classroom. I don't remember the Maths as most of the time I was looking out of the window at the South Downs and the clouds chasing each other across the sky. He was a thick set man in a tweed jacket and an untidy mop of black hair. He was short sighted and wore wire rimmed glasses. He was always doing conjuring tricks and producing eggs from behind your ear and making the chalk disappear and then finding it in your pocket. He was also in charge of the school play and cast me early on as an all singing all dancing waif in a dress. The play was called The Rose and The Ring which he adapted from a Thackeray novel; it was a fairy story about a rose and a ring. There was a real kitted out stage at the end of the gym, complete with lights, curtains and a green room, and I loved the smell and the nerves and the excitement that went with it. Mr Fillingham was a talented man and put everything, including his magic, into the lavish productions. There would be smoke and bangs and flashing lights and sticks of Leichner make up

– there was music and sound effects too, which he recorded from gramophone records and then edited on a big tape recorder. This was then blasted out through enormous speakers on either side of the stage – he was one of Nature's polymaths and inspired me with all he had to offer apart from the maths.

During the holidays when we went to Manchester to see the dentist, I'd be taken off to explore the second hand radio shops by the commissionaire at my father's office – Chief Petty Officer Fleming RN Retired. He had been in charge of the engine room on a frigate escorting the Atlantic convoys during the war. The ship had been torpedoed and capsized, and he and the engine room crew had been trapped in the upturned hull. Those that were left alive kept tapping and somehow were cut out, but the experience had left its mark on him; he was always short of breath and spoke very quietly, but he was also keen on radios and stuff like that, so we would sift through piles of old loudspeakers, headphones, microphones, and rolls of wire to build a basic communications kit. One time I also bought a crystal set and a soldering iron. I'd take all this stuff back to Ladycross and attempt to put it together. Mr Fillingham would help me. Eventually I got the crystal set to work; I was allowed to mess with it during playtime but I also remember taking it to bed and listening to it under the blankets.

I've hardly mentioned work and that's simply because I don't remember doing any. The school reports I've just dug out which smell a bit mouldy now, state generally that I was pleasant enough and quite intelligent but could have tried harder, and then there is a note from the headmaster at the bottom of my last report – I was twelve and a half – which says 'He has stopped growing up.' So that is what arrested development means. I'm shocked. Blimey. How many years have I spent swanning through life aged twelve and a half? Strangely, I've always told people I felt like a twelve year old and I've never read this report until now.

It was always very difficult to nod sagely with an air of maturity and look concerned aged twenty or thereabouts when someone told me that Great Aunt Fanny has fallen over again, or in the context of a wider world that it was quite possible that 'unless we fight, we are going to lose the next Election.' This was a random one that came in from the side as Mrs. Grant, a Conservative to her toenails and our next door neighbour, was kindly driving me to London from Cheshire. I was twenty three and it was the first time I would have been allowed to vote. I said something like 'I think I'll vote for Winnie the Pooh.' We were doing about sixty five in her mini-van on the middle lane of the M1 with cars and trucks thundering past us on both sides, flashing their lights and hooting. Without any warning she swerved across the inside lane on to the hard shoulder, screeched to a halt and turned to me with a look of barely concealed fury. 'I think you should get out and walk.' We were still seventy miles from London.

'Er,' oh shit! 'No, I'm sorry I was only joking.'

'Voting is no joking matter,' said Mrs Grant, emphasizing each word as though speaking to a small child. 'I don't really want anyone in this car who doesn't take it seriously. I really think, Simon, it's time you took a more responsible attitude.' We had stopped just past a concrete bridge on which someone had plastered in dripping white paint 'Marples must go!' Ernest Marples had been Transport Minister back in 1959 when he had opened the M1. He'd also employed a blubber lipped sidekick by the name of Dr. Beeching to destroy the railway network, but I was getting sidetracked.

'No, I understand. I'll think about it seriously,' I mumbled, trying at the same time to work out how they had managed to paint graffiti on such a tall bridge. She pulled out into the traffic without so much as a glance in her rearview mirror. I was quite relieved in one way as I had a hole in my shoe and it was raining. In another way I was slightly worried as she drove like a maniac for the rest of the journey, without speaking.

# 7 – SAVED FROM HELL

Back at Ladycross things were improving. Mr McCurnock and Father Tinker had gone. The food was better. I was not as homesick once I'd been there for a day or so at the start of each term, and I had a few good friends. To make friends was quite difficult as many of them came from France, Spain and Italy and were the sons of serious continental aristocrats, who did not gel readily with Anglo-Saxon commoners. There was a Gereda, son of a Spanish Marquis and closely related to the last King of Spain, a Gelardi from Italy, whose father was grandly Cavaliere Ufficiale della Repubblica di Italia. His family made biscuits or chocolates or something like that. Then there were the four Montalembert brothers, aristos to the very ends of their aquiline noses, who were French. They were designated Montalembert max, ma, mi[16] and min, all short for maximus, major, minor and minimus. Their father, who didn't really do much was quite poor, especially after he had put his four sons through school, but they still

---

[16] Pronounced 'may' and 'my'

maintained an aloofness befitting grand old frayed-at-the-edges French aristocrats. Montalembert min's uniform was particularly frayed by the time it had been passed down through three of his brothers. There were others too from all over Catholic Europe and as far afield as the Philippines. Sometimes it was like the Tower of Babel as a group of boys from the same country would arrive unable to speak a word of English, babbling away in their own tongue. On the other hand there was a French boy, whose name I forget and who looked like a terrified rabbit, arriving aged ten alone and desperately homesick, and unable to speak a word for the first few days. By the end of term he was quite fluent and was making as much noise as the rest of us.

I was also starting to think about girls and from ten onwards had a photograph of my first girlfriend above my bed, together with a photo of Pier Angeli, a beautiful Italian starlet, given to me by one of the Italian boys – they didn't waste time. Both of these loves were purely ones of the heart as no connection had yet been made between them, loins and lust. Father Tinker sowed that seed, so to speak, and at roughly the same time it was the turn of a boy, strangely enough called Rodgers, who introduced me shockingly to the basic essentials of full sexual intercourse, or as he put it rather bluntly 'fucking.' He was well beyond his years and his voice was starting to break. I listened open mouthed as he explained the procedure, first with a gesture involving the fingers of both hands, and when I asked what he meant by that, giving me a short lecture that he had obviously delivered to many other boys already, peppered with words I had never heard before. It was a revelation, and all that had come before was now slotting into place. In fact it slotted into place so well that I spent a lot more time than I should have done in Mr

Fillingham's maths class, day-dreaming and looking out at the clouds chasing each other across the Sussex sky. Occasionally they would catch each other up and become entwined in an inextricable embrace of nebulous passion.

Perhaps this was the moment when I stopped working because it was about the time when the headmaster wrote in my report 'he has stopped growing up'; he also said it was unlikely I'd pass the Common Entrance Exam into Eton. This exam was set by an independent board for boys going on from their prep schools to their chosen public schools. 'Prep school' here means 'preparatory' and a private fee paying school, whereas 'public school' is actually a *secondary* private fee paying school. It's a bit confusing when one compares private education with free public UK state education, both primary and secondary, which accounts for 93% of all our schools. I hope you're keeping up here. State schools are funded for the main part by the state, whereas private schools are funded for the main part by parents. This privileged private education system has never been politicized big time, although there have been efforts to interfere with it; the state system, unfortunately, has been interfered with so much by successive governments, that it has never been able to attain the giddy heights of success achieved by the private sector. Naturally the argument continues, reinforced by the accusations of elitism, money and privilege, but here's the rub: if state education was as good as private, there would be no more argument and no need for the private system to exist. Of course this is a generalization and there are countless independent private schools that don't come anywhere near the high standard of many state schools. It is still a fact though that Oxford and Cambridge universities accept 40% of their intake from the independent private schools when these schools only educate 7% of the children in the UK.

Something is surely wrong here. Is it solely a case of poorer education in state schools? Is it a problem with cost where the tuition fees alone are £9000 a year for each undergraduate? It appears to be a social thing; Oxford and Cambridge are still considered to be elite and only accessible for rich people who can afford them. Of course they are elite, academically elite because only the brainiest children can go there, but it is a misconception to think that clever children with parents on low incomes can't go there too. They can, as both these universities and the state will now subsidise and in many cases pay all their fees. So these two universities stand there with their arms open wide (opened partly by external pressure) saying come on you lot – if you're clever enough we want you. There are no statistics to prove the theory that it is a class thing, but people from poorer working class backgrounds still mistrust what they perceive to be institutions 'designed for bloody toffs – so why don't you get a proper job as a plumber or a bricklayer.' Things are improving but it's a slow process.

Back in 1959 this stuff was way outside my orbit, as I sat looking at the clouds and chewing the top of my fountain pen, trying vainly to translate into Latin 'Caesar marched into Gaul with a large army of ten thousand men on a white horse.' Little did I realize how important this Common Entrance exam was to my father. All I was thinking about was how to get stronger reception for my crystal set. Would the bed springs make a better aerial? Would Pier Angeli ever kiss me? (They did and she didn't). The exam took in Latin, French, English, Geography, History and Maths and possibly Scripture, but I can't remember that for sure. It went on for about a week and a dozen or so of us took it in Mr Fillingham's sunny classroom in the Summer term. The other boys were all booked for Catholic schools around the country; I was the only one sitting for Eton. Working on the assumption that it's better to tell a boy to do his best and go for it than to tell him he hasn't got a snowball's chance in hell, my teachers and father did just that, and I was quite unaware of my shortcomings. Two weeks later the result came in. I'd failed. There must have been a lot going on behind my back that I didn't know about, but it never filtered down to me. The end of term came and so did the summer holidays. On sunny days I would wander round the fields or sit in a hide and shoot pigeons. When it rained I would squelch through a muddy paddock at the back of the house down to the brook, which was not really a brook but a septic drain for the two farms above our house. It had that rather nasty smell and an oily film at the edge of the milky water, but after rain it didn't smell quite so bad. I would get a spade from the garden shed and dig some clay out of the bank and build a large dam, which would then burst as the pressure built up. It was quite therapeutic and I'd sometimes let my brother help.

Then there was the Pony Club camp in some racing stables up the road, where fifty of us would camp for a week, and ostensibly learn to ride better, with my mother and other instructors shouting at us twice a day as we dutifully trotted round them. I had little intention of improving my riding skills, and was only interested in the girls. It was mainly just true love and the occasional kiss, but it was so exciting. At the end of that summer holiday my father drove me up to stay with some good friends who used to rent a lodge in Scotland. He had a long wheelbase Land Rover, and it took us two days and a night to get there. As well as guns and luggage, he also took a small leather case full of maps, which I had to refer to on the way up. There were about seventeen of them for this particular journey and he'd selected them from his collection of eighty six. (I know because I still have them.) We spent the night in a grim hotel in Grangemouth, a noisy oil refinery town with much belching smoke and bright lights on the Firth of Forth. We sat down to eat in a near empty dining room as the rather large and intimidating waitress with big feet brought us the set dinner. All I remember were the runner beans, which came with the main course. They were watery and limp and most of the colour had been cooked out of them. I looked at them and they looked back at me; sticking out of the middle of this lukewarm pile of pale grey sludge was one grey eye – the head of a galvanized plasterboard nail. It was about an inch long and bent. 'Excuse me, my son appears to have found a nail in his beans,' says my father to the intimidating waitress, trying his best not to laugh.

'He looks like he could do with the iron,' says she without hesitation and flounced off, which made us laugh even more as she was rather too large and too old to be flouncing. We wondered whether the nail was a permanent fixture that the chef kept in the kitchen for all Sassenachs[17], who arrived late at night fully expecting a late supper.

Once up at the lodge in Inverness-shire, which was down a twelve mile drive near Grantown-on-Spey and rented every year by our neighbours the Grants, we would tramp up and down the mountains shooting grouse. This was a difficult pastime to master; my legs were very short and the heather was very long. Most of the time was taken

---

[17] Derived from Gaelic 'Sasunnach' meaning 'Saxon' – a mildly abusive term for the English.

up fighting the vegetation. If it wasn't the heather it was trying to climb out of wet peat hags with a loaded gun. Fortunately my father had taught me never to push the safety catch off unless I was about to fire, which I guessed saved quite a few lives. Owing to my very bad aim, quite a few grouse were saved too. Somebody always managed to kill something, which we took back to the lodge to eat for dinner.

The summer holidays were soon over and I went back to Ladycross. I was told that I could take the exam one more time the next summer, but I had to work. This was about as likely as getting a dead parrot to sing God Save the Queen. It wasn't going to happen at Ladycross. I was even threatened with a Catholic public school where the pass mark would have been lower than that for Eton. This was the fate my brother eventually suffered. He spent five more years at a Catholic public school called Douai. It closed down in 1999. But even the threat of five more years being bludgeoned by Catholic dogma failed to make an impression, and a week before the end of this winter term I was called to the headmaster's study after breakfast. 'Your mother is coming to pick you up at lunchtime. You're leaving, Dewhurst.' I was speechless. Wow, and before lunch too! Miss Dock had already packed my case, and all I had to do was say goodbye to my few friends. I said goodbye to my brother too. His reaction was 'you lucky sod!' My mother picked me up and we packed up the car. I couldn't wait to get away. It was all a dream surely? The final scene in Alan Parker's film, Midnight Express, when Billy Hayes walks through the outside door of the prison and off down the street, and then leaps into the air at the end, is exactly how I felt during those last few hours. It was a pinch myself time until we had driven out of the school gates and were back in the real world. I never looked back.

Ladycross closed down and died in 1977 with hardly a

whimper. The headmaster had retired some years before as the supply of new boys under his watch dwindled to a trickle and eventually stopped. Thankfully, his dream to recreate a twentieth century Catholic version of Dotheboys Hall[18] failed. Of course it was never quite as bad as my memory suggests. Nobody died of malnutrition or from being beaten too hard, but I guess the more sensitive parents began to notice that their children were not growing up to be the sons they had expected – either emotionally or academically. Physically we were in better shape after I complained about the food but there was a cost to our parents. In short they were not getting value for money; little by little the word got around that the headmaster and teachers, who were all smiles at Victoria Station, were not quite whom they seemed back in Stalag Luft XIII[19]. In the annual school magazine under the heading 'The Daily Timetable' there was an entry '4.30pm – Milk and Biscuits.' Well, even aged eleven that seemed to me to be stretching things a bit when it should have said '4.30pm – Milk and Bread.' What a difference there is here between these two simple words – bread and biscuits!

---

[18] Charles Dickens' version of scholastic Hell in 'Nicholas Nickleby' and based on a real school of the period.

[19] A German prison camp for airmen in World War 2.

# 8 – THE GENTLEMAN FACTORY

Way back in the December of 1959 as we drove home to Cheshire the memories of Ladycross were forgotten in a flash, well hidden under fifty years of silt, until I dredged them up recently. All I had to think of now were the holidays. Meanwhile my father had been tearing out what little hair he had left, worrying what to do with his wayward son and heir. He eventually found a retired housemaster, James West, from Shrewsbury School, who was willing to take me on as a pupil for six months and cram enough knowledge into my reluctant brain to get a pass in the Common Entrance later in the summer. He was a professional and had somehow got hold of all the information he needed to prove to himself that I was worth teaching. Colonel West was a miracle worker. He taught me how to learn – something I'd never done before. At the end of the Christmas holidays I was packed off to his family cottage near Pontesbury in Shropshire, where I lived for the next six months with him and his wife. They had two daughters, who would come to stay during their school holidays. Needless to say I fell in love with the eldest, who was twenty and at university, but it was all from a distance and I don't think she ever knew. His wife was lovely and bustling and made very good cakes. He was a big man with a grey walrus moustache and he smoked a pipe. He was quite gruff, but when he spoke you had to listen because he said every word with such deliberation. When he said 'Caesar marched into Gaul with a large army of ten thousand men on a large horse,' it became a scene from a film, full of colour and noise. You could hear the marching feet, the grumbling soldiers and the horses whinnying. There was no need to look out of the window at the clouds chasing each other. It was all happening as we sat at his dining room table.

Of course it was one on one teaching and we had a lot of time, but he had the talent to make it all so interesting. It was only head to head for about four hours a day in the morning. The rest of the day was free, apart from an hour's prep in the evening, and as winter floated into spring and then spring into summer, I was allowed to explore the surrounding countryside on my bicycle. Sometimes I would go home at weekends, but the film clips from this time are all from deepest Shropshire and the West family, the buzzing heady heat of a summer when I didn't have a care in the world apart from my teenage crush on Betsy West. In June I sat the exam in a schoolroom at Shrewsbury with some other boys and two weeks later learnt that I'd passed. My mother and father were mighty relieved and later in July we took a trip down to Eton to look the place over. My father hadn't been back for forty three years so it was a Memory Lane trip for him and a chance for us to meet my housemaster, who was responsible, with help, for fifty boys' domestic, physical and emotional well-being during their five years at the school. We spent some time in the tailor's shop as well, where I had to stretch upwards without standing on tip toe, so that my father wouldn't have to splash out on a bum freezer, which boys smaller than me had to wear until they were tall enough.

Splash out on a bum freezer[20]? Etonspeak needs a small dictionary for translation into normal English. I guess it's the same in schools everywhere but this particular school has had five hundred years to develop a unique and arcane language of its own, as well as some fairly odd customs that have been copied and adopted by other schools the world over. Visitors too, from around the world, flock to this small, strange community stranded in between Slough and Windsor, to see boys and beaks[21] continually scuttling in and out of very old brick buildings wearing the oddest looking clothes. The beaks all wear dark suits, which is quite usual, topped by white shirts, starched wing collars and a white bow tie, which is not so usual. At certain times of the day they are required to wear their graduation gowns as well, preferably not while they're riding their bicycles as they tend to get caught in the spokes.

Today all the boys still wear black tail coats, black waistcoat, black pin-striped trousers, black shoes and white shirts with starched white collars. For ties they wear a thin strip of white material with a hole in the middle, which is fixed onto the front stud holding the collar and shirt together, and then tucked in behind the shirt. This material used to be tied as a thin bow tie and the ends shoved under the collar, but this habit died out in the sixties as we were in too much of a rush getting up in the morning. Important, more senior boys were

---

[20]  Eton Jacket – fat white stiff collar over a short black jacket, black waistcoat, pin-striped black trousers, white shirt, black tie.
[21]  Teachers – nearly all male

allowed to wear stick-ups[22] and white bow ties, as did all the boys in Pop[23], who were also allowed to wear coloured waistcoats.

Meanwhile in the tailor's shop my father was no doubt relieved that he was going to save some money on two bum freezer suits, which might only be worn for a half[24] or two. The tail suits could last up to three years, depending on how fast we grew, before buying another set. The last set could be used after we left for weddings and funerals etcetera, or if we decided to become undertakers. Why the school dress is so, I have no idea, and I don't think anyone else does either. It was standardized late in the nineteenth century and hasn't changed since. Around the school it didn't look too odd as everyone else was wearing one but when we went on missions to buy the latest Parade, Playboy or Men Only up in nearby Windsor, we stood out like the toffs most of us were. I suppose it got us used to wearing uniforms so that when we became field marshals, or rear admirals, or the Lord Great Chamberlain walking backwards in front of the Queen, it was a piece of cake. For the thousands of Koreans, Americans and Chinese tourists, disgorging from busses outside the College Chapel, the school dress does still have a quaint attraction, and is therefore a money spinner of sorts. What they really come for is to see and wander through the ancient buildings that were built by Henry VI back in the 1440s. He wanted to provide a school for seventy poor scholars who could then move on to his other pet project, Kings College, Cambridge. This has become somewhat ironic as many

---

[22] Wing collars
[23] The Eton Society – 40 self elected prefects
[24] A term or trimester – at one time there were only two terms a year – hence 'half'.

of the richest families in the world now cough up nearly £35,000 a year to send their children to Eton. To balance this, nearly twenty per cent of boys are subsidized by the school, which has become very rich in its own right. The original seventy scholars are still housed in the ancient buildings for free although most are not as poor as their predecessors. They have to wear short black gowns and they are mostly very clever, something which was not appreciated in my day. The scholars are known as tugs because the other boys used to overtake them in the street and pull on their gowns and then run away.

All the other boys were known as oppidans[25], and twelve hundred of them lived in houses of roughly fifty boys each in the surrounding conurbation that made up Eton.

Now that I had been fitted out with my two penguin suits, we made our way to lunch with my new housemaster, Fred Coleridge. He was a big man in every way. To me he was authority, something I was both terrified of and at odds with. He was six foot tall and wide too with a deep voice and a slightly gruff manner. As Bill Deedes, the journalist, later Lord Deedes, said of him as they went across France soon after D-day, 'Coleridge was a considerable man.' While in Brussels nearing Christmas they decided to have a slap up dinner together, and chose a whole filet of beef and a delicious sauce béarnaise to go with it. They were just starting their third plateful when they were interrupted by an officer, who had been given the job of prising all the officers out of the restaurants and night clubs as there was a flap on, and ordering everyone back to their units immediately. The Germans had invaded the Ardennes. Nothing was going to stop Fred – not even the Germans – especially while he was eating filet steak. They finished

---

[25] From the Latin 'oppidum' – town ie: the village of Eton

their dinner, he rang his superior, and they both got back the next morning.

Nobody messed with Fred but if they did it was never more than once. A good friend who was up to him[26] a few years before me had the temerity to try mobbing him up[27].

'What kind of jam did Caesar have for tea, sir?'[28]

'Clegg, isn't it?' says Fred quite amicably.

'Yes sir, that's me sir,' says Clegg smugly, still totally unaware of his impending fate.

'Well, would Me Sir kindly come up here.' At that Fred pushes back his chair from his kneehole desk with a closed panel across the front. 'Get in there' he says and Clegg gets down on his hands and knees and crawls into the small space under the desk. Fred pulls up his chair and for the next half hour Clegg is pinned between the panel and a pair of enormous knees and lower legs, while Fred rumbles on about the Second Gallic War. At the end of the div[29] Fred pushes back his chair and says 'You can go now.'

After lunch we were shown round the house which had only been built a few years before and was very modern with curving passages on three floors and fifty rooms with central heating. The houses were nearly always referred to by the initials of their housemaster – in my case FJRC. As most of the other houses were very old with coals fires in every room and creaking narrow staircases, we felt privileged. After all, even our own homes were mostly without central heating. Each room had a bed that folded up against the wall, a desk, an armchair, and an ottoman for putting dirty sports stuff in.

---

[26] 'up to him' – in his class
[27] Tease him to test his weaknesses
[28] 'Caesar adsum jam forte, Brutus aderat, Caesar sic in omnibus, Brutus sic in 'at' – schoolboy dog Latin.
[29] Short for 'division' or class

You opened and closed the ottoman lid as quickly as possible for obvious reasons, and it was a good idea to open and close the window during this operation too. Around the wall you could stick up posters of Bridget Bardot and Ursula Andress coming out of the sea wearing very little and hope Fred wouldn't tell you to take it down. He rarely did – I think he was quite keen to promote healthy heterosexuality in an all boys' school. Some boys hung pictures of hunting prints and pheasant shooting to remind them of the holidays and killing animals. At night you could put your shoes outside the door, and Harry the Bootman, would take them away and clean them and put them back the next morning. He was an upright ex sergeant-major who lived in Windsor and held court, talking mainly about football, in his boot room just inside the entrance.

On each of the three floors there was a maid, who kept the rooms clean, made our beds and even cooked our tea if she liked us. For yet more obvious reasons the boys' maids were all over sixty and some were quite frightening, but they all had their hearts in the right place; they had a retirement job for life and were not very well paid, but they had free board and lodging. Overseeing the boys' maids and our health was the Dame, who in olden days had been the landlady of independent boys' lodging houses before they were taken under the wing of the school authorities. We called her M'Dame; ours was a compact little Scots woman called Mrs Logan, whose husband had died some years before. She had her own flat with a small surgery, and although untrained as a nurse, she knew most of the tricks – like putting the thermometer under the hot tap while she bustled away to answer the telephone. A temperature of 106°F wasn't going to fool anybody. Most of the ailments she had to deal with were shortcomings in bodily hygiene, but should they evolve into more serious conditions such as boils, athlete's foot or scrot rot[30], she would send us to one of the two doctors' surgeries in the village. She was also responsible for the food, which varied from house to house. We would eat three meals a day in a large dining room, and the food in our house was very good. The fourth meal was tea, which we cooked ourselves in a kitchen on each floor. This was a pig-out meal and would consist of anything from a boiled egg to roast pheasant, depending on how long we had to cook it, and whom we could trample over to get to the kitchen first. We'd gang up in groups of three or four and mess together in one of our rooms. There was also a chance of a mid morning meal when there was a half hour break. The food shops at the top of Eton High Street did a roaring trade in sausages and chips and pies and stuff, and in the summer ice cream too, including Eton Mess[31] – strawberries, ice cream and meringue, topped off with more cream.

By this time on the conducted tour I began to realize that for the next five years I was going to be staying in a five star hotel or something quite similar. It seemed to me like paradise on earth, and as we drove back up north to our cold draughty house I was beginning to like the place already. I was unaware just then of Thomas Grey's poem, himself an old Etonian, 'Alas, regardless of their doom, the little victims play! No sense have they of ills to come, nor cares beyond today…'

The last weeks of the summer holidays whizzed by. When we weren't riding our ponies – still being shouted at by our mother during pony club camp week, I would

---

[30] You don't need to know
[31] Known as a 'strawberry mess' in the Sixties

spend the time damming the brook with Jonathan, or sitting in my hide in a freshly harvested corn field waiting for pigeons.

My father had introduced me to the killing game a few years before when I was about ten, sometime before our trip to Scotland. The weapon of death was a hammer operated four-ten double barrelled shotgun. It was very old and the inside of the barrels were pitted, but it made a loud bang and frightened many a pigeon. Building a hide out of sticks and straw was fun, and I took a kitchen chair and a sandwich and some chocolate down to the field and sat in it all day waiting for unsuspecting pigeons, which came to gorge themselves on the left over corn. First they would alight on a tree branch and then drop to the ground to start feeding. If I could see them up in the tree through the leaves then – bang! Small branches would fly off all around my aiming point and so would the pigeon. Occasionally I would hit one and it would drop to the ground in a cloud of feathers. Some days it was quite hot in the hide as the August sun beat down, but sitting there for five or six hours was strangely therapeutic and a lesson for future travelling while waiting hours for trains and planes, and sometimes even days for a lift by the side of a dusty desert road.

The killing got more involved when I went with my father to pheasant shoots, where the birds were driven out of the woods over a line of red faced men with guns. In the early days I wasn't allowed to stand with the guns and instead walked through the woods with the beaters, who whacked the undergrowth and trees with sticks and ululated in true country fashion in order to get the birds to fly. They weren't used to flying as the gamekeeper had been feeding them on the ground in their pens for the past three months like chickens, and it was quite a surprise for them to be told they had to fly. Meanwhile, outside the wood, the guns, in a well established dress code of woolen stockings, immaculate plus fours and flat hats or fedoras with feathers in them, would blast away at the squawking pheasants and any other flying fowl that happened to come out of the wood that day. Even ground hugging animals like rabbits and hares would come under fire if they had the temerity to get up and run while the guns were walking to and from the drive[32]. A pheasant, shot at height, resembles a furry cannonball as it falls through the air and hits the ground with quite a thump. Labradors and spaniels held on leads would be let off to pick up these dead birds or look for the wounded ones. Sometimes, when there were literally thousands of pheasants taking to the skies, the guns would be handed a second gun, already loaded up by a man standing behind him, and this process would continue until the barrels got too hot to hold, or the beaters whistle went to signal the end of the drive.

The carnage and noise is difficult to describe – the beaters ululating, the explosions, the whining dogs and the pheasants squawking and thumping to the ground made for a great film soundtrack. All it needed was a couple of helicopters, the Doors and some napalm to complete the picture.

Unfortunately, that never happened.

All this would probably be taking place on a cold winter's morning as the pheasant shooting season only lasts from October to February as it's considered unkind to shoot them during the breeding season. There would often be frost or snow on the ground and the guns out front with their attendant loaders and dog handlers and

---

[32] The location of the wood

wives could get very cold standing and waiting for the first whirr of wings and squawk of bird. After a mid-morning drive, Land Rover back doors would be opened up and an array of warming alcohol in silver cups handed round. Sloe gin and cherry brandy were the morning staples, and later at lunchtime we would drink more of the same, sitting down to enormous piles of rustic country food washed down with beer and wine, and finished off with port. Everyone would then go out again, warm and red faced to kill some more. It has remained a mystery why nobody ever shot anybody else, or even how they managed to stand up for the rest of the day.

I gave it all up when I was eighteen. I just didn't enjoy shooting animals for the pleasure of killing them.

Eventually the summer came to an end and it was time for a new adventure based in a five star hotel. I was really looking forward to it. I remember my father taking me out into the sparsely planted rose garden before we got into the car, and saying these fateful words, 'Well done on getting in old chap – now you can relax and have a good time, but remember there are a lot of silly buggers about.' With that all three of us, including my mother, piled into Vanessa the Vanguard and drove down to Eton. I have no idea what he meant at the time about the silly buggers, but I sure did understand the bit about relaxing and took it to heart. At the end of the first half I was bottom of the school of 1287 boys in trials[33], but there was a lot that happened before that.

---

[33] End of term exams

# 9 – A CHANGING WORLD

At the start of the sixties the western world was changing, and no more so than at Eton which operated within a disciplined yet liberal framework. Free thought and expression was always encouraged from the day we arrived, and always had been. It was very grown up in that respect. Stick to the rules and you would survive the course as long as you did enough work. Break them and be found out, or do no work, and you wouldn't. Mind you, a few of the rules would seem very strange to an outsider and were based more on ritual and tradition than plain common sense. Others varied from house to house depending on the whims of the housemaster, but on the whole these were imposed for good reason.

First off, we had to wear our penguin suits most of the time. In the summer we could just wear a jacket instead of the tail coat and waistcoat, and if we went out we could wear what we liked within reason. At that age though our reason could be different to a housemaster's. We were supposed to wear lace up black shoes, but aged fifteen and being rather small, I took a fancy to Cuban heeled Chelsea boots, and had my trousers taken in so they were as tight as drainpipes like a Teddy Boy. There was another boy in my house, Chris Cazenove[34], who did likewise, and we were always being told off by Fred.

One of the greatest traditions at Eton was fagging. This had nothing to do with homosexuality – well it wasn't meant to – and involved the smallest boys up to the age of fifteen running errands for the Library[35]. The senior boys in the Library would also have a personal fag, responsible for tidying his room and making his tea if the boy's maid didn't cook it. There would also be one to keep the Library clean and tidy too. During certain times of the day senior boys would yell at full volume for as long as they could the single word 'Boy' and the last boy to arrive would get the job – maybe to take a note round to Smith-Cholmondeley in JSBP half a mile away and 'come back as fast as you can with an answer, quick now, move boy!' Sauntering idly along Eton High Street later, having lost the note I was supposed to deliver, I would be passed by other little boys scurrying along, carrying fag notes or even a bag of sausages and chips for their fag master's tea. The justification for fagging in the early sixties was that many senior boys had responsibilities for running things, especially sport and games and didn't have time to do it all themselves, and that junior boys had time on their hands. It only worked as we all knew that we would be able to make our juniors do it too when we got to the top of the house. Unfortunately, from 1960-65 massive social change was taking place in the outside world and, contrary to public perception, Eton was well in the loop. Our own attitudes would change too and by the time it was our turn at the

---

[34] Actor – notably playing Ben in the 80s TV series Dynasty.
[35] Six or seven prefects in each house. They congregated in a common room called the Library too.

top, things were quite different.

There was so much happening in the outside world and even as young teenagers in the rarified atmosphere of a British public school we were well aware of it. The first five years of the sixties saw the launch of the contraceptive pill, homosexual reform, a revolution in communications, the emergence of the Beatles and the Rolling Stones and other bands, the hotting up of the Vietnam War in Indochina, the Cuban missile crisis, President Kennedy's assassination, the Christine Keeler Affair, the first man in space, the imprisonment of Nelson Mandela and the rise of the anti-apartheid movement, the growing Civil Rights unrest energized by Martin Luther King in the US, and left wing student agitation across the western world. The list is a long one. Some of these events and movements were the catalysts for others and many made us stop and think and wonder and were literally awesome. Most of them opened our eyes for the first time and gave us the opportunity to look outwards instead of being blinkered by our own conventions. A few unfortunately, like apartheid, would be prolonged by a stubbornness to accept that human beings were living in a changing world, and would persist for many decades afterwards.

The Christine Keeler Affair deservers a mention. In 1962 it emerged that the Secretary of State for War in Harold Macmillan's conservative government, John Profumo, had been having an affair with a nineteen year old 'model' by the name of Christine Keeler. Nothing wrong with that you might say, but this was over fifty years ago at the height of the Cold War, and Keeler was also having it off with the naval attaché at the Russian Embassy. This was seen as a blatant security risk and the newspapers jumped on it. To start with Profumo lied about the affair, but under pressure resigned from the government and admitted all. It turned out later that there was no breach of security, but for Profumo it was the end of politics; he dedicated the rest of his life working for the poor in the east end of London and became very well respected. This scandal ran and ran in the newspapers; as adolescents we were enthralled by the smuttiness, titillation and occasional mendacity of it all. There were others involved too, and reports of pool parties and other naughty goings on. I remember rowing my boat up the Thames past Cliveden, where the Astors lived, and much of the scandal was centered, wondering if there was anything interesting happening there at that particular moment on a hot summer's afternoon.

Significantly, if they hadn't done so already, people in the UK realized that their elected leaders were fallible, and couldn't be trusted to run an orgy in a brothel. No, that's completely wrong – it was about the only thing they could do. The perception was that the power was falling into the hands of the people, and perception was all we needed to foment the revolution. Little more than a year later, Harold Macmillan resigned, prompted in part by the scandal, and into his shoes stepped Sir Alec Douglas Home[36]. Fred, my larger than life housemaster, was great friends with Home and used to stay with us at Barmere on his way north to shoot the grouse at his pile in the Scottish Borders.

Fallibility and this perception of a power shift from our leaders to the people was felt in America as well. In 1963 John Kennedy was shot and killed by the single bullet from a lone gun man. We had followed the rise of this charismatic man to the Presidency little more than two years before. Fortunately he was the first presidential candidate to use the powerful medium of

---

[36] Pronounced 'Hume' – as in exhume…

television to put himself in front of the electorate and he knew exactly how to make the best of it. Unfortunately, during his short two years as President he was up against a rough little Russian ex-metalworker, Nikita Khruschev, who had risen to power doing quite a lot of work for Stalin. He got off to a bad start with Khruschev, whom he found abrasive, coarse and untrustworthy. Khruschev thought Kennedy was intelligent but weak. If only they had settled down and got drunk one night, and then nursed their mutual hangovers together the next day, what a difference it might have made to world history.

As it was Kennedy had to suffer the shame of the Bay of Pigs fiasco in 1961, when the CIA persuaded him that it would be a good idea to send two thousand Cuban expats, trained up by the CIA, back to Cuba as an invasion force. To give Kennedy his due, he wasn't keen on the idea but had inherited it from the last administration. They expats would drum up enough support to overthrow Castro, who was nuzzling up to Khruschev big time, and frightening the CIA and Kennedy as the Communist leader of a country only ninety miles off the US coast. Unfortunately Castro knew they were coming and clobbered the ex pats soon after they landed, killing five hundred and then ransoming the rest back to the States for $50million. There were a lot of red faces all round, not least that of Allen Dulles, the head of the CIA. A few months after the Bay of Pigs, Khruschev capitalized on Castro's success and slapped up the Berlin Wall, an almost impenetrable border between West and East Germany. He was also planning further challenges to test Kennedy's mettle.

By 1962, it was apparent that the nuzzling between Castro and Khruschev had become even more intimate when a high flying American U2 spy plane took some photographs of a boat steaming towards Cuba carrying nuclear warheads on the end of ballistic missiles, as well as pictures of launch pads on Cuban soil. The next thirteen days were the closest the world has come to a nuclear war, and after tense diplomacy and compromises on both sides, it was averted. Even as fifteen year olds we were intensely aware of the worsening situation, and I can still recollect the zeitgeist of the time. We all had newspapers (I confess here in a whisper that mine was the Daily Mail), and could see the news on M'Dame's TV. When we were fifteen in our house we were allowed to have radios too, so we were always fiercely debating what was going on in a big sad world.

And then on 22 November 1963, when I was sixteen, came the biggest and saddest news of all. We all know where we were on that day. I was leaning on a trolley used by the boy's maid for wheeling stuff up and down the passage, idly looking at some framed photos on the wall at about seven o'clock in the evening. One of them happened to be a group of four boys – perhaps a bumping four[37]. I only remember the name of one boy, Lord Bingham, who had been in Fred's house back in 1952. A year after I saw this photo Lord Bingham became the 7th Earl of Lucan, and last week as I write this, he was declared dead, forty years after becoming the main suspect in a murder mystery that has become a cause celébrè of the late twentieth century. Anyway, a boy called Richard McGillycuddy[38] was walking past and told me that President Kennedy had been shot, and a few hours later we heard and saw that he was dead.

---

[37] Four man crew in a rowing boat.
[38] Pronounced 'mac-li-cuddy.' His full title was 'The McGillycuddy of the Reeks.'

Three days later he was buried and we saw it all live on the television, beamed from America and bounced off the first Telstar communications satellite, which had been launched the year before.

Back in 1960 as thirteen year olds we were thrown head first into the frantic routine of a new boy. There were three other boys who arrived for tea on our first afternoon in Fred's family half of the house – John Robson, Charlie Mann and George Francis. John and Charlie had been at the same school before and were already good friends. I blame them for turning me into an addict of sorts but more of that later. John was blonde and Charlie had black hair – both thin of face they didn't seem to take life very seriously, and neither did I. George was just as funny but he was more serious about life and had more brains than us. He had a thatch of spiky fair hair and could draw brilliantly, and he was the mainstay of our first commercial venture a few years later. There's very little I can recall about that first term. In the house there was the menacing authority of the bigger boys and Fred, the cacophony in the dining room at mealtimes, the frantic rushing up and downstairs when someone shouted 'Boy-y-y-y' from a distant corridor, and the smell of our grey flannel shorts after kicking a ball heavier than lead around a muddy football pitch on a cold, wet afternoon.

The class rooms were dotted all over Eton, but during our first year I had only one about quarter of a mile away. It was a dark room and brown and quite grim with high windows. The other three were in higher divs as they were brighter than me. Mine was Lower F – the bottom division in the school and I was stuck there for a year. We weren't thick, but we weren't clever either. We sort of had half a brain. Teaching us Latin and English and History was a chap called Peter Way. He was new too and was about twenty three, tall, white faced and thin with horn rimmed glasses. He didn't stand a chance with us lot. Perhaps we couldn't spell hooligan in those days, but we were experts in that particular field. He lived in digs in Windsor and one morning on his way to us, he fell off his bicycle coming down Windsor Hill. His glasses were broken and one end of his wing collar had come away from the front stud. There was a hole in his trousers and he'd grazed his head. He was not in good shape and we mobbed him up mercilessly. One day he never turned up at all, or maybe he did, but we were allowed to 'run' if a beak didn't turn up within fifteen minutes of the class starting time. For some strange reason, whenever I think about that gloomy classroom, it reminds me of General Franco, which is weird – half a snippet of a history lesson maybe, remembered with half a brain.

The only other class I remember that first year was the once a week art lesson in the Drawing Schools where a splendid fellow by the name of Mr Thomas held court in a haze of absent mindedness and laissez-faire. You could create anything you wanted in the Drawing Schools, except in year F, when you were only allowed to do it on the paper and paint provided by Mr Thomas. I had an idea – to paint a man lighting a cigarette under a lamp post at night on a dingy street corner. I hadn't a clue about perspective or even how to draw a man, let alone a cigarette, so Mr Thomas drew the outline of the man, the lamp post and the cigarette and for the next ten weeks I coloured it in. I won first prize in the art competition for everyone in the F block of about fifty boys. It was the only picture I ever painted there, which was a pity as I rather liked the all-pervasive smell of oil paint, wet clay and anarchy.

The winter half at Eton was dedicated to the Field Game, a crazy looking mix of soccer and rugby. The pitch is roughly the same size with very small goals at either end. There are eleven a side and the object is to bounce the ball off an opposing team member over his back line and then touch the ball down for a try. The ball can be kicked straight through the goal too but there is no goalkeeper, and if anyone's hand touches the ball on the pitch it's a foul. It was a great game, better than rugby was then, but perhaps not quite as good as rugby is now.

When we won we walked on air and when we lost we could be morose for at least twenty four hours. Games and sport were compulsory in our house until we were fifteen as Fred was keener on brawn than brain, and there were a lot of silver cups on the dining room tables to prove it. It must have been awful for the boys in our house who hated exercise – and there were a few. It would have been a great relief for them, when they didn't have to exercise any longer aged sixteen to go down to the railway arches and smoke a fag with their mates, or wander up to Peascod Street in Windsor and buy the latest Playboy, or stand listening to the Animals and the Pretty Things in the record shop, while trying to look cool wearing a pair of headphones and undulating self consciously to the music in their penguin suits.

Until we were fifteen, and more so as new boys, our timetable was mapped out for us. We had some freedom but just when we thought we could relax and settle down to a pleasant evening of throwing rubbers[39] into waste paper baskets or playing football in the passages, a senior boy in the Library would shout for us and we would be sent on some spurious errand, or else have to

[39] Erasers

clean his room. And then we had the Colour Test to prepare for. There were nearly a hundred colours for the houses, sports and games. They were all different and very muddling to learn, and were used on socks, shirts, caps and scarves. Our house colours were blue with thin white stripes, whereas there was a rowing colour that was white with thin blue stripes. The first XI cricket team was a white blazer with a blue cap and the first rowing eight was a blue blazer with a white cap or was it the other way round? The first XI Field Game team was red and blue quarters and one sock was blue and the other red. Which leg wore the red sock? To a thirteen year old who only wanted to throw rubbers or play passage football this seemed ridiculous. We also had to learn where all the other boys' houses were and where to go to buy a bag of sausages and chips, and what for instance was the Leg of Mutton or Judy's Passage? We had about three weeks to learn all this, and we were then called up to the library one evening where we sat around on the floor and were quizzed by the senior boys.

There was one particular boy I took an instant dislike to – John Lumley. He was the Captain of the House; every house had one and he was appointed by Fred because he was seen to be responsible and grown up and could keep order. To maintain discipline he was allowed to beat us with a rattan cane. He had a large selection of these things with steam turned handles, which must have been mass produced somewhere, probably by the same factory that made the guillotine, and The Tolly from my prep school – Sade Masoch de Paris et Cie. His arrogance and conceit hung from him like Darth Vader's cloak. You could almost smell it as he walked past us down the corridor. He had probably been born wearing it, as had most of the other eighteen year old boys sitting around him on the tatty old sofas in the library on that

dark evening. It was arrogance tailored by an inherited
sense of entitlement, a superiority over ordinary mortals
stitched together over generations from a family
genealogy of prime ministers, slave traders, plantation
owners, generals, rear-admirals, lord chief justices – all
held in place by merchant banks, staggering wealth, lots
of gold embroidered uniforms, vast country estates and
of course the old boy network.

But as I've already said, long after these boys had
disappeared into the outside world, it became
fashionable for us to move in a different direction and
affect an air influenced mainly by the accelerating speed
of modern popular culture. Even our voices changed.
Instead of the languid, slightly adenoidal squeaky little
voices we had when we arrived at Eton, by the time we
were seventeen, we were speaking like the new kid on
the block, Mick Jagger, and making a self conscious
effort to suppress any of the arrogance we may have
been born with. This change in attitude was mirrored
quite surprisingly in what we became when we left.
Whereas there were *seventy three* Old Etonian Members
of Parliament in Harold Macmillan's Tory Party in 1963,
there are now only twenty. Today, instead, there are
more high profile Etonian actors and film stars than
there have ever been before.

Fear was the main emotion we displayed as we sat
there on the lino floor in the library. I hardly knew any
of the answers, but out of bravado nervously attempted
to brush off my ignorance by trying to be funny. This
was a mistake. The other three passed and I was given a
week to revise and then come back again. Of course,
regardless of my doom, I carried on playing and was
called back a week later, and once again failed. Lumley
– I'm sorry I forgot to say that we called each other by
our surnames for the first two or three years – Lumley

called me into the library once more, and leaning languidly with his bottom on the library table and his hands in his pockets with his henchman ranged around him, tested me once more.

'This is your last chance, Dewhurst. Right. Let's go. What are the Field[40] colours?'

'Red and light blue quarters,' quiveringly.

'What are the college beagling[41] colours?' This was the trick question.

'Red and blue quarters – the same,' said with some conviction now.

'Which sock for beagling is worn on the left leg – the red or the blue?' Oh shit. Was it 'red shite on the right' for beagling or football? Panic. Paralysis.

'Blue?'

'You tell me.'

'Red.'

'Wrong.'

And so it went on until the sweat was dripping down the back of my neck and I'd got more wrong than I had right and I was sent on my way. The next evening about nine o'clock, there was a knock on my door and the library fag was standing there. 'You're wanted in the library.'

I'm trying to recollect this after fifty years and it's really quite unpleasant. I mentioned the guillotine a page or two back, and went on to the internet and got a bit carried away, landing up on a page describing Louis XVI's execution and how he walked to the scaffold striding boldly. I trotted boldly up the stairs after the library fag – I can't remember who he was. He disappeared at some point and I carried on. I knocked

---

[40] First XI Field Game
[41] Hair chasing fraternity

hard and purposefully on the door.

'Come in!'

Lumley was in his usual position and so were half a dozen other granite faced boys assuming their normal languid pose on the bursting sofas. One was even pretending to read a newspaper. I stood there with a half smile on my face to try and disguise the piss inducing fear in my belly.

'Despite two attempts you've failed miserably to pass your colour test and you're one of the most incompetent fags that we've ever had in this house. You haven't even tried. What do you say?' I could see about four canes with their curved handles lying on the table behind him.

'No.'

'What do you mean 'no'?'

'No, I haven't tried.'

'You seem to think this is a joke.'

'Not really...'

'No it isn't and because you've failed twice and because of your fagging I'm going to beat you. Bend over and put your head under the table and lift your coat tails up.'

I did and I heard him pick up a cane from above me, move a step back and then – CRACK!! Oh shiiit. The pain was indescribable. The regular visits to the dentist and the Tolly at Ladycross were nothing compared to this. It didn't even hurt Louis XVI this much. My brain was computing faster than it had ever done in its life. Shall I get up and run? Now I'm used to the first one the second won't be nearly as bad. Perhaps it'll only be the one. I started to move my head out. CRACK!! Oh shiiiiit – it was even worse the second time. It felt as though five thousand volts had shot up my arsehole and ricocheted round every nerve ending in my body. CRACK!! This was too much. As the fourth one came down CRACK!! I'd nearly got my head out from under the table. I guess Lumley saw this and not wanting a scene on his hands said 'That's enough, you can go!' and quite frankly I couldn't get out of there fast enough.

From memory, this happened two more times. Caning a boy was a short cut really and served no useful purpose, because it seldom dissuaded him from doing the same thing again. Maybe it satisfied a sadistic streak in the boy who was doing it and was over and forgotten very quickly – a 'short sharp shock' as some politician once said in favour of flogging.

There were much better ways of delivering short sharp shocks to pubescent fourteen year olds. The first lesson of the day was at 7.30 during the winter and summer terms and the boy's maid would come knocking on your door shouting 'Seven o'clock, Sir' and you would crawl out of bed at about twenty past, and half dressed, collect your books and stuff and try to remember, almost sleep walking, where you were supposed to be at half past, which could be in a dusty dark schoolroom half a mile away. If you were continually late for this first purgatory of the day or any other class, the beak would put you on Tardy Book. This involved trotting to the school office, which was quarter of a mile away from our house and signing your name in a big book before Early School. This was one of the few punishments that worked, and I learned how to leap out of bed, throw open the windows and welcome the cool morning with a deep intake of breath and a feeling of oneness with the world. On a particular morning, I got up half an hour early and did this, and there was my next door neighbour, Adrian Hopetoun[42], about to climb in through his window, slightly dishevelled, wearing a

---

[42] Current Marquis of Linlithgow

dinner jacket, and looking rather pasty. He was prone to going up to London now and again for parties.

# 10 – EXERCISE & BURNING FAT

Apart from the field game in the winter and rugby football in the spring, boys could either play cricket or row on the Thames during the summer at Eton. You became a wet bob or a dry bob, or even a slack bob if you hated exercise and preferred to read Latin poetry under the giant elms up on Agars Plough[43]. I opted for cricket my first summer half and was in the bottom game. The inactivity bored me and I was not very good at it, and I was sent out into the long grass to stop any ball that came my way. It seldom did and I would settle down to read the latest Ian Fleming and immerse myself in James Bond's exploits on a train travelling through the snow in deepest Russia with a raven haired girl, who was only wearing black stockings and a velvet choker. Meanwhile the insects hummed and buzzed around me and the occasional cry of 'Owzthat' drifted in from far away to interrupt my concentration.

As someone who liked proper exercise and the

---

[43] A big playing field up towards Slough

competition that goes with it I changed into a wet bob the next summer and learnt to row in long thin boats on the Thames, which was a short walk up the High Street to the boathouse that stood beside the water. You would be allotted your own single sculling boat, starting off in heavy clinker built models and progressing as you got older to sleeker, streamlined fiberglass ones. If you were any good, at around seventeen, you could be chosen for a house bumping four – four boys in a boat with a cox – and for four evenings in May twenty six boats would line up one behind the other with a fifty foot gap between them and a gun would go off; at which moment everyone would row like hell to catch up the boat in front. This was heavy duty exercise and a lot of nervous excitement for us, and the competition was extreme. The object was to climb the ladder until you were head of the river but this might take a few years as you could only get four bumps a year. We got our four bumps and celebrated on the way home in the school pub, Tap, half way back up the High Street. We were only allowed beer or cider and would normally be turfed out after a couple of pints, but it was reward enough.

Rowing up and down the Thames became an obsession, and I soon progressed from a clinker built heavy wooden skiff with a fixed seat to a thin fiberglass sliding seat speed machine called a rigger. This was Morris Minor to Ferrari stuff, and even though top speed was probably only eight miles an hour, it felt pretty good. The boat house was just above a weir below Windsor Bridge, so all of the rowing was done upstream. Spare time in the summer meant free time on the river. Rather than sit at my desk on a warm summer evening trying to get my head round the politics of the French Revolution, I'd slog three miles upstream to the first lock, and then drift back down again, bombarded by the buzzing and the tweeting and the splish splash as another water rat dropped into the river. Beyond the lock was the quietest stretch of black limpid water, trees overhanging on one side and open fields on the other where the green grass came down to the river's edge. On half days – there were three a week at Eton – we could row further up to Queen's Eyot[44], owned by the school, where there was a large shack that sold rough beer and cider and Coca Cola. The journey back would either be a slow drift downstream lying semi conscious close to the river bank, looking up through the leaves of the willow, alder and aspen at the dappled sunlight, or an energy driven slog further up the river to Boulters Lock, depending on whether I had drunk cider or Coca Cola.

And then there were the single sculling races – five boats with five tense boys would line up across the width of the river just below Queen's Eyot on a warm summer's evening, waiting for the starting pistol. Supporters and coaches on bicycles with loudhailers would shout encouragement from the river bank. I only remember one when I was sixteen and still as thin and small as a whippet and about eight and a half stone, but I had the inclination which included stamina, mileage and a competitive streak – rather like a middle distance runner but all done sitting down. This particular race was the Junior Sculling Competition, the second most important race in the single sculling calendar. I had fought my way through four rounds to the final, but I knew that there was no way I was going to beat Borthwick. That morning at breakfast my tablemates made me eat baked beans and at lunchtime mashed potatoes, so even in those days we knew about carbo loading. Fred Coleridge was keener on sport and

---

[44] pronounced 'ate' – Thames speak for a small island on the river.

physical activity than he was on academic stuff, and even though we were continually at odds with each other and he preferred cricket, he was up there on the river bank – his large bulk on his small bicycle.

Borthwick, I don't remember his Christian name, had the arms of an orangutan and the body of a silverback gorilla and must have weighed in at fifteen stone. He was enormous, and even at sixteen far too big to be in the Junior Sculling Competition. Part of his training regime consisted of ripping cars apart with his bare hands and eating a small cow for breakfast. He had drawn the middle of the river and I was next to him towards the trees. The other three were lined out either side of us. He was so big and heavy that his boat appeared to bend in the middle. The gun went off and so did we, trying not to make a mistake with the first few frenzied strokes. For about two hundred yards I couldn't believe it – I was keeping up with him – but then he started to pull away, just a few inches with every stroke. The stern of his boat was getting shorter and shorter in my peripheral vision until all I could see were the puddles of disturbed water made by his oars. Even they began to subside as he drew further away.

It had taken me three weeks of blood, sweat, tears and a sore arse fighting through four rounds to beat the second third and fourth seed, and now it had come to this – second place to a gorilla. It just wasn't good enough. Find some more, Simon, for fuck's sake, you've got to find some MORE! But there wasn't any more. The oxygen in my blood that my body cried out for was being pumped into every muscle cell below my neck at an alarming rate, taking away blood needed for my brain. Everything seemed to slow down, but it wasn't slowing down; it was just going quieter. I could see the three other boys disappearing into the distance up river, and I was gliding effortlessly in slow motion through the black silky water and it felt as though I was flying. I was aware of a muffled thud followed by a sloppy splintering sound behind me. I hardly registered it. Seconds later I couldn't believe what I was seeing coming up on my right hand side. Borthwick, the unbeaten gorilla, seemed to be moving backwards past me, still rowing furiously, but his lower body and his boat were six inches under the surface. His face was a tortured grimace, eyes half closed as he struggled hopelessly against the syrupy black water which was now up to his waist. And then all I could see was his huge ugly back with its massive shoulders still straining on the oars as his boat, with the front end almost snapped off and tilting straight upwards, decided it was time to call it a day and went into dive mode, and the last I saw of Borthwick was the back of his head disappearing below the water like the conning tower on a nuclear submarine with its small bow wave. There was a roaring sound that got louder and louder with every stroke of my own oars. It was either the moment just before unconsciousness and an inevitable death, or the crowd on the bank cheering me on. It was a miracle. The large piece of hidden tree trunk that Borthwick's boat had hit and splintered the front end, had won me the race, and I crossed the line nearly dead but triumphant.

Of course it wasn't like that at all – Borthwick beat me by five lengths. The crowd on the bank did cheer a bit and make some noise, and it was exhausting, but it was an expected result and even being second was quite satisfying. It was the whole craic – the training, the discussions, the nervous anticipation and the races themselves – that was addictive. Of course it was important to win but winning was by no means everything. We learnt to live with disappointment. All but one of the boys in that competition were disappointed, but not for very long. We learnt very quickly how to cope with losing and also how to cope with winning. Neither went to our heads.

As I write this, fifty years later, our attitudes towards sports and games and exercise have completely changed. Successive UK governments have sold off nearly half of our state schools' playing fields – that's well over ten thousand – and they are still doing it! This is an exclamation mark loaded with incredulity at the sheer brainlessness of our elected leaders. Never mind which political affiliation you support. Every government since the eighties has condoned this stupidity, which appears to have been based on fiscal greed rather than common sense.

It's reckoned that just under 20% of our ten to eleven year olds are obese – that's not just fat, that's dangerously fat, life threateningly fat – and a further 14% are overweight, which adds up to one in three eleven year old children being fat. By the time they reach adulthood, the figures are even worse. The UK has the highest level of obesity in Europe with 25% of adults being obese and a further 40% being just fat, which means that two in three of us are fat or dangerously fat. (I suppose this is better than the US where two in three adults are all obese.) Strangely there is a lot of fuss right now about how there is too much sugar in food and drink, and too much saturated fat in processed foods. I say 'strangely' because in the 1960s we were eating the same amount of fat and sugar, perhaps not as much processed food and drink, yet less than 2% of adults were obese.

Since 1960 the average weight of an adult woman has risen from eight and a half to eleven stone, a two and a half stone increase, and for men it has risen from ten stone to thirteen, a three stone increase. So in 2016 women are a third heavier than they were in 1960, and men a quarter heavier.

To cut a long rant short this equates to sixty thousand metric tons of lipid fat attached to human beings in the UK[45]. This stuff could be harvested by some kind of vacuum device and would be far more useful powering the heating systems in our hospitals. This in turn would save a shed load of money, which could be used to provide more beds and nursing staff to look after all the fat people who have progressed to diabetes, high blood pressure, strokes and cancer, problem conditions and diseases caused in the main by being too fat.

Of course the rational answer is to bring children up playing games that involve running around chasing a ball or each other on a grass playing field or in a gym. The alternative is to sit them down in front of a TV screen playing games with just their thumbs and feed them an oversized pizza[46] washed down with nine tea spoonfuls of fizzy, liquefied sugar. Both of these alternatives become life forming habits that can be inculcated at a very early age, but go down the route of the second one at your peril.

Today in the UK it's compulsory for primary school children to do at least seventy five minutes PE a week. This is not nearly enough and many schools are happy to increase the time, but by doing so they bite into the academic timetable. Academic standards, however, don't

---

[45] Lipids are flammable compounds, making up 87% of adipose – human fat. This amount would fill over three quarters of the Albert Hall in London – up to the roof.

[46] Apart from the visible contents here's a sample of pizza ingredients you probably didn't know about: dimethyl poly siloxane, glucono delta lactone, calcium disodium ethylene diamine tetra acetic acid, sodium nitrite and silicon dioxide.

appear to have dropped, and there is considerable evidence that exercise stimulates the brain and to an extent prevents the psychological afflictions that affect so many children today. So the unscientific conclusion is that exercise stops you going mad and keeps you thin.

# 11 – WORKERS OF THE WORLD

The maddest game of all at Eton is the Wall Game. The two teams are made up of boys from College on one side, and boys from the other houses, the Oppidans, on the other. The pitch, which is fifteen feet wide and a hundred yards long, runs down the length of a slightly curved brick wall that divides a playing field from the Slough road. At one end there is a tree with a goal post in the shape of a doorway painted on it, and at the other a small garden door in a returning wall. These are the goals. The opposing teams form a scrum and try to push each other along the wall with the ball against it. It is very scientific and quite painful for the boys up against the wall, who sometimes wear old coats and scrum caps to stop their ears and elbows being rubbed off. It's permitted to use a fist in the face to try and lever an opponent out of the way, but you are not allowed to punch him. There is an area either end of the wall where it's possible to score a shy worth one point when a player or one of his team mates, holding the ball off the ground with his foot, touches it with a hand.

The last goal, worth ten points, was scored in a

formal match in 1909 but teams very occasionally score a one point shy. In 2009, during the formal match on St Andrew's Day, the Collegers very nearly scored a shy, but there was the hell of a fuss when a photographer standing at the end of the pitch, waiting for some action, kicked the ball himself. Poor chap. Without doubt the Wall Game is the dullest game in the world to watch, but for one team to gain two feet over the other during a match, it is considered a triumph, even when the score is 0-0.

In a school of 1300 boys and 120 beaks, there was an eclectic mix of people whose interests covered practically every pastime under the sun including the Wall Game. If you wanted to collect butterflies or rebuild motorbikes there was always someone else to team up with, either in a loose affiliation or an organized club. Today there are about sixty clubs and societies, ranging from the Cheese Club to the Orwell Society, which is a left wing political group. These two probably get together and discuss 'Struggles of Twentieth Century Proletarian Cheese Makers'.

My own interest, among other things, was in film making and the cinema. Aged sixteen I'd managed to scrape some GCE O levels[47] together and was allowed to choose two subjects to specialize in up to A Level. In order not to appear too thick I went for History and English and found I had made a serious error and a lucky choice at the same time. I found myself up to two new beaks, Charlie Barr and Giles st Aubyn, and managed to stir them both into fury and dismay over the next two years in their divs.

Charlie Barr tried to enthuse us with English classical literature, and early on gave us a list of books we had to

---

[47] Equivalent of GCSEs today

read if there was any hope of us getting an A level. At the same time we had to study in depth a few of them in the classroom. I remember two books – The Europeans by Henry James and Emma by Jane Austen. I found both as unappetizing as semolina and Rhubarb and Soda, and could have quite happily burned them page by page. In the fly leaf of The Europeans after leaving I found the list of about twenty books Charlie Barr had given us to read. By the time I left Eton I'd read about three of them. Today, I've read nearly all of them. Here is what he said in one of my reports:

'I think he is the most depressing case I have so far come across at Eton; at this rate there is no point in his thinking of A level English, and he is merely a drag on the rest of the division. I have little hope of better results from him. Whenever we have gone on to essays or more general work he has proved as vacuous as ever. And he continues to sit smirking complacently, not seeming to be worried.

'No doubt he is a cheery lad, kind to animals etc, but this doesn't make his presence in this A level division any more acceptable as things stand.'

Giles st Aubyn was stirred to even greater things in one of my History reports and this was the half in which I sat my A levels:

'When the workers of the world unite I think it would be presumptuous of Dewhurst to include himself in their company ... I did not think much of his notes. They were untidy, incomplete and inadequately set out. In a not especially punctual division, he had the worst record for lateness. I have found a very pleasant person, but lacking in will and self discipline.'

I contend that although they were unable to interest me in anything they had to say however hard they tried, I managed to draw out of them a flash of creativity that they had probably never experienced before or were likely to experience again when it came to writing reports. The upside of the pain experienced by all three of us during this time was a mutual interest in the cinema and film making. Charlie Barr had a cerebral interest in movies and specialized in the films of Alfred Hitchcock. Giles st Aubyn loved the whole technical process of making films, and what's more had all the kit for doing it.

There was also a boy in Fred's house, Henry Aubrey-Fletcher, who loved all the technical stuff too – cameras, tape recorders, wires, loudspeakers and microphones – and we would talk for ages about the relative merits of the Vortexion versus the Ferrograph and the Arriflex versus the Beaulieu. (No, don't worry about it). During the summer holidays in 1963 Henry wrote a film script about a bank robbery. I say wrote – the script was made up as we went along, but I remember he recruited Chris Cazenove and Jeremy Child[48] to be in it. I was a lowly Third Assistant and we filmed in Henry's family flat in London and out at Heathrow. The finished product was called 'The Amateurs' – irony intended I presume. It was filmed in colour with synchronized sound and unlikely to win an Oscar, but it was fun to make. I remember tripping over a great thick cable and fusing all the lights.

Two years later we made another film, this time in black and white with a story line suggested by Charles Barr, so my relationship with him could not have been as bad as all that. It was loosely based on a modern version of Macbeth, but by the time we came to film it had very little to do with the Scottish Play at all and was, from

---

[48] Sir Jeremy Child Bart – Actor – A Fish Called Wanda, East Enders and 100 more film credits.

what I can remember, about a girl meeting a yob in a caff in Birmingham, having a row and then meeting a hoighty-toighty bloke in an E-Type Jaguar who lived in a pile in the country. The moral of the story was that money talks. I played the yob in a black plastic jacket I borrowed from my mother. I couldn't do a Brum accent so I became Kev, a Mancunian who'd moved to Birmingham. A delightful girl called Lindsey Davidson played the girl; we'd never met her before, but she agreed to dive in blindly. She played Jane who left me to meet Algernon, the posh git, played by Christopher Sharples, who is now incidentally Commodore of the Royal Yacht Squadron; he had his career well mapped out even then and refused to play the yob point blank, probably aware that it could be used against him at a later date, should he become Prime Minister or even perhaps Commodore of the Royal Yacht Squadron.

We filmed the classy stuff at Hagley Hall near Stourbridge, the family seat of the Lytteltons[49]. As the Director I was very proud of the long tracking shots we did down the passages at Hagley as Lindsey walked aimlessly up and down looking moody and quizzical in a sort of French way. In fact I'm sure Stanley Kubrick rather liked the tracking shots too and refined them for 'The Shining,' made some years later.

There was nothing funny about this film and we took it all very seriously. Charlie Barr, who raved about the films of Hitchcock, wrote something about flapping birds into the story line as Hitchcock's new film had just come out, and he saw similarities in Macbeth and The Birds. We filmed the odd crow squawking and flapping off the branches of the gloomy, rain soaked oak trees at Hagley, as Lindsey wandered up the drive with a panic

---

[49] Humphrey Lyttelton, the jazz trumpeter, was a cousin.

stricken look on her face. What it all signified, I have no idea and I don't think Charlie Barr knew either when we showed him the finished product. We were so proud that it had all stuck together and hadn't come apart in the projector, and when anyone spoke, their lips moved roughly at the same time as the sound.

Financially the film, now called 'We All Make Mistakes,' was a triumph. It cost £60 to make and grossed £120 in audience receipts on St Andrew's Day when the Wall Game was played, and there were art exhibitions and other creative stuff going on. That was equivalent to around £4000 today. I organized four showings, one after the other and the tickets had to be bought in advance. The advertising campaign was intense for about six weeks beforehand with small fluorescent posters stuck to boys' window boxes. I remember watching the parents' faces coming out after a showing. The fathers had the slightly dazed look of someone who has woken up to find that the lady he's just slept with has stolen his wallet. I didn't ask them what they thought of the film. I didn't need to. Giles st Aubyn, as the Treasurer of the Film Unit took the money, which went into the Film Unit's coffers, no doubt to be spent on the next epic in waiting. I've no idea what happened to 'We All Make Mistakes.' More than likely the one copy is now deep down in a landfill site somewhere north of Slough.

Apart from the Drawing Schools, the centre for all things cultural was the School Hall, a somewhat ornate building with a large dome and cupola, erected at the start of the twentieth century to commemorate Etonians killed in the Boer War. It held 500 people sitting down and had a large stage with no curtain and some rudimentary changing rooms. At the far end above a large balcony was a cinema projection box with two old

35mm carbon arc projectors. Concerts and school plays were put on in the hall and it was used on important days for making speeches, and every week day morning too, for all the beaks to gather like a senate to be addressed by the headmaster.

Towards the end of our first half a dustbin appeared on top of the eighty foot high cupola. Initially, nobody knew who had put it there or how they were going to get it down. After a few days of working out what to do, steeplejacks with ladders and ropes climbed up and with much faffing, managed to remove it. Recently the explorer, Ran Fiennes[50], owned up to the crime in a book. Even now as a novice climber looking at a picture of the dome, I don't know how he did it without crampons, and suffering as he does from vertigo.

During my last two years I joined the Film Society and together with Henry Aubrey-Fletcher and a few others got to work in the projection box, overseen by Mr Notley, who was the school electrician and didn't say much. We showed obscure foreign films and English language films of repute chosen as often as not by Charlie Barr, as well as the latest blockbusters at the end of every half. We'd print a thousand un-numbered tickets for a two night showing, and then sell them in advance. Once I discovered that there were too many boys in the audience for the number of tickets sold, and even with our tight security couldn't work out how that could be. I went through all the tickets, and discovered some brilliant forgeries, complete with pictures. Where are the forgers now, and all the other criminals that Eton produced, I wonder?

One summer money began to disappear from boys' trouser pockets left hanging in the boathouse, while they went rowing. None of mine was nicked because I seldom

---

[50] Full title – Sir Ranulph Twisleton-Wykeham-Fiennes Bart OBE

had any. Somebody with acute perception figured out that it was probably the work of thieves, so an invisible dye, which turned green on fingers, was smeared on to one pound notes and left as bait in the odd pocket. It took a few weeks to discover the thief; the culprit was a boy in our house, who actually used green ink in his pen and told Fred that his fingers were all green because his pen leaked. He was flogged[51] and then sacked and the last time I heard about him he was rather aptly tending the garden in an open prison somewhere near Colchester – a green fingered tea leaf.[52]

---

[51] Administered by the headmaster. Birch twigs bound together were used to thrash the victim's bare bottom – painful.
[52] Rhyming slang for 'thief'.

# 12 – EAR WHISPERERS & NOSE TAPPERS

By now you may be wondering why I have hardly mentioned homosexuality. So am I. Perhaps it's because I didn't really experience much of it. Whether that was because I tended to fancy girls more than boys, I'm not really sure. It certainly didn't have anything to do with what my father said about 'silly buggers'; at the time I had no idea what he was talking about.

Way back in 1533 Henry VIII made buggery between two men, and between a man and a woman, and even between a man and an animal, a capital offence. Even with the threat of execution there always remained an ambivalence about homosexuality in the UK. It was accepted and it wasn't accepted. The golden rule was to obey the eleventh commandment 'Thou Shalt Not Get Found Out' by keeping a low profile, your nose clean, and your head down – so to speak. If you were caught with your trousers down *in flagrante*, it was a good idea to show remorse or have good connections. Do this and you could avoid execution. One of the first notable people to experience this draconian law was a chap called Nicholas Udall in 1541, and guess what? You've got it! He was the headmaster of Eton. Fortunately for him he wrote a letter to the right people, who were close to Thomas Cromwell, Henry's ear whisperer, and got away with a year in prison. He later became the vicar of Braintree and finished up as headmaster at Westminster.

There were, however, men less fortunate. Buggery was a capital offence until 1861, as was stealing a sheep, and spending more than a month in the company of gypsies,[53] and a lot of other minor stuff such as blowing your nose in a railway station[54]. Between 1800 and 1861 fifty six men were executed for buggery in England and Wales although there were around nine thousand prosecutions.

In 1861 the law was changed and the maximum penalty for buggery was now life imprisonment. Evidence that penetration had actually taken place was hard to come by, and acts of fellatio, masturbation and other non-penetrative acts were not included in the new bill. Something more comprehensive was required to mollify the protestations of the bible thumpers, and these peccadilloes were later included in a 'gross indecency' amendment of 1885, but any offence under this updated law was now reduced to a misdemeanour, punishable by a maximum prison term of two years, with or without hard labour.

The last high profile trial for gross indecency was Oscar Wilde's in 1895. The 9th Marquess of Queensbury, not known for being a man of high culture, left a calling card at Wilde's London club writing on it 'For Oscar Wilde posing as Somdomite.' It was well known at the time among the chattering classes that Wilde was having an intense affair with His Lordship's son, Bosie

---

[53] This is not made up – it was a genuine capital offence.
[54] This is made up.

Douglas. Wilde made a mistake of suing for libel. The jury accepted that what his Lordship meant was 'Oscar Wilde posing as a *Sodomite*,' accepted too that he *was* a sodomite, and he therefore lost the case, breaking the golden rule. The poor fellow was then tried for gross indecency, found guilty and sentenced to the maximum term of two years with hard labour. Physical exercise was not his forte and he was broken on the treadmill, dying five years later in Paris, reputedly declaring in his last breath, apropos of nothing here, 'Either this wallpaper has to go or I do.'

Oscar Wilde's may have been the last high profile trial for homosexual offences but certainly not the last prosecution. By the end of the Second War prosecutions were generally dealt with by a magistrate, who dished out a nominal fine. It was quite usual for the defendant to give a false name, and in 1953, the actor John Gielgud was arrested for gross indecency in a Chelsea lavatory. The surname Gielgud is very rare. He was taken off to Chelsea police station where the Sergeant, who knew him quite well, asked him as a matter of routine for a name, expecting him to say something like 'John Smith'. 'Arthur Gielgud,' replied the actor. Arthur was his second Christian name. The fuss that ensued in the press caused him a load of grief for many years afterwards.

In 1960 there was another seven years to go before homosexuality was finally decriminalized; the word 'gay' in common parlance still meant light hearted and carefree; its other meaning was restricted to the still half secret world of nose tappers and full club members.

At Eton the words were used were 'queer' and 'queering' in a semi derogatory way, and with my contemporaries aged fourteen or so calling someone a 'queer' was a common insult or a joke. 'All those who can't whistle are queer,' I remember saying with difficulty, swallowing quickly and starting to whistle Colonel Bogey as three of us sat round a table at teatime stuffing Rice Krispies into our mouths. Just try whistling with a mouthful of Rice Krispies. But there was ambivalence here too. Until very recently I was under the impression that there were no boy on boy relationships in my house, and it came as quite a shock at an old boys' dinner last summer when I sat next to John Robson, not having met him for fifty years, and he started to tell me about the goings on in our house.

Eton generally reflected the sexual inclinations of the outside world apart from the fact there were no girls there. Since the sixties there have been occasional experiments to allow girls into the sixth form, but without much success. It was inevitable that the excess testosterone starting to pump round fourteen year olds was bound to fire off feelings for other boys. Scientifically though, it would be difficult to prove whether these feelings prevailed after leaving, and produced a higher proportion of gayness in old Etonians than anywhere else.

It's more than likely boys were buggering each other from the front, the back and maybe from the side, and probably some of them continued to do so after they left Eton, but it was hardly different from the rest of the world. I suppose it has something to do with prolonging the species, but I have always considered that the sweet aromatic perfumes coming from a lady's front garden must be infinitely more preferable than the occasional malodorous down draught emanating from a gentleman's back passage.

A small thirteen year old boy with blonde curly hair wearing a bum freezer was particularly vulnerable and would invariably be referred to as the school tart. It was quite common for these boys to take up boxing in an attempt to avoid further abuse. In fact any kind of abuse or bullying had to be dealt with by the victim himself, because to tell someone in authority was the worst sin you could commit. If a housemaster did suspect that a boy was being abused or bullied it was a different matter, and unlike Tom Brown's Schooldays, justice was swift.

Having said that, Eton was tough and it was up to boys to come to terms with their new surroundings. Of course most boys had been sent away to prep schools four or five years before and were quite used to coping with temporary family alienation, and the pressure cooker they now found themselves in. Eton was different to their prep schools though. It took away a lot of the imposed discipline and guidance a boy had been used to, and made him take on responsibility for himself. Most boys responded well and were able to cope in the main, but a few found it troublesome. I found it easier the older I got. After all, I'd been to the mother of tough schools at Ladycross.

As new boys we were rude and aggressive to each other, but this mutated into something bordering on respect, and we even learnt to cope silently with enmity. It's a common misconception that the rich and privileged who progressed through Eton had their arses wiped for them, and could never cope with being thrown into the real world. On the contrary, most old Etonians find the real world, and even the harsh world of prison, a piece of cake after learning how to survive at Eton. In my time there were a few boys who were pathologically inclined towards hubris and arrogance, but this was generally beaten out of them, sometimes physically but mostly by the emotional pressures put on them by other boys and the demands of the system. If these proclivities weren't beaten out of them at least they learned to suppress them while they were still there.

As the testosterone of adolescence started to grumble and bubble inside us we had other problems to deal with, apart from the faceful of zits that would erupt without warning. Most of us relied on the two Ps – well thumbed copies of Parade and Playboy. Parade was only 1/- (£1 today) and mostly in black and white. The girls looked as though they were just trying to earn a few quid and their underwear was always a bit grubby. Playboy, on the other hand was real class but very expensive. When someone felt the urge to splash out 8/6 (£8 today) on Playboy, then it would be handed round, well thumbed; all the photos were in colour on glossy paper with lots of tits and bums and the girls were spectacular. Fred would usually come round each evening to check on us and to discuss our progress. We could hear him coming along the lino covered passage, and he would always pause politely for a few moments before pushing open the door and standing there, his bulk taking up most of the doorway. He gave us plenty of time with his noisy approach to cover up the said magazines as we sat deskbound, pretending to ponder the intrigues of Jane Austin's Emma and – red in the face – frantically chewing on our pens. I say 'our,' assuming that all the other boys were doing the same as I, but after John Robson's admission a few pages back, I'm beginning to wonder now what the others *were* doing.

During the daytime there was loads of other stuff to be getting on with. By 1965 with only two more terms to go and after thirteen years, my scholastic career was coming to an end. It never occurred to me that I should be making plans for the rest of my life. Opportunities appeared that I liked the look of and I grabbed them. If I didn't like them, they were discarded or endured with a kind of mental sulk. My mother insisted when I started out at Eton that I should have extra religious instruction and for a couple of years once a fortnight on a Saturday afternoon I would traipse down the High Street to the little Catholic chapel and listen to the poor Augustinian priest, who was just as bored as I was, drone on about the Virgin Birth and allied stuff. I think he gave up first and a great weight dropped away.

There were about fifty Catholics at the school and we only had to go to this Italianate chapel once a week on Sundays. It had been built in 1915 to some opposition from the authorities, but it was quite a pleasant place. I had a feeling that the other boys who turned up there weren't much interested in God either. There was a certain Anglican aura around the boys, and although there was a smell of incense and the sound of jingling bells, it was all rather low key. At least we were excused the daily ritual of going to College Chapel as were the orthodox Jews, the Hindus and the Buddhists. The extra twenty five minutes was a peaceful time after breakfast when everything went quiet and I could stroll off to the next class without the mad last minute rush. In fact there was only one Hindu, Prince Birendra of Nepal, and no Buddhists that I knew. I would invariably meet Birendra each morning as he stepped out of his own house. He was a couple of years older than me; we would exchange smiles and the occasional mumble. Little did we know that thirty five years later when he was the king of Nepal, he would be shot and killed by his own son at a family dinner in the Royal Palace in Kathmandu.

Meanwhile I was starting my last half at Eton. My father, with Fred's agreement, wanted me to go into the army and with this in mind I prepared for a civil service exam which would start me off on the road to a short service commission. This was an escape route should I fail the A levels, as there was little chance of passing them. I still had the maturity of a freshly made cheese – and about the same amount of interest in becoming a soldier – but I acquiesced. I think it was also compulsory to have Physics GCE at O level too but I'd failed this exam three times. I remember the complexities of trying to determine the specific gravity of a nut and bolt way beyond me.

I was much more interested in the rowing, making the film, and getting involved with Henry Aubrey Fletcher in all the technical stuff for the concerts staged in the School Hall. During the last year I'd also joined a theatre group that had two allotted classes a week called extra studies with a beak called Ralf Payne. He was the equivalent of a housemaster, looking after the Collegers in their ancient lodgings facing the College Chapel. He was tall and tousle haired with tortoiseshell glasses and an air of vagueness, a chain smoker who never seemed to open his eyes, but he saw everything and was a very good director. With half a dozen other boys we put on Shakespeare extracts in the ancient cloisters, and the acting flame was re-ignited.

During the summer half of 1965 I helped Henry with recording and amplifying the sound at a special concert in School Hall. There were a couple of warm up bands, which were awful and then Marianne Faithfull[55] walked on and sang for an hour, accompanied on a guitar by her husband-to-be, and then very soon afterwards not-to-be, John Dunbar. I remember trying to be cool like everyone else, but like everyone else I fell in love with her, just like Mick Jagger did a year or so later, beginning a highly publicized relationship during which she was discovered wearing just a rug at Keith Richards' house in Sussex

---

[55] She had a hit song 'As Tears Go By' and appeared in films most un-notably 'Girl on a Motorcycle'.

during a police raid. She appeared so serene and had a delicate and fragile beauty which was well expressed in her songs; it was hard to imagine how she became the queen of the swinging sixties rock chicks, swept up by Mick on a wave of sex and drugs and rock and roll. It is even harder now to imagine what happened after the said raid; she took to cocaine big time and later heroin, lost her son by John Dunbar into care, and after breaking up with Jagger was discovered by an old friend two years later living on the streets of Soho – a bag lady. She began a slow recovery and the delicate nightingale voice had dropped an octave and now sounded like a digger bucket being scraped over gravel. But she survived and is still performing.

The five year holiday at Eton was now coming to an end. I was the oldest boy in the school with about as much to show for my privileged education as a pocketful of sweet wrappers. I didn't even want to go into the army. I knew that my History and English A levels were going to show two big fat zeros, although I had passed the army exam, which only meant I was eligible for applying for the officer school at Sandhurst. In fact two years before Fred had encouraged me to join the Corps[56] and I'd been thrown out of it after six weeks for dropping my rifle in some complex and forgettable manoeuvre on the parade ground.

The last summer half seemed to flash by. I found myself in the third rowing eight. They shoved me up to the front of the boat as I was very small and light and should really have been the cox, but I must have been quite useful. We rowed against another school over two miles in a race, and I remember nearly dying at the end of it and thinking that I could cross rowing off things to do again.

---

[56] Pronounced 'cor' – the Eton Army.

It really did seem like the end of a holiday that we all knew would never be repeated – rushing round saying goodbye to beaks and boys, packing up stuff that had been festering in cupboards and dark corners for five years, and exchanging photos of ourselves with other boys for reasons I have not yet been able to fathom. Perhaps they were supposed to be aides mémoires in later years when we met on the street. I met some of them at the reunion last year, fifty years since we'd last been together and I only recognized one of them.

# 13 – ADRENALINE

And so we went forth into the real world – some of us back to our estates or royal palaces, some of us to family businesses and merchant banks, and some even into the world of entertainment and the media. I went home still not knowing what the word 'future' meant. The movie clips are coming fast and furiously now and I can't believe how so much was crammed in during the next five years.

I'm now on the back of a semi retired but reliable racehorse called Mersey Boy, riding in a point-to-point steeplechase at Eaton Hall in Cheshire. Ten other jockeys and horses are galloping towards the first fence at thirty miles an hour and for a few seconds I'm terrified. Penned in by the others, all around me are the jockeys' nodding bottoms and the snorting horses, and there's no way I can get a glimpse of the first fence. Unbelievably, my horse takes off and we glide in a slow motion parabola through the air and the terror subsides into an almost warm glow and a fleeting thought 'Gosh, that was fun' as we thundered on towards the next fence.

I remember little of the training, enforced by my

mother, which included getting up at sunrise to exercise the horse, and going for runs at sunset to exercise me. I do remember lying across the horse's withers towards the end of that first race like a sack of potatoes; the horse was in the same state, but it was a fantastic buzz. There were a few more of these excursions to racecourses all over the country and Mersey Boy and I came in second once, much to my mother's displeasure, who said I should have won. In one race south of Birmingham, I made a bit of a bollocks and forgot to let the reins out as Mersey Boy landed over a fence. This meant that I went straight over his head and I flew like a fruit bat from six feet up onto the grass below. There was an excruciating pain as I slithered front first to a halt. The pain was centered around my knackers and I got up clutching them and pirouetting round and round on the same spot, whimpering. Within seconds a lady appeared from the St John's Ambulance service and she made me lie down on a stretcher and I was driven back to the medical tent, where she insisted I take down my breeches so she could inspect the damage – nuts bruised and willie stretched – damage minimal.

My brother, Jonothon – he'd now changed his name because he was fed up with people asking him to spell it – had a much hairier career as a jockey. He was much better on a horse than Gemma and myself but there was a problem. The horses he rode, unlike Mersey Boy, belonged to my mother, and there was usually some defect, sometimes obvious like refusing to jump fences, and sometimes something hidden. She had been given a really intelligent but quite useless old racehorse a few years earlier, called White Faced Jeff, and put Jonothon on him one time. We called him Facey – he was bright orange, euphemistically known as chestnut, with a large white star on his face and four white socks. He would have had a brilliant television career as Roy Rogers' horse, Trigger, but he failed the audition and Trigger got the part. I made friends with him and when I was bored or had problems would go and lean over the fence, and talk to him. We got on quite well and could converse intelligently on all sorts of things. He would snort back in a sympathetic or derisory way, depending on his mood, or mine.

I was away at the time but it happened like this. Facey got about half way round the course, having resigned himself, out of politeness I suppose for the free board and lodging my mother gave him, to a pointless twenty minutes of galloping and jumping. Like Oscar Wilde, he had the same view about over exertion. 'If I feel the urge to take exercise, I sit down and wait for the urge to pass.' So, half way round he took off over a fence, had a heart attack in mid air and dropped dead – on top of Jonothon, who sat there somewhat confused but alive. Within minutes my mother and father are there standing over him, and checking that the horse is dead and their son still alive, my mother says 'You've killed my horse!' and my father says 'You've ripped my boots! I've had them for forty years! Good god, you've broken my whip too!'

For the next few days Jonothon is a little glum and his neck hurts and he can't move his head, and after much persuasion he asks if he can borrow Woodie, the Mini Traveller, to drive to the hospital. He is sitting waiting for the results of an X-ray, when a nurse rushes up and says 'Mr Dewhurst? Don't move! Don't move! You've broken your neck!' He spent the next twenty minutes trying to persuade my reluctant mother and father to come and pick him up, and the next six weeks in plaster from his chin to his waist. He too gave up being a steeplechase jockey.

One evening, late in the Spring of 1966 I found myself in an old Methodist chapel in Chester that had been converted into a theatre. It was pouring with rain the night I went with some friends. A repertory company had been operating there for a year and it was obvious they were having a bit of a struggle to keep the place going. I don't remember the play but I do remember the water dripping into a bucket next to me. Afterwards I went backstage and asked if they needed any help, and I got my first serious job, paying £1.10s.0d a week, only it wasn't serious. It was hilarious. My official title was Assistant Stage Manager, doing the donkey work with furniture and buckets etc, and sawing up last week's scenery to make next week's. Soon I was promoted to minor parts, and because of a shortage of actors I once had to do both butlers in 'The Importance of Being Earnest.' Usually there was an audience of at least three people sitting there unsmiling in their overcoats with their arms folded, but occasionally during the school term we would play to a packed house. After I'd ridden out on Mersey Boy, I would drive into Chester for morning rehearsals and then leave late at night after rollicking around the pub in hysterics. It was a heady time. The whole company had been trained at acting school and acted properly, according to the book, and I got continual bollockings for doing it all wrong, like upstaging the others instead of remaining still and motionless when it wasn't my turn. Picking my nose as the butler at the back of the stage and then throwing a challenging look to the audience while the principal at the front of the stage was delivering an emotional speech, was not well received by the rest of the company.

The lead actor was a chap called Bryan Hunt who had teamed up with a girl called Jayne Someone. They were the Couple, very responsible, and spoke in melodious and perfectly pitched tones until they'd had a few in the pub and became raucous like the rest of us. Jayne was all floaty scarves and very serious about – about the Craft darling. There were a few hissy fits rumbling under the surface, and a scapegoat in the form of a girl called Lizzie Adam. She was attractive and comely, and had nice hair but she mainly played herself. With this in mind, the director Gavin Sutherland, who was also the set designer, carpenter and stage manager gave her the smallest parts in most of the plays, 'but darling you're made for the part – it would be such a waste to give it to someone else...' Gavin was also one of the funniest men I had met up till then. He was quite large and bald and his father owned a pub. He was keen on the amber nectar, and had us in stitches all the time. Finally there was Wendy Eyton, a few years older than me, whom I took rather a fancy to, but I don't think she reciprocated. She had lovely hands and large beautiful eyes and was a bloody good character actor.

The most hysterical moment of all, though, was on stage during a performance of 'The Importance of Being Earnest.' There was surprisingly a full house as it was compulsory stuff for GCE O level English in many schools and there were well over two hundred people crammed in. I was playing the butler Lane, and Bryan as Algernon, had just said to me something like 'Where are the cucumber sandwiches, Lane?' and I had replied 'There were no cucumbers in the market, sir, not even for ready money,' and then he said something like 'Never mind,' and dropped on to the sofa. There was a sound of splitting wood and one of the legs came off, tipping Bryan backwards on to the floor next to me. All the audience saw were his legs disappearing. All I saw was Bryan as he leapt back up, almost in the same movement, with the audience raising the roof, shouting 'I told you to sort out that woodworm Lane!' I had collapsed behind the upturned sofa, and was weeping with laughter but otherwise catatonic. As the laughter died Bryan managed to say something like 'Go and get a hammer, Lane,' and after about a minute and a half trying to get over my catatonia, I eventually sauntered off with a serious look, and returned shortly with a hammer and a block of wood on a tray. Bryan had known all along that the sofa was going to go, and wanted to make a political point, but there was no money really to do anything after paying our paltry wages, which we spent in the pub, laughing all the more. But it didn't matter. It was the roar of the greasepaint and the smell of the crowd[57], and it could have gone on for ever as far as I was concerned.

The Methodist church has gone now and so has most of Queen Street where it stood, and over the past fifty years I've toyed with the idea of going back into acting, but visiting Wendy's cramped damp flat in a boarding house all that time ago put me off. Acting is a vocation like nursing or the priesthood or being a jockey where the poverty is of little consequence as everyone else is in the same boat, and I would not have coped with it or the discomfort. It's all consuming too – you live it and sleep it and for me there was other stuff to be doing. But over the years I have done a lot more here and there, in a very amateurish way, and there is nothing to compare with the nerves and anticipation as you stand in the wings, nearly wetting yourself, before walking out on stage. Even now, just walking on to an empty stage with an empty auditorium puts the hairs on the back of my neck up, and I feel I'm turning into someone else. And if I happened to

---

[57] Award winning 1965 Broadway musical 'The Roar of the Greasepaint – The Smell of the Crowd'.

be playing to a full house and a good audience the buzz when I came off was almost better than riding in a race, jumping out of a plane, skiing fast down a steep mountain, falling in love, and far more exciting than eating lobster with a good Bâtard Montrachet.

There was so little margin for error that it was dangerous in a non-fatal way. It was not as bad as messing up jumping from a plane, or making the wrong move on a horse, but it was still buttock clenching. It was a tightrope walk between euphoria and embarrassment. A cock-up in front of three hundred people was all there was between triumph and oblivion. Perhaps that was part of the attraction – living on the edge of the cliff.

Apropos of nothing, five hundred years ago a courtier noisily broke wind as he bowed low to the passing Queen Elizabeth. In acute embarrassment he left the court for he was a sensitive fellow, and was only persuaded to return seven years later by a friend. Her Majesty noticed his return as he bowed low once more, mumbling some sycophantic apology for his absence. In front of everyone she said quite simply 'My Lord, we hath forgot the Fart.' The story is more than likely scurrilous and made up to bitch about a social adversary[58] but it makes the point – death by gaffe!

Driving home the seventeen miles late at night and happily tipsy after a wild time in the pub was never a problem. This was a time when a policeman would ask you to get out of the car and walk down the white line in the middle of the road, or even ask you to stand on one leg for a bit without falling over.

I was driving a second hand Austin A35 van which had seen better days. She was called Nellie. I'd passed

---

[58] Possibly Edward de Vere – occasionally thought to have written Shakespeare's plays.

my test a couple of years before in Woodie, the Mini Traveller, that was my parent's second car. Car number one at that time was a fluorescent green thing. She was called Vanessa the Vanguard. The day I took my driving test my mother suggested I put her bull terrier, who was called Tootle[59], in the back. Tootle was so laid back that you would have thought he was on drugs to see him tottering along and quite often walking into things. He would stand there with a confused look on his face before finding a way round the obstruction. He spent most of his time asleep in a haze of flatulent and foetid air in front of the fire, but when awake could strike terror into those who did not know him, simply by just standing still, and because of the reputation of the breed to which he belonged. He was also pig ugly. My mother always had a penchant for bull terriers – usually benign but unpredictably ferocious – and I have the scars to prove it. She obviously didn't think I had a hope of passing unless there was some implied threat to the examiner, and indeed this proved the case when the first thing he said on getting into the car was 'Is the dog all right?' and I said 'He's all right at the moment,' putting the emphasis firmly on 'moment.' It worked and I'm still the worst licensed driver in Europe bar the Belgians, and have been for the past fifty years. Shortly after passing I was driving Nellie the van round quite a sharp bend on the drive up to the back door. There was no gravel or tarmac. It was just earth with a few brick ends and on this particular day it had been raining. I was going too fast and slammed on the brakes and the van skidded quite a long way and was stopped by a cast iron down pipe against the house which shattered as I hit it. The

---

[59] Short for 'toute à l'heure' meaning 'presently' as in 'he's a bit slow – he'll be here presently'.

noise was deafening as thirty feet of drainpipe, now reduced to shrapnel, dropped on to the bonnet of the car and stove it in. In the relative silence I heard a hissing coming from the radiator, and there was an ugly black shaft of pipe sticking out of the bonnet. A few seconds later my father rushed out, thinking that we had been attacked. I'd banged the top of my nose on the rear view mirror and I was staggering around with lots of blood dribbling from a tiny cut, but it saved me from a bollocking. Of course I wasn't wearing a seat belt – nobody did back then.

It is almost unbelievable that it took ten years from the first draft of a compulsory seat belt law for front of car passengers to eventually get it through Parliament in 1980, and another eight years for rear seat passengers. In 1965 twenty two people a day died on the UK roads. In 2015 that was down to five people a day. Looking back today it seems so obvious; we were in denial and refused to accept that compulsory seat belts would save thousands of lives. Instead we said that it was the beginning of the end and would restrict people's freedom to do as they pleased. We were right in a way because seat belts did indeed restrict our freedom – to fly through the windscreen.

Denial is a powerful motivating force that papers over rational thought processes, especially when it comes to drugs. Just think how long it is taking to ban cigarettes and how we will eventually be able to look back on a total ban in a hundred years time, and say how ridiculous we were back in 2016. Presently tobacco is responsible for killing 100,000 people a year – yes that's every *year* in the UK. Ride on lung cancer, heart disease, strokes and dementia, at least they're keeping the National Health Service busy and the 720,000 who work there. Right now, tobacco kills about half a million people a year worldwide, and without banning the stuff it's estimated that this century will see one billion deaths from diseases directly related to smoking. Is it some grand plan to keep the population down, or do we just have the brains of building blocks?

Of course with tobacco the answer is greed. Tobacco companies harvest the leaves and make the cigarettes. They justify this by saying they are giving jobs to people in third world countries. They then sell the cigarettes mostly to people of low social backgrounds and mostly to the same third world countries. The companies are based in the more affluent areas of the world such as North America and Europe where, of course, most of the shareholders live. Some daft shareholders even smoke themselves to death together with their unfortunate non-smoking friends should they be cornered by them. But hell, I can rant as much as I like. We're making money out of it and that's what counts, isn't it? Not only are we keeping the population down, we're also killing off those who aren't much use to us anyway. Progress, progress, you can't stop the market!

Meanwhile, outside the back door back in 1966 I was suffering from a bruised ego and bleeding to death from a tiny cut in my head. Both of these were good things in an indirect way, as my driving got marginally better with the dial moving away from suicidal to occasionally careless, and I started to wear a seat belt long before anybody else did.

Lou Coffin, who owned the garage up the road, came and took the car away to repair the bonnet and radiator. The irony of his name was a constant reminder to those who visited his garage. His father had built it back in the thirties after the family retired from the coffin making business, which apparently they had been doing since the Domesday Book[60]. Back in the sixties it looked very like someone had transplanted an old gas station from the desert in New Mexico next to the main road in Cholmondeley – minus the tumbleweed. It was an untidy mix of corrugated sheeting and rusting hulks of old cars and random bits of metal, but round the back there were a few gems. Lou was allowed by the Rolls Royce factory in Crewe to repair their cars, and had access to much information about second hand Rolls Royces and Bentleys, which he bought and sold. He got on well with my father, who rather wanted to own one, but couldn't afford it. One school holiday in the late fifties, we came home to find two Rolls Royces in the stable yard. I think they were called Silver Ghosts. One was made in 1928 and the other in 1930. Only one worked – the black one. The other, almost the same but in grey was there for spares and for us to play in. The black one was for pulling the horse trailer, but I never found out why my father needed a Rolls to do this or what sort of a deal Lou Coffin did to persuade him to take two. The closest noun to describe Lou was a rogue. He knew that we knew he was a rogue as he sold us cars with that quiet voice and a naughty glint in his eye, but he was charming with it and we were putty in his hands.

It must have been a strange sight seeing a gleaming black Rolls Royce purring along the main road with a horse trailer being towed behind it. Most people used Land Rovers or a sleek estate car, but no, we had to be different. As children we loved it. We would sit in the back behind a sliding glass window pretending we were royalty and shouting down a bakelite microphone with nonsensical orders at whoever was driving.

One cold winter's afternoon in January we were

---

[60] Collated in 1087 by William I

coming back from hunting the fox and the Rolls was struggling to pull the trailer, full of ponies, up a steep hill on the main road. It was snowing hard and the back wheels were spinning hopelessly. We were walking up the side of the road for some reason when we saw a cattle truck coming the other way over the top of the hill. My father, who was driving, could do nothing as the truck began to skid, veering from one side of the road straight into the Rolls. There was a very loud bang as the front of the cattle truck stove in. The lady kneeling down on the top of the Rolls' chrome radiator housing didn't budge, but apparently this gem of a car was a write off, and both of them disappeared.

By this time, Barrow the groom, had been replaced by Shorto, the new groom and gardener. Leslie Shorto had arrived with his wife, Hilda, and son, Peter, at almost the same time as the Rolls Royces. He had been a commando in the war and naturally as fellow soldiers there was common ground and he got on well with my father, whom he called 'the Colonel,' while he called him 'Shorto' so we all did. Shorto, as a commando in the war, had landed on Sword Beach on D-Day. Bombarded by German shell fire before even hitting the beach, he had spent the next four hours lying in the sand, overcome by fear with his dead and wounded compatriots lying all around him. He was a small wiry man and upset nearly everyone by turning most conversations into a fight. He was stubborn too and would only take orders from my father, so my mother – as Commander of the Horse and used to giving orders in that respect – had to go through my father if she wanted Shorto to do anything. Not blessed with a great intellect, he nevertheless had an opinion about everything, guided mainly by the Sunday Pictorial and the giant chip on his shoulder. He could not come to terms with his social position in the world either, and looking back now I don't blame him.

One day, when he was taking Gemma and Jonothon somewhere in the Rolls with their ponies in the trailer behind, he had just got into a short fifty yard one way stretch on the main road, where there were some repairs being done. This was before traffic lights and there was a large lorry coming the other way and many cars behind it. Both vehicles stopped and the burly truck driver suggested in no uncertain terms that the Rolls would have to be reversed, as there was a long queue behind the lorry. Shorto refused point blank and eventually took out his sandwiches and sat on the running board washing them down with a thermos of tea. Gemma and Jonothon sat regally in the back of the Rolls and couldn't believe it. One by one the cars backed out and eventually the lorry. By this time Shorto had finished his lunch, cleared away the crumbs and was ready to drive on. He could quite easily have been killed – by the truck driver.

Fast forward to the Spring of 1966 and Shorto's War was a jaundiced version that he hadn't yet told me about; in a few month's time I was going to join the army too. Looking back now it was almost pathetic. I didn't want to join the bloody army; I was only doing it to please my father. I was blissfully happy in the theatre, and one day had the courage to tell him, and he told me 'I don't want a mummer for a son!' and that was that. I stupidly thought a mummer was his slang for a homosexual, and I didn't want to appear to be one, but as I wasn't one anyway, what did it matter? Perhaps I thought I might turn into one.

During a break in theatre activities I went down to Westbury in Wiltshire to take the entrance test for officer cadets. It was four days of physical and intellectual testing which would determine whether I was suitable material for an officer. I was physically fit and dived through all the fake windows and climbed all the ropes with ease, but still with the social maturity of a twelve year old, there was no way of passing. When a crusty old tartan-trousered colonel asked me whether I was going into the cavalry or infantry and I replied 'the infantry,' he then wondered why I was trying to get into the Royal Scots Greys – a cavalry regiment.

The inevitable letter came three days after I'd come back home, and of course I'd failed. It was decided I should go and train as a squaddie[61] up in Catterick, Yorkshire. After a final evening treading the boards as a mummer in the theatre, and a completely wild night in the pub afterwards, I said goodbye to my fellow luvvies. A few days later I drove to the Recruiting Office in Whitchurch, and joined the army. I was told to report to the cavalry training regiment at Catterick in Yorkshire two weeks later.

---

[61] ordinary soldier – a trooper

# 14 – TRAINED TO KILL

I had been thinking for some time after leaving school that it might be a good thing to cut loose from home and find a place of my own like most other people did. This idea had been bubbling in my head for some time and one day I was chatting to Hugh Rocksavage, who ran the Cholmondeley Estate for his father at the time, and had rented out Barmere to my father for the past twelve years for a pittance. I asked him if I could rent a cottage on the estate if there was one free. He lined me up with one, which is even now just a hundred yards from where I write. We didn't discuss rent because Hugh didn't really understand the concept of money; he relied on other people to deal with that sort of thing. He had been born into the rarified atmosphere of the English aristocracy just after the First World War.

His father was the 5th Marquis of Cholmondeley who lived in the family pile, Houghton Hall, in Norfolk. Houghton, a massive house even by stately home standards had been built on the proceeds of somewhat dubious deals in the early 1700s by Robert Walpole, Britain's first prime minister, and Hugh was directly descended from Robert, whose daughter had married a Cholmondeley in the 1720s. The Cholmondeleys were a canny lot when it came to marriage and invariably made a good job of it; Hugh's father had married Sybil Sassoon[62], while he married his next door neighbour in Norfolk, Lavinia Leslie, in 1947, and they came up to Cholmondeley in the early 1950s, where Lavinia whipped off all the dust sheets, redecorated the place and started to reinvigorate the forty acre garden, which is now one of the most spectacular in Northern England.

One day at lunch I had overheard Hugh talking to my mother, who had little idea about how money worked too, and it went something along these lines. 'Do you know what – we've discovered this thing called a Morgidge – yes a Morgidge. It's a loan from a Building Society and it means we can sell some of our cottages to our tenants instead of renting them out. They get the money from the Building Society to do it so then we have a lump sum to repair other cottages. It's a bit like a bank when you borrow money.'

Whereas Walpole had been a scoundrel and an accumulator of wealth at other people's expense, Hugh was happy to run the seven thousand acre Cholmondeley Estate, after his father died in 1968, with an unusual benevolence and magnanimity. Realizing that most of the tenants on the estate were not as well off as him, he tended to offer them low rents and made sure that he only rented houses out to those whom he liked. He was also very keen on roulette and one of his favourite places was the Casino in Monte Carlo, a short hop from his

---

[62] The Sassoons – Siegfried was a cousin – were one of the richest families in the world in the nineteenth century. Of Bagdhadi Jewish origins, they made their fortunes from trading, originally in opium, from China to Western Europe.

family holiday home in Cap Ferrat. I guess he lost far more than he won, but on a particularly good night when the numbers were running his way, he made enough to build a swimming pool and a rather grand balconied loggia overlooking it attached to the castle. Basically he was an accountant's nightmare, but everyone on the estate was very fond of him. Tall and good looking with the charm to go with it, he had fought in the war and reached the rank of Major, and been awarded a military cross for gallantry.

Apart from roulette, Hugh had one or two other peccadilloes, one of which was food. He had an official job at Court, as Lord Great Chamberlain, and was in charge of all Royal visits to the Palace of Westminster. Every year when the Queen came to open the new Parliament, he was responsible for making sure everything was tip-top, walking backwards in front of her holding a long stick without tripping over, and giving her a gin and tonic in the ante room after her speech. The problem was his scarlet and gold thread embroidered uniform that was made to fit in 1968 but a few years later was getting a bit small, so he would disappear from Cheshire in late October, ostensibly to check out the Parliament Opening in early November, but really to check into a health farm with a friend where they would starve for a week, and he could get into his elaborate coat and not be throttled by the high collar because his neck was too fat.

So I said to my father that Hugh had found a cottage, and he said 'What do you want to do that for when you've got a perfectly good house here – and where are you going to get the money to pay for it?'

I sighed inwardly and climbed into Nellie the Van, after chucking in a small bag of clothes, a map and the pieces of paper telling me to report to the Queen's Own

Hussars, D Squadron, Catterick Camp, Richmond, somewhere in furthest Yorkshire. It's strange but I remember very little of the next 187 days. All I can see again are more short film clips with little or no plot to hold them together. It was one of the most boring six months of my life. But in hindsight it was the hell of a lesson in social experimentation, and however much I loathed it at the time for its sheer tediousness, it was an invaluable experience.

Catterick Camp was, and still is, the largest British army garrison in the world. Surrounded by open moorland and with few people to annoy with all the loud bangs, it was freezing cold in the winter and freezing cold in the summer – the perfect place to freeze our knackers off and soften us up for what was to come. The Queen's Own Hussars was assigned for two years to train recruits who wanted to join a British cavalry regiment. It was not a great posting for the regiment, but one up from the grim plains of Northern Germany, where in 1966 one squadron was still left, contributing to our NATO commitment against the perceived threat of Communism.

My first lesson in social anthropology, army style, began about two days in, after we had been shown our barrack rooms, dished out with about four complete sets of clothing down to socks and shreddies[63], and had most of our hair cut off. I was ordered to report to my platoon commander, a certain Lieutenant Johnnie Bulkeley. Holy shit! Two years older than me, he had been in my house at Eton! He was not a close friend but I'd known him quite well and he had known me. Small and well built with curly fair hair, he was a keen amateur jockey in his spare time. He sat at his desk with his platoon sergeant

___
[63] underpants

standing behind him. The sergeant had a slight smirk on
his face. Johnnie, I mean Lieutenant Bulkeley, spoke out
of the corner of his mouth rather like Prince Charles, and
the conversation went something like this:

'Now look Dewhurst. We may have been at school
together, but now you're at the bottom of the pile and
you'll get absolutely no favours from me or from
Sergeant Crippin here. Do you understand?'

'Yes – SIR!'

And that was that. I didn't see him again. So much
for the old boy network …

For the first three months of basic training the new
intake, about sixty men in all, were allotted barrack
rooms with eight to a room. There were communal
bathrooms and lavatories on each floor of the new
buildings, and they were light and airy with large
windows that looked out over the adjacent moorland.
There were eight of us in my room and seven had never
been away from home before. We were all roughly the
same age; perhaps the oldest was twenty one. For the
first few nights I was astounded to hear stifled weeping
coming from some of the beds. Most of these boys were
desperately homesick and after a few days one
disappeared, never to be seen again. He'd resigned and
gone home. For a reason I've forgotten – perhaps it was
my accent – I was known as 'Proff' as in 'professor.' It
may have been a perceived intellectual advantage.
Whatever there was of that I did my best to keep to
myself out of self preservation. More likely it was
because one of them was writing home and wanted to
spell 'homesick' and I helped him out.

What I did twig right from the start was how vital it
was to say the right things and never to start an argument
or make an enemy. Some of these men were potentially
very dangerous, and yet we all became mates, bonded

intentionally by the system and unified by the discomfort and compulsory hard work. The chap opposite me was tall and well built with short reddish hair and freckles and spoke with a Shropshire accent. He didn't want to join the army but had been arrested and charged with actual bodily harm, and after being pulled up in front of the magistrate, had been given a choice between the army and prison. He'd chosen the army, and luckily told me this early on. The Duke of Wellington is often misquoted as having said of his soldiers 'I don't know what effect these men will have on the enemy, but by God, they terrify me.' Whoever made this quote up understood well the qualities of the British squaddie. He came from a social background where the only acceptable way to deal with a problem was to fight his way out of it. Logical disputation? What the fuck does that mean? Added to this he was now being trained to kill with machine guns, rifles, hand grenades and other assorted paraphernalia. It was definitely a good idea during our training to take all the weaponry back off us at the end of a firearms lesson as quite a few recruits would have been killed or maimed as feuds arose. I was put in charge of this lot as room leader, a meaningless title that got me the blame when a communal job wasn't done properly, and caused grief when I tried to cajole them into scraping a bit more non-existent dirt off the perfectly clean lino floor before yet another inspection.

I remember very little about Catterick apart from the barrack room and the men who lived there. The marching, the running and the standing still took up most of the daylight hours and some of the night time too, and when that was over it was back to our beds to sleep, knackered, even in the middle of the day. In the evenings and sometimes into the night it was cleaning, scrubbing and polishing with Sergeant Crippin shouting stuff like

'I want that fuckin' floor so fuckin' shiny that I can see the reflection of your fuckin' ugly mugs in it you 'orrible little people.'

I guess we were burning up about twenty thousand calories a day or something similar, probably the same as a termite after an ant eater breaks in. Even during our lunch hour we were coming back from the canteen and going fast asleep on our beds. Surprisingly, the food was really good, served up by a team of trainee soldier cooks, and supervised by chefs from the Army Catering Corps. Good food and the army had not always gone well together and indeed the tins of constipating stodge we had to take with us on exercise, were pretty awful, but back in barracks it was a different kettle of fish. After a report by a chap called Sir Isidore Salmon in 1940, a new national catering school was set up, and during the war civilian advisors were brought in to try and improve things. I can imagine the first meeting and the word 'garlic' being mentioned, and some crusty old general retorting that garlic was for the savages across the Channel. Napoleon had said 'an army marches on its stomach' and coming from him this would not have improved matters. In 1965 the Army Catering Corps became a totally independent unit a year before I arrived at Catterick, and morale could not have been higher. For the first time men interested in cooking joined voluntarily, and took the place of ordinary squaddies who previously had been forced to cook.

Meanwhile we were being physically and mentally broken down and remoulded to the army's way of thinking – one step back and then two forwards so that at the end of three months training we were very basic soldiers. Not all of us in our barrack room made it. One day, about six weeks in, we came back from lunch to find clothes and equipment being thrown from a jagged star shaped hole in one of our windows. Upstairs, screaming curses at nobody in particular, was one Keith, a squat little chap with spiky fair hair, just about to hurl another boot through the window. We calmed him down and he too disappeared and that night there was one more empty bed. Was it a girlfriend, boyfriend, family pressure, army pressure? I never knew. Another man from another room eventually took his place. Perhaps this new fellow was the only one left in his own barrack room. He was called Phil and was a dark haired good looking chap, who spoke with a Brummy accent. He had been a dancer in civilian life and had appeared once on TV. He didn't appear to be gay, but then I had a pretty naïve view of what constituted gayness. Once again the word was not yet part of the vernacular, and homosexuality was still a year away from legality, so I presume anyone who was gay in the army was very careful about how they came across. But as recruits, we suddenly found that we had no interest in sex anyway. Was it the bromide they put in the tea? This was a recurring theme and strongly denied by our superiors. It was more likely that our sexual urges were severely diminished by the day's end because we were completely fucked.

Back to Phil. He got on well with all of us and was unusually intelligent and funny. One evening I went to bed early, and was in the depths of a dreamless sleep. I heard all this later but around ten o'clock, Phil had gone to the bathrooms to clean his teeth. Two other soldiers from outside were waiting for him, and while one held him, the other went to work on his face with a Stanley knife, cutting through both his maxillary arteries. He had staggered back to his bed leaving a trail of blood and the others had tried to stop the spurting with his sheets. I was in the next door bed, and it wasn't until the medics

162

had arrived and taken him away that I woke up to see the red and white sheets – more red than white to be honest – and a smeared trail of blood leading out of the door. We never saw Phil again, and we never heard why he had been attacked.

Violence was never far away and one of my final memories of the twelve weeks basic training was a fish and chip shop one Saturday night.

I'm queuing with the others after a beery evening in the NAAFI, where we're allowed to go at week ends and socialize. A small dark wiry man pushes in front of me and I say to him, being a bit pissed, something like 'Oi, what the fuck do you think you're doing?' and a mate standing behind me, gets hold of me and pulls me out of the chippie sharpish before I can say any more; there's a taxi outside waiting for us.

'Think we'd better go – Proff's causing trouble,' someone says.

'But that little wanker jusht barged in front of me,' says I, swaying on the pavement.

'That little wanker might just fucking kill you – he's a skin.'

'He's a what?'

By this time I'm being pulled into the back of the taxi and as the door closes, the little wanker comes up to the window and is trying to open the door and mouthing something at me as someone leans across and tries to pull the door shut as I'm trying to push it open.

'Why won't you let me hit the little fucker?'

'He's a fucking Iniskillin' and you don't mess with them,' someone says, and that was that.

I'd been saved by my mates. The Royal Inniskilling Fusiliers were a tough regiment from Northern Ireland, all Protestant. The Duke of Wellington once told someone that he'd had more Inniskilling Fusiliers flogged than everyone else in his army put together, so their reputation had gone before them. Two of them had been killed by the Southern Irish Catholics in the Easter Uprising in 1916. I wonder what that ferrety little fellow would have done to me if he'd known I was a forkin' taig[64].

You will have noticed that 'fuck' has been used as several different figures of speech in the last few paragraphs – as a noun, a verb, an adjective, an adverb. Just like the letter 'e' being the commonest letter in the English language, 'fuck' and its attendant derivations was the commonest word in the army. It really was. It beat any other word by fucking miles. Forget 'march,' 'rifle,' 'shoot,' 'kill,' 'dead,' 'next-of-kin,' 'coffin.' It was believed that the sergeants and especially the RSM[65], who shouted at us the most when we were learning how to march on the parade ground, sat in their mess of an evening making up things to bawl at us the next day. The sergeant-major always carried a hinged pace stick under his arm. It was like a geometry compass, and used to fix the length of our marching stride. It was commonly known as a swagger stick. He would often come up to one of us if we'd made some interesting move like turning left on the order 'Right turn!' while everyone else had gone the other way. 'Listen to me Dewhurst! If you don't pull your fuckin' socks up and fuckin' listen, I'm going to stick this stick up your fuckin' arse and march you round the parade ground like a fuckin' lollipop!'

Of course some of these aphorisms stuck and were handed down to be used sparingly with each new intake

---

[64] Fucking Catholic
[65] Regimental Sergeant Major – the highest non-commissioned officer in a regiment. Not to be messed with.

of recruits. Once Sergeant Crippin came up to me after a spectacular cock-up, standing so close that he was shouting down vertically at the top of my beret and lacing it with spittle. The tirade usually started in a sympathetic and seductive tone and finished with a hysterical crescendo of well rehearsed invective. 'Not a lot of people know this Dewhurst, but if they'd invented wanking as an Olympic sport, you'd have about six gold medals lined up on your mantlepiece. Now tell me, you horrible little turd, how tall are you?'

'Five foot seven – S'AR'NT!'

'Do you know what' – building into the crescendo and polishing it off with a falsetto scream – 'I'VE NEVER SEEN SHIT PILED SO HIGH IN MY LIFE!'[66]

At the end of twelve weeks we finished our basic training, and I don't even remember the passing out parade. The others would have all gone on leave and then to their respective regiments. I moved into another building and joined a room full of potential officers, who had also finished their training with other intakes. We were here to do weapons training and map reading, as well as eighty mile forced marches across the moors blindfolded, carrying three hundred pounds of gubbins and stuff in a rucksack.

We had two new nannies – Lieutenant Cannon and Sergeant Bull. David Cannon had the right name for a soldier, but I have the feeling he would have been happier catching butterflies and writing poetry. He was fair haired and thin and spoke very quietly and was not much older than us. We hardly ever saw him. Pete Bull on the other hand was a big man, about six foot two and well built. He probably kept dumb bells in his toilet and ate three chickens a day because he had a massively

---

[66] This was Sgt Crippin's version of a well used insult.

ripped upper body and a tiny waist; he walked on his toes with his arms held out and a bit of a swagger. He was a lot more friendly than the other sergeants and usually had a smile on his face and we called him Sarge. He liked to give the impression that he could kill just by looking at somebody.

I can only remember three of the others in my room. One was Richard Russell who wanted to ride in the Grand National and win it. I said that I wanted to make an Oscar winning film, so there was a bet that neither of us won, but it was a good thing to have the drive and optimism. He was far too tall to be a jockey, but after leaving the army he went on to train racehorses. He was a friendly fellow and took everything that was thrown at him without really caring about anything at all.

Then there was Chris Joll. Well, he liked to be called Christopher Joll and he'd had a rough time as a recruit. He was a pleasant fellow but I got the feeling that he wasn't prepared to let go of the conventions he'd accumulated over his short life. Whenever we went to the pub he'd dress in cavalry twill trousers, a yellow check waistcoat like Rupert Bear, and a tweed jacket, while we were all in jeans. By the time we were all quite merry and taking the mickey out of each other, he was happy to join in too, but metaphorically he took some time to unbutton his waistcoat. We got on well and I must have kept in touch with him, because my sister, Gemma, remembers being dated by him and going to a Sandhurst[67] Ball. He had joined a cavalry regiment that still wore spurs on the dance floor. Gemma says her dress was ripped to shreds. She took him back to meet my father, who didn't like him because he was Jewish. That was going some from my father, who had Jewish

---

[67] Royal Military Academy

blood at least down to where his legs forked.

Then there was Mo, short for Malcolm, whose second name I've forgotten. He wanted to be a rally driver and was going to join a tank regiment. He was quite small, which is a good thing if you're going to drive a tank as you tend to bang your head a lot if you're tall. He drove a small minivan furiously to the pub and back, trying to steer the perfect corner, which apparently was difficult to do in a minivan. We used to go to The Bull at Moulton (no relation to Sarge) and drink lots of squaddie shorts like rum and blackcurrant, while Christopher Joll drank gin and tonic – all mixed with a few pints of beer.

I was coming back from the canteen one time with Mo. We were wearing our overalls and berets and mooching along kicking the odd stone as one does, with our hands in our pockets. There was a sergeant we didn't know coming the other way, and we nodded as he passed. He stopped, turned his head and barked 'You two!! Come here now!! At the double!!'

Shit.

'What the fuck do you think you're doing?' He was frothing at the mouth and his face had turned quite red.

'We were just walking back to our – '

'You were AMBLING like fucking officers with your hands in your pockets. You're not fucking officers – you're still soldiers. And YOU' – pointing at me with a quivering finger and getting into my space rather too closely I thought – 'Take your fucking hands out of your pockets and stand to attention – NOW!! What's your name you little turd?'

'Dewhurst, Sergeant.'

He glanced at my beret. 'Well well, Dewhurst, I see you're going into the Royal Scots Greys huh?'

'Yes Sergeant.'

'Do you know about that eagle, Dewhurst?'

Eagle? Oh, my cap badge. I didn't know much about it except I'd spent hours taking it off my cap, polishing it, and sticking it back on. I was aware also that it was the insignia of the regiment I was going into.

'Not really Sergeant.'

'Not really Sergeant. I don't suppose you even know what sex it is, do you Dewhurst?'

'No Sergeant.'

'No Sergeant. Well, I'll tell you what sex it is – it's a female eagle. And do you want to know why it's a female eagle?'

'Er, yes Sergeant.'

'BECAUSE IT'S GOT A RIGHT CUNT UNDERNEATH IT! – NOW FUCK OFF – AT THE DOUBLE!'

One day when I had a bad hangover Sergeant Bull told us we were going to practise killing people with hand grenades[68]. After an intensive and repetitive lecture on how to use them, and what they did to a human being when they exploded, we drove up to the range. These things were like small pineapples, four inches long and two and a half wide with a curved sprung handle held against them with a split pin on a ring; you pulled the ring pin out, got into the throwing position, and threw as far as you could. From the time you let go of the handle and it sprang open, there was roughly four seconds before the thing made a very loud bang and hurled bits of iron shrapnel for over a hundred yards in all directions, including back over you as you dived to the ground. It was as heavy as a rock of the same size, roughly a couple of pounds, and I'd never been able to throw stones, let alone rocks. I was used to

---

[68] The Mills bomb was invented by a chap called William Mills in 1915. It killed people with great efficiency for the next seventy years.

guns and rifles but these things scared the shit out of me. Anyway there we were in the freezing cold, standing behind a wall as a gale howled around us in mid July. In front of this wall was another shorter wall. The plan was to stand in front of the short wall with the instructor when it was your turn, while everyone else settled down behind the big one. When you'd thrown the grenade, together with the instructor you'd move quickly behind the little wall to avoid the shrapnel. We all wore one of those tin helmets shaped like flying saucers, which were very uncomfortable, and a meagre concession to safety. My helmet didn't fit very well, was loose and kept coming down over my face. Sergeant Bull called my name and I was given a grenade by a corporal squatting beside a box full of them. I joined him round the front of the wall.

'Ready, Dewhurst? Remember the drill – pin out – back – throw – move. Got it?'

'Yes Sarge.'

As instructed I stood sideways like they did in the comics we used to read at school, with the grenade in my right hand and my left over the ring pin. Panic struck, I tried to remember the drill. Take out the pin with the index finger of my left hand, and in a fluid movement, lean backwards, letting my empty arm point skywards and moving my other arm down and backwards in the opposite direction, and then bring the body up, swinging my right arm over, and let go of the grenade. Suddenly there was a loud bang. My helmet had fallen off and clattered on the stony ground. Thinking I'd dropped the grenade, I rushed round behind the wall trembling with fear and just stopped short of crapping myself. Shit! I've taken the pin out! It's going to blow us all to bits!

'Where the fuck d'you think you're going?' Sergeant Bull thundered from the other side of the wall as I looked down befuddled and saw I was still holding the bloody thing with the pin in. I sheepishly walked back to pick up my helmet and try again. This time I got it right but the grenade only went about twenty feet and I scuttled behind the wall as did Sergeant Bull. There was a loud explosion and I heard the fuse cap zinging back over our heads.

'Well done son, that should have killed a few,' says Sergeant Bull out of the corner of his mouth. 'Unfortunately, most of them would have been on your side,' he added rather unnecessarily. That night, still suffering from my hangover, I took three aspirins and went to bed early with my headache.

It was not all physical as a potential officer – once a week we had an hour in a classroom with the education officer. He was one of the few people who had quite an influence on my political leanings, which at that time were somewhere in between the editor of the Daily Mail and Genghis Khan. I cannot put a face on him, but he had the gift of the gab and we listened opened mouthed as he told us of the dangers in the world of geopolitics, army style. He had a large black and white map of the world on a blackboard behind him, and he pointed to the Far East where China and North Vietnam had been coloured in red. There were large black arrows pointing south and west, and he told us in no uncertain terms about the 'yellow peril' that was set to spread west across Asia, and that's why America was throwing all it could against the North Vietnamese, and what we didn't know at the time, against the Cambodians and Laotians as well. He then whipped the map over to show us a new one – the same world but the red had now spread westwards and the arrows too, into India. Of course there was an irony here. The British Empire's red or pink on the globes and atlases of the world were nowhere to be seen on this map. I left that particular lesson feeling that the Americans were doing the right thing, and that Communism had to be stopped at all costs. Two years later I was cheering Vanessa Redgrave in Trafalgar Square as she railed against the Vietnem War.

Apart from out initial interview, the only time I remember meeting our platoon commander, the one and only Lieutenant Cannon was late in the Spring of 1966. We were lounging on our beds when Sergeant Bull strode in.

'Stand by your beds, gentlemen! Quick sharp! Mr Cannon[69] to see you!'

You could tell that Mr Cannon didn't really want to see us at all but there was a flap on.

'Good morning chaps. There's a flap on. The wubbish tip at the top of the woad has been invaded by cwows and they're causin a bloody nuisance, flappin awound and annoyin passers by.' The only passers by were the recruits who had to run up to the top of the hill and back every morning. I'd have thought there were far worse things for recruits to put up with than being squawked at and being shat on by a crow, but like the others I stood to attention by my bed and said nothing.

'So you chaps have all volunteered to come with me and build a cwow twap to catch them.'

Sergeant Bull looked at his watch. 'Right men – three minutes to get your boots on. Meet us at the front entrance at 0930 – MOVE!' and out they went.

As we approached the rubbish tip in the back of the troop Land Rover I saw an old crow, lifting off on wings that had a few feathers missing, with a crust of bread in his beak. Sergeant Bull leapt out of the driving seat full of bounce and optimism.

---

[69] First and second lieutenants were officially known as 'Mister'

'Right lads, chop chop! Get that netting out, and the rest of the stuff. Mr Cannon will tell you what to do.' Whereupon he climbed back into the Land Rover, gave us a wink, reversed with a squeal of rubber, and drove back down the hill. Mr Cannon slowly unfolded a large piece of white paper, the same size as an architect's plan, on which was drawn a picture of the crow trap. It was just a sketch really – a cube with a cylinder on top. And that was it. We spent the next three hours making this pathetic thing and nobody really had a clue what they were doing.

After a while we didn't notice the smell from the rubbish tip, although the stink stayed on our overalls for the rest of the day. By half past twelve, with pieces of wire, wooden stakes and wire cutters, we'd built something that looked vaguely like what Lieutenant Cannon had drawn. I remember thinking to myself 'Holy shit, we're supposed to be trained killers, dogs of war preparing to be unleashed against the yellow peril and the red tide of Communism. What the hell are we doing building a bloody crow trap on a rubbish tip? What am I doing here? Shit, I'm leaving!' and I made the decision there and then, squelching around in the wet garbage under a threatening grey sky, with cold fingers and a dripping nose. The army wasn't for me. I was bored stiff!

A week later the date for a second visit to Westbury for the Regular Commissions Board exam came through. This time my superiors were pretty certain I'd pass, and then I'd be expected to sign on for a further three years as a cadet and then officer. But I'd made a decision. Boredom completely fogged the career path I'd found myself stumbling along and I couldn't see a yard ahead of me, let alone where the path might lead. I decided to leave while I still could. A week after building the crow

trap I was officially discharged and took all my kit back,
shook hands with everyone, collected my severance pay,
climbed into Nellie and drove home with no idea what I
was going to do next.

## 15 – FILTHY LUCRE

My father was not happy and from the moment I arrived home he gave up on me – well not exactly on me but on his mild ambitions for what he hoped I would be. He never told me to my face what he felt but I was told by others. I guess he realized – perhaps a little too late for his own peace of mind – that he had adopted the wrong attitude, and he then made a pragmatic decision not to bother with what I did, and just appreciate me for whom I was.

Of course my mother and father made a few mistakes with us, but like most of us they weren't psychologists. They were just parents. They did all they could, limited by the conventions they themselves were governed by. Philip Larkin nailed it[70]. One of the greatest errors my father made was giving me some of his money.

---

[70] 'They fuck you up your mum and dad. They may not mean to but they do
They fill you with the faults they had and add some extra, just for you.
But they were fucked up in their turn by fools in old-style hats and coats,
Who half the time were soppy-stern and half at one another's throats.
Man hands on misery to man. It deepens like a coastal shelf.
Get out as early as you can, and don't have any kids yourself.'

Whereas my brother was always quite careful with what he was given, and had a more responsible attitude when it came to a career, my pocket and my bank balance was always empty. It was the same with my sister. Mention to me the word 'career,' and I'd react like Dracula being confronted by a wooden cross and some garlic.

When I went off to Eton my father gave me £3 a week and set up a bank account with a cheque book. Within months I became one more hand rubbing statistic for the gnomes in Lloyds Bank, and when they weren't rubbing their hands, they opened their arms wide and invited me in to drink from the Trough of Perpetual Overdraft, from which I've been drinking almost ever since. But my father never bailed me out, and somehow I've survived without going bankrupt.

There was a Scottish chap called Lord Erskine who died twenty years ago, always short of money and always in trouble with the bank. I was at school with his son. In his will he was reputed to have left his testicles to Barclays Bank because he said 'they had no balls of their own.' I had the same kind of relationship with my own banks as they refused to lend me money for the next business venture, which was a good thing although I didn't realize it at the time, or else they let me run up a huge overdraft and then took my house away, which was a bad thing. I guess I'm no exception when it comes to debt, and with the experiences I've had in the past sixty years I could write a self-help book on how to deal with it.

As I write, the latest published figures at March 2015 show that the average household debt in the UK stands at £13,500. If mortgages are included this comes to £54,600. This second figure doesn't seem so much as the banks make sure the value of your house exceeds your debt, but lose your job, and poof – you can lose your home and quite possibly your wife and your well being. Add every household debt together in the UK and the total comes to a mind boggling £1.4 trillion – that's £1,400,000,000,000[71]. I was going to put an explanation mark at the end of this figure, but I'm thinking what's the point – it's only a figure isn't it? Is it real? Should we be shocked or upset? After all, I can probably see more grains of sand from where I'm standing just now, as I start walking towards the sea with my pockets full of large stones, hopeful that it will soon be over... I don't know whether we should be shocked or not. I personally know that for a long time I never really understood money or how to use it. If it was there I would spend it, and just as we all were, we were encouraged to spend it. A hundred and fifty years ago, I would have spent half of my life in a debtors' prison, or would I? Brought up to only spend what I had, perhaps I'd have had a different attitude and never have got into debt in the first place.

Today we are encouraged to accumulate debt, and I'm certain there are very good reasons for this. Someone who understands debt better than I do would say that debt is a good thing because certain kinds of debt are an investment. A banker lends you money to buy a house and this keeps the giant wheel of commerce lubricated and turning, and he, the banker skims off the interest and trousers it while you work your little cotton socks off to pay it back. While you work, your boss pays you a lot less than he can make from your own endeavours working for him, and he in turn spends the proceeds on expensive holidays and a large yacht, and he invites onto the yacht the bankers from whom he has borrowed the money to start his business in the first place.

---

[71] Slightly more in the US but not much. This figure is also roughly the same as the UK *National* Debt!

One reason for accumulating debt is to provide a control mechanism and hook us into the capitalist system, a system which suggests to us that we can all experience the good life. Weighing the benefits against the downsides, this is more perception than reality. I'm not really saying that we are being controlled. We perpetuate and accept the idea ourselves and the subsequent denial actually becomes a motivating and positive force to keep the wheel going. After all, look back a hundred years ago and we were all dirt poor and look at us now with all our big cars, our big houses, our big holidays, our big televisions and loads of other stuff and it matters not that the debt gets bigger. As long as we can keep digging all this stuff out of the earth we can keep ahead of it and go on producing these rewards for our efforts.

In years gone by, it was an early death and the Kingdom of Heaven that was the reward for hard work. Nowadays it's a Porsche Cayenne and a 72 inch plasma television on the drip[72]. All I need to do here is ask a simple question – are we happier?

Another reason to promote debt is greed, and here we're in denial too. Speculate to accumulate says your boss. I've laid my cock on the block for you guys and taken all the risk. Be thankful I've given you a job. I know many millionaires and the odd billionaire and none of them say whatever goes into my coffers I'll share equally with the people who work for me. The greed is not just restricted to those who lend the money and take the interest, or build the properties and take the rent. We too are greedy for the tidbits we are encouraged to buy on credit, and convince ourselves that we deserve them

---

[72] In days gone by this referred to hire purchase – now a credit card or bank loan

as rewards for the work we do.

Finally and quite simply, real wealth can buy power. How that power is used becomes the whim of the individual. At one end of the scale some choose to give some of it away. Others unfortunately, realizing the susceptibilities of human nature, use it differently and exploit even further those they have already exploited.

Whether or not you aspire to this kind of capitalism, here's the rub. I've said 'we' for the past few pages, and discounted 'them.' Currently just over 20% of the populations of the UK and US live in poverty – that's 13.5 million people in the UK and over 40 million in the US and guess what? The irony is that in the US as I write, one of the fat cats, a man who has made his billions exploiting his fellow countrymen, and on occasions us as well in the UK, seems likely to be voted in as President of the United States, carried along on a growing tsunami of disaffected, poor Americans. His rise is similar to that of John F Kennedy's in 1960, but Kennedy had been moulded by the political system which he joined shortly after the war. This man, Trump, is exhibiting raw power fuelled by his own money, devoid of diplomacy and any sort of political convention. Like an unstoppable badger snuffling across somebody's lawn, he is undermining the system and exposing a mother lode of discontent and barely suppressed hate, and turning it into a simple and beguiling mantra, 'We Will Make America Great Again.' His blunt ability to tap into the thoughts of the masses, to get their agreement and support, makes his power base even stronger. His growing millions of supporters are thinking and saying – he's a good man, he's one of us. He looks in the mirror and says 'I'm a great man. Just like I've always done, I can use them.' Donald Trump has less regard and respect for the white trash whose cause he apparently espouses than most people have for a dog turd. He is very dangerous.

Hitler did it through oratory. Trump has done it with negative oratory, money, television, and appearing to be devoid of intellect. This has given him a distinct advantage with his followers over the high falutin, presumptuous conventions of the Washington power base. He has also touched what we think of as two basic human instincts – fear and aggression – just as Hitler did. Although he's ignorant, he's not stupid; he's cunning and that word again – 'beguiling.' Make the lie big, make it simple, keep saying it, and eventually they will believe it[73]. Make America Great Again! Watch out world. If you thought George Dubya and Tony Blair and the henchmen they gathered around them were dangerous, and that this guy Trump is just having a go, think again. In our shrinking and volatile world, he's dangerous with a capital F.

Enough ranting! At about the same time as I left the army, there was a trust fund of my grandfather's that produced a wad of cash that momentarily cleared the overdraft, so for a short while I was carried along on a wave of money and spent it as fast as I could, thus making my somewhat late contribution to the economic post-war miracle that Harold Macmillan referred to ten years earlier by saying, 'You've never had it so good.'

For some time I had been trying to improve the quality of the music I listened too. Prosaic obsession? I guess it was – somewhere in between train spotting and

---

[73] Adolf Hitler – Mein Kampf 1925. Hitler also said 'In a hundred years time, perhaps, a great man will appear who may offer them a chance at salvation. He'll take me as a model, use my ideas, and follow the course I have charted.'...

building model aeroplanes. A few years before I'd bought like everybody else a portable, mains operated, record player that could get through about twelve vinyl records you piled up on a long spindle. I think it was called a Dansette. The records could be either 45s or 33s. The first ones were singles and went faster at 45 revs per minute than the twelve inch long players which went at 33.3 revs per minute. How odd!

The first record I bought was Frank Ifield's, 'I Remember You,' aged fifteen and I listened to it all day, mesmerized by the yodeling and the actual noise coming out of the built in loudspeaker. After a few days of listening to this I got bored – hardly surprising – and lobbed out another 6s 0d (30p) on 'Tell Laura I Love Her' by Ricky Valance and listened to that for 322 times, and then went and bought some more. Well before I'd got this windfall, I'd already ripped open the back of the record player and wired it up to a big loudspeaker, which was built into a large chimney pot that had fallen off the roof many years before. I'd found it in the kitchen garden and it had had been used to grow long delicate stems of rhubarb. After finding it, the rhubarb that Shorto picked and brought into the house was decidedly short and stubby, but it tasted the same and the new sound from the Dansette was quite impressive. With the extra money I could now buy the best kit on the market, but for some reason, I decided to make the loudspeaker cabinets myself, perhaps because the best ones were just a bit too expensive. These things ended up being twice the size of a washing machine, and there were two of them. Instead of building them outside in the garage I began sawing up the wood in my bedroom so that I could get started in the morning immediately after sliding out of bed, still in my pyjamas. The mess was exceptional and there was blood everywhere from cut fingers and once from my knee when it got in the way of a wood chisel. I shouldn't really have painted them in the bedroom either. After a week they were finished and I managed to get the door open. They were so heavy that it took three of us to get them down the stairs, and I put sofa castors on them to help wheel them around.

Spend, spend, spend! Within a few months I'd bought my first car, a Morris Minor, taken up photography with a Pentax 35 mm camera and all the lenses, built a darkroom in our old nursery, and magnanimously offered to pay Mary £10 a week rent, which was readily accepted. But after a few months at home I started to feel uncomfortable. Most of my friends had gone off to London and had responsible jobs. Even the ones up in Cheshire were working. We spent a lot of time going to the pub and parties and being generally dissolute but there was something missing. After all, this was 1966 and the Swinging Sixties were just starting to swing a bit and I didn't seem to be swinging at all.

I didn't even have a girl friend. I hadn't really been in love since I was nine. There had been a few girls I'd had crushes on at Pony Club Camp when I was about sixteen, where we would kiss a bit, but after a clandestine meeting with Sue Cadwallader in the hayloft I kind of shelved all hope of romance.

We'd arranged to meet one night after lights out. I slid some jeans and a shirt on and crept out of my stable in the boys' area where we were separated from the girls, and made it to the stable where all the hay was kept. She was already there lying in the hay wearing a blue baby doll nightie and some matching knickers. The baby doll nightie was trimmed with blue fur and was transparent, but it was just too dark to see what I would really have liked to see. I sat down and put my arm around her and then it hit me. Her breath. It was awful. It took all my will power to kiss her on the lips in a desperate attempt to hide the smell. But that seemed to make it worse and the excitement and anticipation and fantasy evaporated in an instant.

Now, four years on and still a virgin, I made the second big decision since leaving the army – get a life man and go to London! Only it didn't work out quite as I thought. My mother suggested I could go and live with my grandmother in her dark overstuffed two floor flat in Queen's Gate. It was at the Kensington Gardens end, a minute's walk from the green grass and flowers of the park. She had bought it twelve years ago after my grandfather died. I wasn't sure about that idea, but I didn't discard it completely.

Grandma was a city person, who did not really like the country very much. She had agreed to raise her three daughters in Cheshire but her heart was always in London, where she didn't have to drive anywhere, and much preferred taking busses and taxis. There was a good reason for this. She was one of the worst drivers in the world, bar the Belgians and myself.

In Cheshire you couldn't go anywhere without a car, or a horse, or a bicycle, and she had never wanted to get on a horse or a bicycle. She was small, dark haired and Jewish but with some Irish blood too; the Jewish side of her family had escaped from Holland in the late 1500s. I can't ever remember her laughing, but she was very kind to all of us. She spoilt us really and when we were small our mother would take us to Tilston on Fridays and we would swim in a green painted swimming pool filled with green water with our cousin Nigel, and my mother's sister Aunt Myra. Green was Grandma's favourite colour and the inside of Tilston was all green – green carpets, green paintwork, green curtains and a lot of onyx ornaments. The only change in this colour scheme was the scarlet lipstick she always wore which looked quite startling superimposed on her white powdered face, and the bright red jelly we had after swimming. She would get very cross when Grandpa, who didn't appear very often, came downstairs for tea, sat at the head of the table and smacked the jelly very hard with a large silver spoon. One time it exploded out of the bowl on to the light green tablecloth and Grandma and Aunt Myra and my mother got very cross, while we looked at each other, barely being able to see over the table top, and giggled.

Twice a week she would go shopping in Tarporley, the village a mile down the main road. She would generally get Culshaw, the chauffeur, to take her in the Rolls, but Grandpa, rather daringly, let her drive their second car, a battered and clapped out old [74]Austin 7 on local journeys. One morning she drove the Austin 7 to Tarporley as Culshaw had taken the Rolls to the garage for a service. She needed to buy some meat from Mr Milward the butcher and parked up outside the shop. I forgot to say that she could be quite absent minded. She came out of the shop with the meat and climbed into the back of the Rolls Royce, saying as she did so 'You can take me home now,' and there, sitting on the back seat was a very large lady she didn't know, obviously waiting there while her own chauffeur was picking up *her* shopping.

'Oh dear, I'm so sorry – wrong car' said Grandma, having realised why Culshaw hadn't opened the door for her. She climbed out and made her way to the Austin 7 and weaved off down the High Street with the

---

[74] The UK utility car of the '20s and '30s similar in purpose to the Model T Ford.

spluttering exhaust leaving a trail of blue smoke.

We never knew our grandfather Ocky, and only saw him for tea. He had been badly shell shocked in the First War, having spent nearly four years in the trenches of eastern France. After school at Eton he went to Cambridge where he was Vice President of the Footlights and Captain of the Cambridge Football team. I have a large framed photograph of the team on my wall, and I look at them and imagine how many never made it to 1918, and of those who did, how many were traumatized as badly as my grandfather was for the rest of their lives. What I can't imagine is how they put up with the slime, the filth the dirt and disease, not to mention the bombardment and going over the top, making pointless attacks through wave after wave of bullets and shrapnel that were coming the other way, seldom achieving anything apart from an early grave, or waking up in a hospital with an arm or a leg or the side of a face missing. When he was dying at home in 1954 of liver cancer, the nurse brought him some medicine and his last words were 'I don't want any more fucking medicine' and that was that. Perhaps in another form it could have been an apt epitaph for the war he had taken part in.

My paternal grandfather, Cyril, fought in the trenches in France too, and as a major was the battalion commander of the West Yorkshire Regiment. He was much older than Ocky, and when he was forty five on a sunny Saturday afternoon in June 1916 a shell exploded in his trench near Bertrancourt. His second-in-command, Captain Edward Depledge, was killed immediately. Grandpa Cyril was badly wounded and the first thing he discovered after coming round in hospital was that he no longer had a right leg below the knee, so thankfully for him that was the end of his war. He then had three pairs of wooden legs made for him – two for every day use, two for dancing, and two for riding his horse and hunting.

Unfortunately he had inherited the Dewhurst Impulse Gene from his grandfather George. It wasn't really a gambling gene in the sense that we know it – it was more an impulsive risk taking gene executed on the spur of the moment, without weighing up the possible results.

After the war he acquired a very good steeplechase horse by the name of Conjuror II and in 1922 it won the National Hunt Cup at Cheltenham. After the Grand National this was the most prestigious race in the UK, and was restricted to amateur riders. Jig, my Uncle Peter, was the jockey, and on the strength of this win they were entered for the Grand National the following year. To everybody's delight they came third and Grandpa Cyril reckoned Conjuror would have won with a better jockey on board. Goodness knows what Jig the poor fellow thought; this probably contributed to the reasons for escaping to Canada a couple of years later. Anyway, a jockey by the name of Harry Brown was engaged to ride Conjuror the following year. Now the Grand National is a fickle race; there's always a possibility that the best horse in the world, being ridden by the best jockey in the world, won't win it. Conjuror started at 5-2, the shortest priced favourite ever known for the race. The odds may have been affected by the amount of money Grandfather Cyril put on the horse – £50,000. This was a staggering amount of money in 1924 and I've no idea what went through his head. In today's money that comes to £2.7m.

All seemed to be going well with Conjuror and Harry Brown well placed in the middle of the field for the first circuit, but then disaster struck. At Becher's Brook the second time round a loose horse ran across them on the landing side and Conjuror was brought down. What went through Granfather Cyril's head at that moment? A much older cousin of mine, Ben Brind, remembered staying at Tilston shortly afterwards and my grandfather wandering round the house mumbling 'Where's it all gone? Where's it all gone?' It must have been awful for him and his family – but he did survive. The family moved from their very large house near Tarporley, and for the next five years lived in a pub in Whitchurch, while the coffers re-filled themselves. Not surprisingly, my father never mentioned the story.

So, six months after leaving the army at last I saw a way out of shedding my guilt complex about doing very little. I was about to escape to London with what remained of my wad of cash and get a job. I went to Chester in the Morris Minor and bought two cheap suits. I didn't have a job, but I'd heard you could go to an employment agency and they would find you one.

I was helping quite a lot at home, mowing the grass and pushing wheelbarrows full of coke[75] round the house from a twenty ton pile that would be delivered three times a year to fuel the boiler that heated the water. One morning I went to the garage to fetch my father's latest addition to his stable of automobiles. They seemed over the years to have reflected the ups and downs of his own fortune. After Rodney the Rolls (feeling rich) he progressed to Vanessa the Vanguard (feeling poor) and then to Bimbo the Bentley (feeling rich again).

Bimbo the Bentley felt the pain one day when we were driving up to London and my father inadvertently opened the door at seventy five miles an hour. Unfortunately it opened from the front and was ripped

---

[75] Not the stuff you put up your nose. This was a smokeless form of processed coal – used in power stations.

off its hinges. Fortunately it was mid summer and warm and we drove the rest of the way with a door missing to Grandma's flat in Queen's Gate. People walking the pavements of Knightsbridge must have been a little puzzled as he drove sedately past in an immaculate pin striped suit and a spotted bow tie as though nothing was amiss. I hid down below the windows on the back seat.

The next car was Robin the Reliant (feeling poor again). This was bright blue and a three wheeler made of fiberglass and it could only go on short journeys as it was deafening to drive and was very unreliable at cornering. I drove it out of the garage in a cloud of foul smelling blue smoke and round to the front door where my father was waiting with a shopping basket. We were on a mission to Goodwin's Supermarket[76] in Whitchurch to buy his weekly supply of crisps and something for cleaning drains that Mary wanted. I steered right a little too hard and the bloody thing tipped over, upside down. There was an appalling grinding noise as the gravel scraped away a corner of the roof and a few loose stones rattled into the hollow interior. I switched off the revving engine, and in the silence undid my seatbelt and climbed out through the window. My father was catatonic, standing there with his basket, but he recovered enough to help me tip the thing the right way up and we drove off to Whitchurch with a piece of the roof flapping and whistling in the wind.

I knew my days permanently living at Barmere were coming to an end. If things progressed like this, soon I would burn the house down. That, incidentally, would come later, but it wasn't really my fault.

---

[76] He pronounced it 's-ewe-permarket' – like a female sheep.

# 16 – MEN IN WHITE COATS

Grandma's flat could have been worse; in fact it was a whole lot better than the smelly boarding house where I spent the first four nights. This was somewhere in Pimlico and on day two I rang my grandmother up and asked if I could come and stay after all.

The flat was two floors up in a rickety old lift with noisy metal scissor gates that only a couple of people could fit in. The place looked out over the leafy Queen's Gate thoroughfare, and as it faced south the front rooms were quite light and airy. But as you went further back it got very dark and gloomy and it was furnished with what was left from Grandma's house in Cheshire – dark green. It wasn't really a flat at all; I guess it was a duplex being on two floors and it had two sets of stairs, and I moved into a separate little flat up the back stairs, overlooking the Albert Hall and the Royal College of Music. Everything up there was green except for the sheets, bath, sink and lavatory, which were a welcoming virgin white. They could easily have been avocado. Even the carpet and cupboard were green. I don't know why because it's the primary colour of the countryside, but it made the flat very dark and was depressing.

Grandma was welcoming. She had been there about twelve years and had learnt how to cook in her own way – have it delivered, ready made from Harrods and heat it up in the oven – simply wonderful darling. Added to this she also knew how to do vegetables, especially frozen green peas. Everything would be slathered with masses of butter, but it tasted good and I was unaware of liver overload at the time.

Although she had lots of friends she would go and play bridge with, I think she rather welcomed someone in the flat and was a bit lonely. I found it quite stressful at the start and became someone else, pretending to be relaxed but inwardly always uncomfortable. She was after all over eighty and had very strong views and not a great deal of intelligence, so I had to agree with her and dispose of the little voice in my head that kept calling me a liar.

I would be out all day during the week at work but if I wasn't going out in the evening we would sit very formally in her drawing room watching some game show on her black and white television with the sound turned up full as she was a bit deaf. After making her a large gin and helping myself to an even larger whisky this wasn't as bad as it sounds. Occasionally she would book tickets to the theatre and we'd go in a taxi to the West End and sit in the front row watching her old friends in some drawing room comedy, and then go round backstage to meet them and drink some gin, and I'd listen to them talking about the old days darling. Once a year at Christmas she would have her party and invite many of these actors and musicians and dancers to the flat and there would be lots of champagne. She was actually very good at having parties, and they were far more relaxing than living with her on my own. She was often tipsy and would bounce erratically off the walls of the dark green corridor, but she never fell over.

I signed on with a temps agency and soon had a suited job in the city as a bean counter. Well it wasn't really counting beans. It was far worse.

By 1966 computer technology had gone through a sea change. Before 1960 a computer needed a building the size of a block of flats to house it and a small power station to fire it up. One byte consisted of a valve the size of a small milk bottle, but by the sixties tiny solid state transistors reduced the size and increased the performance considerably and a computer could now fit into a large broom cupboard. You could feed pieces of card full of holes into one end, and out the other end would come half a mile of paper printed with thousands of names and addresses and other information, depending on the holes in the cards that went in.

I worked for a start up company that sold unit trust portfolios to the general public. They advertised in the national press to the effect that you, yes you, the working man could own shares and become a capitalist by investing with us in the stock market! Literally hundreds of thousands of people filled the forms in, cut from the tabloids and the Radio Times, and they arrived at the office in sack loads to be processed. My job was somewhere in the middle of the operation, and I spent four months filling pieces of paper divided into tiny squares with either zeros or ones. I was the equivalent of dropping a small rock into the gearbox of a perfectly tuned car engine.

I didn't know then and I certainly can't remember now what my instructions were. Most of the time was taken up laughing and joking with all the others and concentrating rather too much on my next door neighbour, who was very attractive with blond curly hair and was half German; she wore loose flowery tops without a bra, and a mini skirt that looked more like a curtain pelmet, and occasionally asked me or one of the others to help her for a few moments to carry some boxes down into the filing room.

It wasn't long before I was demoted and sent to the outer fringes of the office complex, which took up a few buildings down a narrow street near the Bank of England. For the last two months as a city slicker I sat in a dark and dusty garret room with three middle aged men correcting the thousands of mistakes that people like me had made in the first place. I always wondered who corrected what I cocked up a second time. I didn't wonder for long because I got the sack. This was infinitely better than staying in that gloomy attic office with those others to be discovered, lost to the world and mummified, fifty years later.

I went back to the temps agency at the start of 1967 and they said there was no office work for me. More than likely the unit trust company had told them that I was useless. They did have a vacancy for a cinema projectionist, however, which wasn't really their bag but I'd said I was interested in films in my original interview, and would there be any point fixing a meeting? Within hours I was sitting in Maurice Parkin's tiny windowless canteen drinking tea in the bowels of the Columbia Cinema, Shaftesbury Avenue, and telling him why I would make a good cinema projectionist. After all I'd done it before – at school. Really? What school has carbon arc projectors then. Eton. Eton? You mean Eton College?! Hey, Brian, we got a right one 'ere. Brian was the Assistant Chief Projectionist and a ferrety little middle aged man with thinning fair hair, buck teeth and a wandering eye, perhaps caused by trying to look through a very small window at the cinema screen and his projector simultaneously. He wore a white coat that was about seven sizes too big for him. He had been there many more years than any of us and said very little.

Maurie Parkin, the Chief Projectionist, whom we had to call Chief at all times, was very dapper. Tall, with swept back crinkly blonde hair, he was what you'd call a ladies man. He had a very long thin nose, and always wore an old fashioned but immaculate double breasted grey suit with a white shirt and a flashy tie. He lived 'out of town' in some place like Pinner, which wasn't really out of town at all, but he liked us to think it was. He was a perfectionist – a perfectionist projectionist – and over the next six months he came to haunt me. He had no sense of humour and when he smiled, which was not often, it turned out to be more of a grimace and quite frightening. He took me on, not because I'd had some experience – I turned out to be useless – but because I'd been to Eton. He was a pathological snob. It must have been quite painful for him to try and marry my apparent stupidity on the job with his view of what Etonians should be like. My incompetence sprang mainly from panic, as buttons had to be pressed and levers thrown on the millisecond according to Parkin's Rules. If he didn't appear everything would run smoothly, and I soon found that my panic was directly proportional to his proximity. If he was at home in Pinner everything was chilled and went well. If he was standing behind me and breathing down my neck I went straight into panic mode.

There were two others working there, my age, and our job title was something like Junior Assistant Projectionists. One was Mike Lemmon, a cool black haired chap, who was a good looking version of Liam Gallagher. The other was Ray Moore, stocky and friendly, who bustled around and dusted a lot, something Maurie Parkin was very keen on.

The job paid £8.10s.0d a week, so little that I was thankful there was still some of Grandpa's cash left, for London is an expensive place. We worked in six hour shifts, two on two off, and covered midday to midnight seven days a week. Maurie Parkin would cover for us occasionally and definitely come in on important evenings like Royal Charity Premieres. The Columbia was underground and had a state of the art air conditioning system in the auditorium, but nothing in the projection box. The season progressed into a warm summer in London and often the huge carbon arc projectors and the rectifier equipment to power them would raise the temperature in the room to the mid nineties. It was compulsory to wear our white coats, so the three of us would often strip down to our underpants and go barefoot, unless of course Stalin was there, in which case we would sweat cobs, all shirted and trousered and shooed, and have to drink gallons of tea.

In the six months I was there we only showed two films, but they were both very good in their different ways. One of them was The Deadly Affair which I must have watched about ninety three times. It was based on John le Carré's first novel about Smiley and was directed by Sidney Lumet with James Mason, Maximilian Schell, Simone Signoret and Harry Andrews. It was dark and moody and wonderfully depressing, not just because of the story, but because the negative film had been pre-exposed to give a grey washed out colour to an already wet, gloomy London backdrop. I loved every bit of it, and mesmerized by some minor detail would forget to switch from one machine to the other for a second or two, and Stalin would sack me. I was sacked about seventeen times during the six months I worked there.

The second film was Franco Zefirelli's Taming of the

Shrew, a complete contrast to The Deadly Affair. It was exuberant and loud and full of laughter and the colour and the costumes were exceptional; it was a feel good film. With Richard Burton and Elizabeth Taylor as Petruchio and Katerina, it didn't stick exactly to Will's script but it was just fun and moved along at a cracking pace. We must have watched this film about a hundred and ninety three times, and once again there was always some little nuance to catch. Reading Richard Burton's diaries recently, I would never have guessed how much he disliked making it and how contemptuous he was with the arrogance, histrionics and voracious homosexual appetite of Zefirelli. Burton really hated acting but what kept him going was the booze and the money, and his beloved Elizabeth.

After several months working underground, Mike and Ray and myself decided that we needed some fresh air. It was getting on for mid July and the projection box was getting hotter and hotter. I'd been planning to leave before I was really sacked. One night there was a Royal Charity Show with a house full of the rich and worthy including Princess Margaret. On Premiere nights Stalin would give me the sack-you-if-you-fuck-up routine, and then stand front of house, no doubt grimacing obsequiously at all the celebrities. Once they were all in, he'd stand at the back and quietly tell us when to go, via an intercom. On this evening of all evenings, after all the time working there, he thought it would be fine to let me open the show. Somehow I managed to put the last reel on first, and a rowdy crowd scene erupted on the front of the curtains before I'd even turned the lights down. I got into a terrible muddle but eventually closed the curtains, and pressed the right button for the lights to come up again.

This time Stalin had a total breakdown, and instead

of shouting at me hysterically, I found him in the tea room ten minutes later, head in his hands sobbing silently, a broken man, his career no doubt in tatters. Feeling somewhat sorry for him, I realized the best I could do to save his reputation as King of the West End Projectionists was to resign, so I did. He looked up and staring into the middle distance said 'Yes … yes … yes,' and he then smiled a proper smile for the first time, almost beatifically, hardly registering that I was sitting there, 'Yes … yes … what a good idea … what a good idea,' dreamily, as if it was the first time he had ever thought about it. I backed out of the room silently, slowly, like a film going backwards, and left him alone to grieve into his mug of tea.

# 17 – A SHORT BIKE RIDE


Mike and Ray left the Columbia Cinema soon after me. We'd become good friends and we decided in the pub one lunchtime soon after we left that the best fresh air we could get was to buy three bicycles and set off across Europe. This was after a couple of pints mind you. Mike had been on a camping holiday to Southend with his parents when he was sixteen, but Ray had never been further from his home at 136 Camrose Avenue than the top of the Edgware Road, where his Uncle Reg had a caravan, tucked away in a spinney on the edge of the A41. But he was a bikey sort of a chap and we went to see his friend, Don Farrell, who made racing bicycles in his shop close by. Ray already had one so Mike and I bought one each and had Don fix panniers and bags over the back and front wheels. Mine was a sleek red and green affair with white mudguards. We then set off on a hot August morning from Ray's home about six miles from the caravan for a practice run. By the time we got there we were knackered. We made some tea and had our sandwiches, but Ray got quite itchy, and wanted to get home as soon as he could. I think it was agoraphobia of some sort, but we put it to one side. We planned to leave at the end of August, taking the train and ferry and then train again to Paris, where we would start cycling down through France, Spain and Portugal to finish up in Gibraltar.

I don't know how it happened but the first thing I remember about the trip was standing on the quay on a hot summer's morning in Calais as the bemused French sailors, Gualoises hanging from their lips, hoisted a six hundredweight net, full of equipment and other stuff, off the boat and on to the concrete. Included in this huge pile were two dozen rolls of toilet paper, two dozen cans of baked beans, several bottles of fruit juice cordial, including Lucozade, several packets of Mornflake porridge, a large movie camera, a coil of washing line, some rope, two boxes of tea bags, a large carton of Daz[77], a lavatory seat, and a lot of first aid kit, including bandages, medicines and pill bottles of every description. I forgot to say that Ray was a keen body builder and very concerned with his health. When it came to hypochondria he could beat me with his hands in his pockets, and he took his diet and bowel movements quite seriously in a very English way. Most of the stuff was his and most of it had to be left behind and sent back to England. I haven't a clue what the rope was for and I didn't ask. It took quite a long time to organize the return of all this stuff. Even after several trips to France, hitching around and going on a sailing course off the west coast of Brittany in the school holidays, my French was still awful, and it took the rest of the day to sort things out and eventually hoist our sleek racing bikes, each weighed down by sixty pounds

[77] Washing powder

of kit, on to the Paris train, including a canvas tent in a large kit bag on the back of my bike.

The next morning we started out from a flea pit somewhere near the Place de la Concorde and headed south. Ray was not happy but Mike was quite cool and took on everything that came his way. Ray was hungry; in fact he was always hungry. The only time he wasn't hungry was while he slept, but even then he probably dreamt about food. Wobbling round the Place de la Concorde, which was cobbled then, during the Parisian rush hour was not something I'd recommend. How we got out of Paris without landing up in a morgue I don't know. The aim was to reach Versailles the first day – about twelve miles – and once we were in the suburbs we stopped for breakfast where Ray wolfed down about nine croissants, a lot of salami sausage, and an enormous block of cheese. At the same time we bought some water and a bottle of wine each to go in the two bottle holders we had on the front of each bike. The wine was a mistake. It was dark red and smelt of nail polish remover, and was the sort of stuff car mechanics use to loosen stubborn wheel nuts. By mid morning as the sun beat down Ray found that he had a very bad stomach pain, and while Mike and I lay dazed and exhausted by the side of a busy D road south of Paris, Ray floundered around in the woods looking for somewhere to evacuate his turbulent bowels, cursing that we had sent the toilet paper back to England. He was rapidly declining with us two not far behind as the red wine rendered us near speechless.

We eventually wobbled on to Versailles and late in the afternoon, tired and emotional, we found a grim looking campsite. We were not in top form; we were all drunk and dehydrated with throbbing headaches, and Ray was moaning quite a lot, and while he sat there on the ground staring blankly into the middle distance, no doubt wishing to be back in 136 Camrose Avenue with a bag of chips and a glass of milk, Mike and I put the tent up. It had probably started life somewhere behind the lines during the First World War and had been in my family ever since. It was all thick wooden poles that slotted together, hand carved wooden pegs and lots of rope, and smelt like a sack in which many generations of mice had once lived. When dry it weighed about twenty five pounds and all wrapped up in its green bag, it stuck out a foot from the back of my bike rack. It came complete with a large wooden mallet for banging in the pegs. I don't know why we decided to camp rather than stay in youth hostels. Camping didn't just mean a tent. We also brought along a stove, a frying pan, a saucepan, camping gas, sleeping bags, a large groundsheet, blow-up mattresses, a gas lamp, plates, mugs, eating implements, and that was before we loaded up spare inner tubes, a spare tyre each and all the tools needed to repair the bikes. There wasn't any room for clothes, but we didn't really need many as it was very hot, and the further south we went the hotter it got. There was so much stuff we had to pile on the bikes every morning, and it took so long to get moving, that we only ever did about twenty miles a day. The logical option would have been pack mules – or to have stayed at home – but it was a bit late for that.

After a shower, or more to the point a dribble of cold brown water from a pipe half way up a bare concrete wall, we cooked some potatoes and a tin each of heated frankfurters and tomatoes and retired to our communal boudoir in a state of near paralysis as darkness fell. Of course August is the holiday month in France and the campsite was full of squealing children and grumpy parents, and occasionally a plastic football would bounce off the roof of the tent, accompanied by tittering from the children outside. Inside, the groaning, breaking wind and buzzing mosquitoes completed this wall of sound. The campsite must have been close to a malarial swamp because the mosquitoes were prolific and of course we'd forgotten the insect repellent. Early the next morning, dazed, with our faces covered in red welts, we ate breakfast straight from the tins – frankfurters and tomatoes with no potatoes as Ray had finished them the night before. We eventually climbed on to our bikes, and deciding that a cultural tour round the Palace of Versailles was not going to happen, we headed down the map towards Gibraltar.

We rode south west, almost in a straight line to Bordeaux, where we arrived about three weeks later. Where we could we chose the D roads, avoiding the traffic and passing through quiet villages, where we bought bread and tomatoes and lots of salami, cheese and fruit. We must have been burning up about nine thousand calories a day and although Ray didn't really like the food, he still ate twice as much as we did. About a week from Paris we stopped off at the Chateau le Lude in the Loire Valley. My mother knew the people who lived there – some French aristos – and I had telephoned them the day before to say we were coming. This involved going into a quiet village bar about twenty miles away and shouting as politely as possible in bad French into the microphone of a large bakelite handset, while clamping a separate single headphone to the other ear. Even then it was almost impossible to hear what the other people were saying, let alone understand them.

Luckily they were expecting us and we put the tent up in the dry moat, had a shower in their swimming pool hut, found a shirt and a pair of trousers each in the bottom of our panniers, and then ate a bizarre dinner in a huge ornate dining room with twenty members of the family and an army of flunkeys in white jackets. They produced three bottles of 1924 Chateau Margaux, and we drank it with great ceremony. It should have been good but for some reason it was over the top. Ray wondered later why we had to drink something that was forty two years old when we could have had a nice cup of tea instead.

I only have three photographs of the trip and they are all slides. The first is a picture of the tent in the moat, the second is our underpants hanging on the washing line in a forgotten campsite, and the third is Ray mending a puncture on my bike. As it got hotter the further south we went it became an endurance test; we didn't exactly start hating each other but we retreated into our own heads while we were on the road, and sometimes we were miles apart. Only frequent stops for more fodder and water brought us back together again.

By mid September we arrived in San Sebastian on the southern side of the Pyrenees in Spain. For the first time we stayed in a youth hostel where Ray said that he'd had enough fresh air and wanted to go home. The next day someone stole Mike's bike, and the day after that they both caught the train back to London and I was on my own. They took the tent back to England, which was a relief, and I carried on through Spain towards Portugal, at last staying in youth hostels or sleep-bagging it out in the open air. Because I was now carrying less than half the weight that I had before, I could go about forty miles a day, but it was getting hotter ... and hotter. Even moving along at fifteen miles an hour wasn't providing enough breeze to keep cool. Soon after midday, I'd be looking for a shady tree to go to sleep under, and a couple of times, after a bellyful of bread and tomatoes and salami and lots of chocolate, I nodded off, only to be woken an hour later by a loud bang. I'd parked my bike in the shade too, but as the sun moved round on to the tyres, an inner tube exploded. By the end of the trip the inner tube looked like a patchwork quilt and I could mend a puncture in about five minutes. I quickly learnt to let the air out at lunchtime to stop the early wake up calls. There was no need for a watch. I did everything by the sun; it only rained once during the next three weeks.

I headed south west towards Portugal, passing through or around the towns and cities where a hundred and fifty years before Wellington had fought with Napoleon – Vitoria, Burgos, Valladolid, Salamanca, Badajoz, Ciudad Rodrigo. There was very little traffic on the main road to the Portuguese border and even fewer people. I'd pull off to look for food in a village and as long as it was before the hottest part of the day when everything would close down, I would buy enough food and water and wine to last for the next twenty four hours. If I arrived at a sleepy village during the siesta, the only living creature I'd come across would be a dog lying in the shade of a building not even bothering to bark, or quite often a slightly surly Guardia Civil policemen who would appear from nowhere, wearing his strange looking patent leather hat and a menacing air. This was still the time of Franco and old rural Spain, and I was well off the tourist track. I felt I was an intruder sometimes and was occasionally viewed with suspicion, and often I would be asked to show my passport. I avoided the cities as best I could, but the attraction of a shower and a good feed was sometimes hard to resist. At other times I would come across stone troughs known as albercas, close to the road and fed by crystal clear spring water coming from a pipe sticking out from the side of a hill. If there was no-one around, I'd be off the bike and diving in without even taking off my clothes.

One night after cooking something unmemorable in my saucepan and drinking half a litre of vino tinto, I bedded down in a shallow ditch and sank into a dreamless sleep. Towards dawn I did start dreaming – I felt the full weight of a beautiful young and naked Spanish girl sitting astride me and massaging my chest with her lovely slim hands. Her nails were painted a brilliant red and her half open lips moistened with her pink wet tongue were ... there was a sudden thump and something crashed on to my legs and I woke to a familiar smell and then saw the face of a sheep about three inches from my own, and the back end of another as it climbed from the trench. The one on top of me was struggling to get up, but was having trouble. I tried to get up too and with a loud bleat it managed to scuttle off. I thanked it; the dream had been quite pleasant but it was a pity that it had ended so soon. The shepherd bringing up the back of his flock looked a little surprised, but we exchanged what I hoped were early morning pleasantries and he moved on. My sleeping bag was now covered with brown blotches and smelt a bit, but after drying it in the sun, the smell more or less went away.

A week later I arrived in Lisbon after a long three thousand foot climb up to the city of Guarda some miles inside the Portuguese border. It had been hard work and hilly but a relief from the monotonous plains of central Spain. The people I passed were more friendly and curious too, but they appeared to be a lot poorer.

For the past thirty years both Spain and Portugal had been ruled by dictators, General Franco and António Salazar, who for all their faults had attempted to drag their countries into the second half of the twentieth century from places of illiteracy and poverty, but the Catholic Church still had a stranglehold on most of the people. In fairness, the dictators' legacies were mainly beneficial, although Franco would probably be hauled before a war crimes tribunal today as he was responsible for the deaths of hundreds of thousands of political prisoners. I only mention the dictators because within an hour of arriving in Lisbon, somewhere near the university, I was approached by a guy my own age, who asked me where I was going and the end result was a bed in a student flat for three nights where I chewed the cud with my hosts, went to art galleries, and one evening saw a staging of Macbeth in Portuguese. After getting drunk in a bar the first night, I felt I knew these friendly people well enough to mention Salazar, and they all went into the spy movie routine and pretended I hadn't said anything, and then told me quietly that they were all for a revolution and wanted him out of the way and we shouldn't mention him again, because there could be people listening, so I didn't. They didn't know it and neither did I, but the following year Salazar had a stroke while he was getting out of the bath, and although someone else took over, those around him carried on talking to him as though he was still their leader. He died two years later in 1970, and five years after that a bloodless revolution, a constitution, and an elected socialist government brought Portugal into the club of western democracies. Coincidently, in 1975 Franco died and by 1978 Spain too had a new constitution, which included a return to the monarchy and free democratic elections.

After a long weekend of culture, beer and politics, I climbed wearily back on my bike and headed south once more. Eight days later I was sweating up the last thousand foot high hill from the beach out of Tarifa on the south coast of Spain, nearly two months since leaving Paris. It seemed like two years, and as the summit got closer and closer I swore this was the last time I'd get on a bike.

From the top of the hill I could see through the haze across the Straits the north coast of Africa, and down below just a few miles away, the Rock of Gibraltar.

Riding down Main Street two hours later on the way to the youth hostel I stopped at some traffic lights and a chap came up to me and asked if I knew Don Farrell. Don who? And then I remembered I was riding one of his bikes and his name was plastered all over the frame. This chap had heard of him and after about thirty seconds agreed to buy the bike for £25, which was half what I'd paid for it, but it had come a long way and there was a knocking sound from the front forks every time I went over a bump. I was mightily relieved, and went and bought a rucksack.

Gibraltar was a strange place and I'm sure it still is. Barely two miles long and a mile wide it's little more than a great lump of limestone fourteen hundred feet high at the entrance to the Mediterranean, but politically it is one of the most strategic lumps of rock on Earth. And the Spanish would very much like it back. Since Britain took it off them in 1704, they have grumbled ever since and quite rightly. It's a bit like finding the end of your middle finger belongs to somebody else, and all they can do is stick that finger up in front of your face. But that is the way of the world. As a consolation Spain has the enclave of Ceuta on the other side of the ten mile wide entrance to the Med and this should really belong to Morocco. Spain, however, is not going to get Gibraltar back anytime soon, bar an all out war, and especially if the locals have anything to do with it. When I was there they were more English than a rolled umbrella.

Everywhere was painted red, white and blue – even the curbs edging the pavements. The policemen wore helmets, there were red telephone boxes, pubs selling revolting Watneys Red Barrel and Smiths Crisps, and quite a few fish and chip shops. I got a job as a waiter in one of them. It was a nightmarish plaice run by a large dark haired bully of a man with a very bad squint and appalling breath. His wife wasn't much better. She had the body of a retired Russian shot putter with dyed blonde hair and a white coat that was too tight. Her voice sounded like a bag of shingle being dragged over corrugated iron. They both chain smoked and came from Yorkshire. The only reason I took the job on was because I could eat as much as I wanted and get paid £2 a day in wages. On the second day I tripped over a protruding tile and a plateful of cod, chips and mushy peas went flying through the air to land in a customer's lap. She was wearing a dress, and it was quite a delicate job to scrape it all off without being accused of molesting her. On the third day I got the sack and a £5 note in wages, which was a lot better than a slap in the face with a wet fish.

I'd arrived in Gibraltar with the equivalent of £5 in pesetas, and telegrammed my bank in London asking them to send £15 to a local bank, so with the £25 from the bike sale, less what I'd spent on the Rock, I was all cashed up and had nearly £40. I was rich. The next day I left the Rock and took a boat to Africa from across the bay in Algerciras. I'd haddock nuff of Gibraltar.

# 18 – ONE GOAT LEFT

Arriving in Ceuta on the north coast of Africa was a shock. The smells and the noises were quite startling. Here we are they said, get used to us. It's a long time ago now, but if someone was to bottle the smell and hold it under my nose I would go straight back to that first landfall. My recollection is a sweetish mix of cooked spices, exhaust fumes, prickly pear cactus, the smoke from hashish pipes, and day old human shit. And the noise was quite different too. Battered trucks with men standing in the back would come thundering past, men would shout at each other in a guttural language I'd never heard before, donkeys would bray, and policemen in smart uniforms and white hats would blow whistles and wave their arms at cross roads. Women would glide past covered in dark material from head to foot with just slits for their eyes, and the children would materialise from nowhere and cluster round, grinning dirty faces and curly black hair, trying to sell me stuff – beads, hashish, wooden carvings and even kaftans.

In 1967 Morocco was on the hippie trail. If you had an old Volkswagen you headed for Nepal, but a cheaper version was a rucksack to Morocco or in my case a bicycle then a rucksack. There were boys and girls from all over Europe, the States, Canada, Australia and New Zealand, making this pilgrimage to nowhere, mainly for the marijuana and the vibe man. Our mode of travel was hitch hiking and the occasional bus if we were rich. It was mostly lifts in cars and as we went further south into the desert we had to rely on trucks.

I felt rich to start with but got poorer the further south I went. Incapable of budgeting I started off staying in grubby, fly infested youth hostels, but ended up sleeping rough, out in the open under the stars on many nights during the next six weeks. I would meet up with others and we'd travel together in twos and threes for a day or a week and then drift apart like leaves being blown around on an autumn lawn. We stood and sat at the edge of dusty roads for an hour or a day or even longer and wait for a car or truck. It was a slower pace of life than a bicycle but I was OK with waiting.

One day south of Marrakesh on a hot October morning, I was sitting by the side of the road with a fellow traveller, a large bushy bearded Canadian called Matt. He didn't say much but he was an affable fellow and we got along fine and he was patient too. We sat on the kerb opposite a butcher's shop. At least we thought that's was what it was. On a table outside this single storied concrete block of a building were the haunches and even the skinned head of some dead animal. The blood was still dripping on to the ground so it could not have been dead that long. An old man appeared from the dark maw of the shop; he was holding a plastic sheet. The meat was covered in flies and he shooed them all up into the air, then deftly slung the plastic sheet over the meat. The flies landed back on the sheet and wandered around, obviously perplexed, searching for nice fresh meat to lay their eggs on. The man went back in and came out seconds later with an old fashioned fly spray with a pump and a reservoir shaped like a small can of baked beans. He pumped it up and sprayed a cloud of poison over the plastic. The flies buzzed around, dying in their hundreds, and he took the sheet off and walked back into the shop.

I didn't like Morocco much. In the towns and cities it was dirty, smelly, and we were continually hustled and hassled. It improved as we went further south into the desert where there was less tourism, but the lifts got more difficult. We saw very few women, and if we did they were completely covered. There were very few women travelling too, unless it was with their boyfriends. There were always rumours flying around about girls being sold into slavery or raped in the youth hostels but it was mostly piffle. There was a lot of petty thieving though, and it was a good idea to keep a close watch on what meagre possessions we had. One night Matt had woken up to see a Moroccan youth trying to cut the cord he had used to tie his rucksack on to the end of his sleeping bag. He couldn't get out of it, but he roared at the Moroccan who ran off without the bag. No one stole anything of mine; I even managed to hold on to my camera for the four months I was away.

For the last three weeks in Africa I survived quite happily on a diet of tinned sardines, tangerines and bread. The £40 didn't last long and it was just about impossible to get any money out from England, so the alternative was to sell blood, which I did three times in Morocco. We all did it as we ran out of money, but it was only the big hospitals in the cities that would buy it. Half a litre was the normal amount and we'd be paid just over £2 which would buy enough food for three weeks, by which time we could sell another half litre without dropping dead from blood loss.

The final lift that Matt and I took was on the back of a truck down to El Aaiun in the Spanish Sahara, another chunk of land the Spanish had appropriated and colonized with little more than a military presence since 1884. It lay on the northern part of the bulge of Africa's west coast and consisted of sand, rock and scrub, and was inhabited mainly by Berbers and Arabs who fished and bred camels. It was unusual for travellers to go there and I had somehow got a transit visa from yet another Spanish enclave at Sidi Ifni a hundred miles north of Morocco's southern border. The most frequently used routes across the Sahara to equatorial Africa were further east, but Matt was going to carry on round the bulge to Mauritania. I wanted to spend the last month before Christmas on Gran Canaria, which was a short flight from the African coast. We sat in a fly infested village fifty miles north of Tarfaya for four days waiting for a final lift on the back of a large truck. It arrived early on the fifth morning, piled high with lots of stuff wrapped in sacking, a few tyres and bits of machinery. Wobbling around on top of all this stuff were two kid goats. We climbed up with them and during the next thirty six hours had some interesting if limited conversations with the goats. They weren't that happy as they had been taken from their mother that morning, and when not talking to us, they nibbled at the sacking. They were quite agile and while we hung on for dear life as the truck bounced along the un-mettled road with a great cloud of dust trailing behind, they seemed content to wander about, tethered on the end of cords. We were helped off the back on the second evening and so was one of the goats. We ate it for supper, while the other goat looked on from the top of the truck. At one point I was given a jaw bone complete with teeth to gnaw on and Matt was given an eyeball, but the men were having a laugh and admitted that they never ate these bits themselves. They were keeping the other goat for their return journey.

In El Aaiun, which was little more than a large village with a small army garrison, I bought a ticket to Las Palmas for the equivalent of £3.10s.0d and flew in my first plane to the Canary Islands. After a night in a youth hostel and some advice on where to go and stay without having to spend any money, I headed south to Maspalomas, a mini desert with real sand dunes and a hut on the beach selling drinks. Some bright sparks in Las Palmas had imported a few camels with their Berber handlers from the Sahara and arranged day trips in busses from the smart hotels, complete with packed lunches, down to the deserted beach where the guests climbed on a camel, went round a sand dune, and then sat and ate their packed lunch – or didn't. Down there I met a few other vagrants, and we made our own ramshackle huts out of palm fronds and sticks and rummaged through the rubbish bins at the end of the day when the trippers had gone home, leaving their unopened packed lunches behind. We would feast on cold chicken, hard boiled eggs and potato salads and watch the sun go down and then light a camp fire, and someone would produce a guitar. I fell in love with a beautiful willowy Swedish girl with long blond hair, but unfortunately she was with a great ugly Swede so I was left to dream.

After ten days of chicken salad and not talking much to a beautiful Swedish girl, I left Maspalomas and went back to Las Palmas, having decided I needed something different to eat. I went to the hospital and sold some more blood and then had a slap up meal. At a bar afterwards I met a large Irishman, whose name I've forgotten. He was an alcoholic and gay as a ribbon counter, but I gathered that he owned a villa up in the mountains and needed help building it – free board and lodging? I took my chance and slung my rucksack into the back of his jeep and off we went. Fortunately he had a boyfriend up there and there were several others, all men, working in the garden and on the house. I was up there for three weeks, and we hacked away at the rocky ground with pick axes and spades, but it was now the beginning of December and I wanted to be home for Christmas. The gay, alcoholic, kind Irishman gave me the money for a flight from Las Palmas to Malaga, and a few days later I headed back to Europe.

There was a fierce wind blowing in Malaga and it was very cold, and it had snowed there the day before. I went straight to the hospital where I sold a final half litre of blood to keep me going till I got back to England. It took me about eight days to hitch up through Spain and France and it got colder all the time. South of Madrid I remember standing on the side of the road in four inches of snow, waiting for a lift and thinking what a change it was from a few months earlier. The good thing about hitch hiking in the cold is that people stop. And it was getting close to Christmas and that made it easier too. One night in France I stayed with a family just north of Limoges and the next night knocked on the door of a farm and they let me sleep in their barn under the hay.

By the time I arrived back in London in mid December I was down to my last pound. I'd called my grandmother from the station to say I was coming back. She was pleased to see me but suggested straightaway that I should have a bath. A couple of nights later was her Christmas party, which went with its usual swing, but I was feeling ill and was sick every time I ate anything, and thought it was best to go back to Cheshire for Christmas. Back home I would eat and be sick and then I noticed that my eye balls had gone yellow. Because I was so brown, nobody noticed my skin was yellow too. The doctor said I had Hepatitis A. I thought I was going to die during the next two weeks. All I could eat was dry toast. By that time and with simple deduction I'd worked out that the cause must have been a dirty needle in the Malaga hospital, or contact with the virus from food. I slowly recovered but couldn't drink any alcohol or eat much fat for nearly a year afterwards.

Unfortunately, about a week after I'd managed to get out of bed my father had caught it too. He was 68 and I remember going into his bedroom as we all stood round the bed and he lay propped up on the pillows and I thought to myself oh shit, I've killed him. He knew how to be ill too and he lay there all yellow, hardly able to talk, knowing that he was going to die. Only he didn't die. It took him a lot longer than I had to recover. He told me later that in the war when the army was in Eygpt most of the officers got jaundice but none of the other ranks, and they worked out that was because the officers shared their food and eating implements and plates in the officers mess, while the other ranks ate from their own mess tins. He avoided it that first time and thought himself lucky. It might have been better if he had got it as we can't catch it twice, and recovery is usually 100% in the young, whereas there is an increasing mortality rate the older we get.

# 19 – THE LIGHT FANTASTIC

The next year is all a bit of a blur. Still unable to settle and get a proper job, I got one instead through friends with a start-up printing company as a mini van driver, and was expected to deliver heavy packages of trendy stationary and business cards to smart addresses in Knightsbridge and Mayfair. We were based somewhere near Berkley Square, all very posh, and I got to know my way round the West End pretty quickly. Working as a secretary was a pretty girl called Judith Mann, and I got to know her pretty quickly too. She was small and birdlike with a body similar to Goya's Maja Desnuda. She had dark curly hair and was a couple of years older and bossed me around a lot. I quite liked this in a masochistic sort of way. After all, I'd spent most of my life being bossed by my mother and Mary, and I missed it a little. Jude laughed at my jokes and was very funny herself, which was even more important.

I don't remember how it happened but it was in a ground floor flat in a cavernous room somewhere in Redcliffe Gardens, on the floor with the light from the street coming in through the tall Victorian windows. We

214

had both been to a party and we came back to her place quite pissed at two o'clock in the morning. What I do remember were the carpet burns the next morning on my elbows and knees. I'd never read about that possibility in the instruction manuals, which up till that time had consisted of Lady Chatterley's Lover, ('... rain dripping off his balls as she lay beneath him on the damp leaf mould of the forest ...'), long winded articles in Playboy and Penthouse about the G-spot, and the short sharp couplings of James Bond. No one had mentioned carpet burns, and for a few minutes after waking the next morning next to Jude, I thought perhaps I'd contracted some hitherto undiscovered sexual disease. Jude laughed and then laughed some more, and then we made more whoopee and the carpet burns didn't get worse and then she asked me how I'd got to be so experienced and I said that this was the first time and she said I bet you say that to everyone and then I realized that I'd been spending so much time with the said instruction manuals and allied smut that I must have been living in what we now call a state of virtual reality. Our relationship was never love; it was more lust and passion and a good shag when we wanted it, and we got along well and carried on laughing about everything, which of course suited me fine.

For a while Jude lent me an element of her brain that was missing in mine – the ability to make decisions instead of dithering in denial. Thanks to her, I made the first major decision of my life aged twenty one on a sunny Sunday morning in Kensington Church Street, and it was like walking through a thick pea soup fog at the top of a mountain and suddenly coming down into a bright sunlit valley.

At the start of this story I lash out with some contempt at my mother's passion for her god and her efforts to pass the parcel on to us. Included in the package was a sense of guilt, wrapped up conveniently in the natural human instinct of superstition. In simple terms this meant we all inherited the original sin committed by Adam and Eve when they ate the apple after God had told them not to. This blot on their soul was inherited by all of us like a faulty gene and we were born with it. The only way to get rid of it technically was by being baptized, but emotionally we still retained this sense of guilt and like Jesus Christ, carried our sins and the sins of the world with us. Wrapping it up with superstition was a clever idea as this really is a natural instinct and incredibly difficult to get rid of. If you are a Formula One racing driver and you believe that wearing the same pair of underpants that you wore during the race you last won will ensure victory in the next one, what hope is there for fanatical atheists like myself to rid humanity of religious belief?

I had been toying with disbelief for years and was sitting on a hot Sunday morning in the middle of August, listening to a priest droning on about the Blessed Virgin Mary and her Assumption[78]. The church was full being Sunday Mass, and with the smell of incense and expensive perfume and the heat, I was just dozing off, quite comfortably with my squeeze next to me, when she suddenly stood up and in a loud sotto voce trilled 'FUCK! I can't stand this TWODDLE any longer!' She pushed passed me adding 'I'll be waiting outside!' It's a big church and only the people around us heard her. Nevertheless, I went quite red in the face and looking towards my new next door neighbour shrugged pointlessly. The air calmed and during the next minute I

---

[78] When Mary the Mother of Jesus died, all of her, including her body went to heaven. When us mere mortals die only our souls go to Heaven – or Hell.

came to a positive decision. I stood too, and padded out of the church trying to be invisible.

Jude was leaning against the wall ranting and seething with indignation at our stupidity. I felt a great weight lifting. It was over. I was free – free to think for myself. There would be no more kneeling in a confessional, telling an unseen face that I had committed an impure deed the week before, no more standing, sitting, listening, singing and speaking in a language that I did not fully understand every Sunday and feast day. I had resigned from the club and its cosy reassuring Sunday get togethers! Only for me it was never that; it was an overpowering, suffocating, mind altering, cultish, time wasting pursuit. To shut her up and in a state of euphoria I kissed her on the lips and we went and celebrated our freedom with a good lunch and a quality shag. I never told my mother and continued to go to church with her, as did my brother and sister, but I'm sure she must have known my heart and spirit were no longer with her god.

Jude and I were sort of together for the next six months but I never took her back to Grandma's flat and didn't move into Redcliffe Gardens. Ours was a light switch relationship, either on or off. She'd let the genie out of the bottle and I didn't intend hanging around that long, but we always stayed close friends. When the printing company folded, she found a job as a personal assistant to Wolf Mankowitz, who was a well respected British screenwriter. His major achievement was putting Cubby Broccoli and Harry Saltzman together to form what became the most lucrative film partnership ever – producing the James Bond movies. Perversely, he collaborated on Dr No and then asked for his credit to be withdrawn, and instead wrote the screenplay for Casino

Royale – a rival production of pure garbage that was supposed to be funny but wasn't. It made a lot of money and Wolf Mankowitz briefly famous, and Jude was brought in as an efficient organizer to protect him from hoi polloi. She rather took to working for slebs and went on to become PA to Richard Harris[79], but the drink was too much for her and drove her away, and she later landed up working for Princess Caroline in Monaco, where she lived for the rest of her short life.

One time, a year or so after we had broken up and before she went to work for Harris, she was staying in a flat I shared behind Harrods. She had been invited by a very famous English cricketer to accompany him to a sporting awards dinner in the West End, and had asked me if she could come and stay for a night. It had been another sweltering summer's day in London and the heat was still throbbing off the pavements and buildings. The flat in Lennox Gardens was on the top floor and with all the windows open, at least there was a soft breeze blowing through it. I was lying in a bath of tepid water, cooling off and listening to Jude as she got ready in my room down the corridor. There was a silence and then she glided into the bathroom wearing a long white cotton gauze dress with transparent white bra and panties underneath. This was the swinging sixties after all.

'Well, what do you think of this?' and she did a twirl. She'd already told me where she was going and who with; despite this, I thought for an instant about rekindling our relationship. After all, we were alone in the flat. I had to sit up in the bath quite sharpish.

'Well' I gurgled, 'the dress looks really nice but your underwear looks a bit – untidy.' She glided out and a few moments later glided back in without the bra.

---

[79] Irish actor

'Well?'

'Urm – still untidy. Try it without the knickers.'

This time she took them off in the bathroom. I tried not to gulp but she knew what she was doing and she also knew that I knew what she was doing. For a moment I thought that the dinner date was a set up and she looked like she was going to climb into the bath with me. But it was all a tease.

'That looks really cool. That's impressive. Go like that. You look amazing,' all said with my face about a foot away from the see-through dress and the dark triangle of her pubic hair. She left, just like that, practically naked, and behind her the echo of her tinkling laugh and a whiff of Chanel No 5. She wasn't even wearing shoes. I couldn't believe she had taken my advice, but I think she only wanted reassurance. The cricketer was furious and tried to send her home, and there were photographs in one of the tabloids the next morning. His wife was very annoyed too. Jude never told me why but I think she didn't really like him very much and wanted to get her own back for some slight from the past. She was quite capable of carrying it off without a hint of embarrassment, and would have relished his own discomfort. She was a loyal friend but a formidable enemy, and in an earlier life would have revelled in the power games of ancient Rome.

The swinging sixties were really getting a move on by 1968, fuelled by the music coming from the west coast of America and the UK. In fact it wasn't until the mid seventies that the swinging sixties finally came to an end, when Punk Rock and Johnny Rotten arrived like sharks in the bay to cause severe disruption among the peaceful harmonies that that had lasted for ten years.

This was when I met a long time friend, Peter Roundell, at a party and he wanted to set up a mobile disco, and did I know anyone technical who knew about the machinery because he knew a lot about the music, and I said yes I do know somebody, and we set up a business partnership of sorts that lasted nearly five years. We took seventeen singles to the first party and only one turntable and charged £15. I set everything up and he was the DJ. We were quite different from each other but we got along. He was very tall and thin and had a professional career all sorted as an insurance broker. I was quite short and had a day job as a van driver. He was very grown up and lived with his girl friend in a posh flat near Buckingham Palace. I hadn't yet grown up and was living with my – no I wasn't living with my grandmother any longer because about this time I answered an ad on the front of The Times and moved into a penthouse flat with a great bunch of guys round the back of Harrods which was a smart address too. In reality it was more of a garret, but it was light and airy. My grandmother didn't mind me moving out. I had to really because it was difficult to get anyone past her and up my stairs without her knowing.

One evening the inevitable had happened. I'd invited a very attractive and agile blonde girl back to my bedroom while my grandmother was out playing bridge. She came back early at the worst possible moment, and came tottering up my backstairs calling 'Darling darling – are you there?' Of course I was bloody there with my trousers gone and a black stockinged leg belonging to the agile blonde clamped to each ear. And of course I said 'I'm just coming' and the blonde girl said 'A bit soon for that' and then spluttered in hysterics below me with my hand over her mouth, and I went through the whole theatrical farce of trying to pull my trousers on and hopping and hoping against the odds to reach the open door before Grandma hit the landing at the top of the stairs and walked in – which luckily she didn't as she was eighty two and moved quite slowly. Yet another decision was quickly made and I moved out soon afterwards.

Meanwhile Twiggy, that's Peter Roundell because he was tall and thin, went and bought some more records with the £15. All the money from my grandfather had run out, but on my twenty first birthday my father, displaying the fiscal recklessness of his own forebears, made over a large settlement and I could now splash out on a van and some more kit for the discotheque. The bookings started to come in and at week ends I would typically drive down to some huge pile hidden away in deepest Hampshire, where a car salesman from the East End – let's call him Ken Trimble – had settled after making a few million in cars and property and wanted to play the country squire, and give his daughter a leg up on to the accessible if-you've-got-the-bottle upper class merry go round.

This has always been a rarified place where even now new money scrabbles to get a foothold on the same rung as old. Arrivistes, flashing their cash and expensive paraphernalia and unable to comprehend taste, imagine they have made it. They haven't. It takes at least one generation, and more likely two, to be accepted. In fact, what has happened recently is that these people have created a brash and socially corrupting class of their own, fuelled in part by sleb television. Many of them don't give a toss about taste and joining the posh people. They have their own code – a stable full of cars, fuck off yachts the size of small destroyers, and like jackdaws, houses full of dreadful art and a lot of shiny trinkets.

The trappings of old money are acquired at birth just like language, and for new money it is still a long, steep learning curve of tortuous social rituals and etiquette. In fact there are people actually teaching the basics in a diluted form to the children of very rich Russian, Chinese and other foreign nationalities, thereby creating another class who think they've made it.

Let's get back to the generic Ken Trimble, who had changed his name to something like Kenneth Fawcett-Downe, and had a daughter called Caroline. That's a good start. He could have called her Swallow or Amazon or Chardonnay. He realized that it was going to take a couple of generations for his children to make it, but he was going about it the right way. After all he had engaged us for the princely sum of twenty five guineas[80] plus travelling expenses. He had put Caroline through North Foreland Lodge (motto: 'To Do Good and Be Happy'), a sporty high class public school where the girls were allowed to keep their pet rabbits for an extra fee, and where rumour had it they encouraged each other to use long handled hair brushes as AA batteries were in short supply. After leaving North Foreland at seventeen with no academic qualifications, Caroline was sent to a finishing school in Chateaux d'Œx[81], Switzerland, where she added skiing and shagging the local montagnards to her list of sporting proclivities. These already included foxhunting, tennis and salmon fishing, and if she had any Sapphic tendencies, shooting pheasant and grouse. Being eighteen, and having learnt how to leave a trail of long adenoidal vowels behind her whenever she spoke, it was time for her to come out as a deb and do the season.

Coming out in this instance has nothing to do with being gay. Originally it was a rite of passage for

---

[80] A guinea, still used today when selling racehorses, was £1.1s.0d – £1.05 today. In the sixties it was used as an affectation to indicate you had something smart to sell.
[81] Pronounced 'day'

aristocratic virgin girls to enter society and the marriage market, and until the end of the fifties they would be presented to the Queen at the Queen Charlotte's Ball. They were known as débutantes and by the mid sixties were expected to have their own grand ball and go to all the big events of the summer season as well as all the other girls' dances. The season started in March with the Boat Race and included Cheltenham, the Chelsea Flower Show, Wimbledon, the Henley Royal Regatta, the Eton v Harrow cricket match at Lords, Royal Ascot, Glyndebourne – ad nauseam, finishing with the opening of the grouse shooting season on August 12th, when the winter killing season began.

To entertain these girls and hopefully marry them, were the debs' delights, young men, sometimes of a dubious nature and background, who were sniffed out by mothers and put on a list to be invited to all the balls and parties too. To qualify without any questions asked they were usually guardsmen or sons of peers of the realm. Lloyds' underwriters were just passable. Disc jockeys were dubious – for god's sake they're connected to the music business. They were further sub-divided privately with acronyms – for instance GITs (Gropes in Taxis), POMs (Plenty of Money), NAFs (Nouvo and Flash), FLARs (Fucks Like a Rabbit) – you get the idea. The last one was probably made up by the girls themselves.

Mummy had bought Caroline a pearl necklace and got her a full page photograph inside the front cover of Country Life. She was quite attractive in a horsey sort of way, but tended to sweat up a bit on the dance floor and get a bit breathless. She had a job somewhere near Berkley Square on one day a week where she was PA to a darling man in PR called Rupert, and where the most important job was painting her nails and then answering the telephone when Rupert, recently retired aged twenty three from the 11th Hussars and without much of a chin, called from his father's lodge in Scotland to see how things were going.

Daddy splashed out and had every intention of giving her the best coming out dance of the summer. There was an enormous marquee in the garden, far bigger than the tent the previous Saturday at the Digby-Templeton's (old money). Caroline's boss, Rupert, not as useless as you may think, had lined up Paul Jones and Manfred Mann as the headline band, and The Music Box, that's Twiggy and me, to play smoochy music in the nightclub.

I arrived from London mid Saturday afternoon, and erected all the gear in a cleared room in the house. The lighting was minimal for obvious reasons, although I fixed up an ultraviolet tube, which was turned off most of the time and we only had a tiny light above the turntables to see by. That week end I'd brought along a girl called Joanna. Well, she'd asked herself along but I thought she could help me and be vaguely useful. I'd met her at a party a week before and made a terrible mistake. Very drunk, I stupidly invited her back to the flat in Lennox Gardens. I must have had a brain seizure; she had long greasy hair and spots and my flat mates didn't like her either. She looked like a water rat when she closed her mouth as you could still see her two front teeth. She smoked like a chimney, drank like a fish, and smelt like a garlic clove. As metaphors go she was a complete mess. She only came back for the night, but after a week we still couldn't get rid of her.

Twiggy arrived soon after we had set everything up. He always did but we thought it looked cooler that way as he was DJ-in-Chief and always assumed an air of reliable authority. During the night, I would be allowed to take over for a few sessions while he had a break. In fact, thinking about it now, I did most of the work anyway.

I can't remember exactly how it happened, but Hey Jude was playing on one turntable and I'd lined up Those Were the Days on the other. Joanna, whom I hadn't seen since the party began, appeared in front of me and tried to introduce me to the poor unfortunate chap she was now dancing with, but she was three sheets to the wind and having trouble speaking. She suddenly threw up all over Hey Jude. It's hard to describe the noise coming out of the speakers as the needle ploughed on; it was certainly different and a lot worse than the original. Joanna's slightly green, spotty face then disappeared as she dropped unconscious to the floor to be cleared up by her dancing partner, while I cleared up the turntable. There was a result. She disappeared and I drove home early in the morning without her; I smelled faintly of vomit, but I didn't see her again. Twiggy was a little upset as this sort of thing was not good for our image.

We did all kinds of parties off and on for the next three years. At the other end of the scale was some sort of rave out in the East End of London – West Ham I think it was – in a large old dance hall. We set up on the stage to start at eight and about six hundred people turned up. Most of them were blokes with shaved heads, braces and shiny Doc Martin boots, and some of the girls had crew cuts too and looked a bit frightening. Our fee was £16 cash for four hours. We'd been told to play reggae and Jamaican music only, and of course we said yeah no trouble, but we only had a couple of Bob Marley records and one by Des Dekker. By the time we'd played The Israelites six times and some other mainstream stuff the crowd was getting a bit menacing and making no attempt to dance, and we were beginning to sweat. What we didn't know was there were two rival gangs in that night and just after nine o'clock they kicked off. We thought they were coming for us but it was a home match between West Ham and Millwall football fans. Within a few minutes there was beer and blood all over the dance floor, the girls were screaming and beer glasses flying. When one landed on the stage we reckoned it was time to make an exit. We managed to get the curtains closed and started to dismantle the equipment, thinking we could be in real trouble, but guilty though we were about the music, no one was coming for us and a little chap with curly hair appeared with the £16 and apologized for the fight. We were back home by ten o'clock.

One cold December night towards the end of 1969, I drove all the gear up from London to a house on a Welsh mountain. It was a twenty first birthday for an old friend, Tim Bacon, whose mother was splashing out on a dance for him. The house overlooked the Cheshire Plain and could be seen from Chester about ten miles away. Nearly fifty years ago, if you were having a dance it was the custom to get your friends to have people to dinner first, and then they would drive to your dance afterwards, all pissed. This was and wasn't a good idea. It saved feeding and watering everyone and you could spend more money on the marquee and the music, but it was pretty bad for car crashes.

So I arrived about seven o'clock, on my own this time, to set the gear up before we all sat down for dinner. I looked around the marquee which was enormous and empty. The Bacons had invited about two hundred people and it was all lined very stylishly and there was some well placed lighting and chairs and tables and a stage for the disco. It was warm too and I could hear the muted hiss of some gas heaters against the walls. Attached to the main tent was a smaller one with all the drink in it, which was still in boxes. I went inside and

226

said hello and asked if someone could help me get the heavy stuff out of the van.

It all happened very quickly. I walked outside with a couple of guests and as we got round the corner of the house, I saw flames licking along the apex of the marquee about twenty feet up. The tent was perhaps thirty metres long by twenty wide. Within seconds a hole appeared in the roof and it expanded rapidly and a small furnace-like gout of fire began to roar through it. The first thing I thought was save the drink. The second was call the fire brigade. One of the boys shot inside and the two of us started to get the crates of wine, champagne and other boxes out. Within two minutes, with help from some others we moved all the stuff outside but it was getting very hot – I was nervous too about the gas canisters exploding – and now with the whole roof ablaze, the fire was spreading to a small marquee tunnel joined to the house. Hose pipe! There was already one attached to a tap outside the back door so I pulled it inside and we turned it on, aiming at the French windows in the drawing room where the curtains had started to smoke even with the glass doors closed. The moment the water hit the hot glass it cracked into a hundred pieces but didn't break. Looking through the glass was like watching a disaster movie on a large TV screen. Pieces of burning fabric were falling from the roof like enormous blazing tongues, the tables and chairs had caught fire and then the roof collapsed completely because the ropes that held the tent poles up for all of ten minutes had now burnt through. The drawing room was getting very warm, but I kept the hosepipe squirting at the windows and they still held as the water turned to hissing steam.

Shortly afterwards the fire engine from Chester arrived. By now, what was left of the tent blazed away merrily on the ground with the odd chair collapsing in a silent explosion of sparks. The firemen had got the call and seen the fire all the way from Chester about eighteen minutes before, which was good going. Once there, they didn't hurry; there was no point, but they started to water down the side of the house just in case, and as the flames died down, dowsed the gas canisters and what was left of the charred lawn.

We cleared as much furniture as we could out of the drawing room, rolled up a damp carpet, opened a few bottles and the party started without the marquee. Mrs Bacon sobbed for a short while but although there wasn't much left of the creepers and roses up against the wall, at least the house was intact. There was a bit of a squash on the dance floor but the party went well. I must have played it about ten times but it got everybody going. It was the hell of a song and people had to go outside afterwards to cool down. It was a one hit wonder from The Crazy World of Arthur Brown – 'Fire! You're Going to Burn! Burn! Burn!'

# 20 – BROKEN LUNCH

'Come on Stanley, haven't we done enough for tonight – it's after three o'clock?' She said it with a smile and Stanley smiled back and kind of shrugged, and he said something to his Assistant Director I couldn't hear, and they mumbled quietly for a minute with the Second Assistant Director. We all stood around hoping, and then the Second AD in a loud voice said 'OK ladies and gentlemen – that's a wrap – you can all go home now.' And after queuing to sign our release sheets we all made our way to the entrance of the large toy shop where the night shoot was being filmed, stepped over the thick tangle of cables running to the generators, and walked out into the cold London morning.

Nicole Kidman had made a good call. With her then husband, Tom Cruise, she was working on Stanley Kubrick's last movie, Eyes Wide Shut. Kubrick had wanted to make this film for the past thirty years and now he was. The end result came out in 1999 and was not one of his best. The story line was predictably week and feeble, and like most porn films had about the same amount of erotic content as a house brick[82]. By the time it was finished Stanley Kubrick was too, and he died soon afterwards. It was not really a fitting swansong for one of the greats, but making films is like baking a quality cake – forget one ingredient or put something in it that doesn't quite taste right and the whole project can go tits up.

I'd been working on and off as a film extra for six years, and the phrase 'broken lunch' is taken directly from the carefully worked out pay structure in an extra's contract. Extra work is a microcosm of my own life – short bursts of physical activity and work interspersed with long periods of doing nothing or little of any use, laughing a lot with similar folk and frustrated performers, who become friends for a short time and are then discarded, earning a pittance and always hoping for a little more, getting bored very quickly, longing for the end of the working day, and eating a lot. The food was very important to alleviate the boredom. Just as Napoleon had said 'An army marches on its stomach,' the moment we arrived on location we'd quite seriously ask 'Who's doing the catering?'

A typical call time would be 7am and we would normally be contracted on a nine hour day rate, with an hour off for lunch. Lunch had to be called and taken before five hours elapsed. If it wasn't and the director wanted to do another take after the twelve o'clock deadline we'd get an extra fee for a broken lunch, which was £12.75, even if it was only two minutes past when he called a halt. There were many additional fees for other odds and ends like having a haircut, saying a few

---

[82] This wasn't entirely Kubrick's fault as the distributing studio digitally altered some sex scenes to get a lower rating in the US after he died.

words, handling domesticated animals, stripping naked, being rained on and simulated sexual intercourse. If you did all these at the same time you could earn a small fortune for a day's work and probably catch pneumonia.

The most I ever earned in a day was on Shakespeare in Love where it rained, there was a broken lunch, I had a haircut and the shoot went into overtime. In addition the food was good and I got to see Gwyneth Paltrow with a moustache. As a courtier to Judi Dench, I mean Elizabeth I, I also got to wear the most elaborate costume – a beautifully made doublet and hose complete with an erect codpiece in matching material. This was a movie that gave the impression it was going to do well, although nothing at the shooting stage was ever certain. We used to discuss this on each new film. This just feels right. This is complete crap. Some big budget studio movies we worked on were never even released and millions of dollars went down the pan.

It's easy to say it in hindsight but Shakespeare in Love appeared to have all the right ingredients, even while it was being made. Making feature films is a team game that often starts with just one person and an idea. In this case it was the American screenwriter Marc Norman, who had an idea back in the eighties and by the time it came to shooting nearly eight years later, a team had been put together with great care to ensure that there were no flaws, no glaring howlers that could potentially wreck the project. At the top was the manager, the producer, the money man, Harvey Weinstein. He was an astute operator, responsible for engineering the whole project. He put together the writer Tom Stoppard, the director John Madden and an inspired collection of actors (and of course extras), who could potentially deliver more than the sum of their parts.

Weinstein, incidentally, was an intimidating

character. When he appeared on the set late in the night at two in the morning, everything came to an abrupt halt and the atmosphere in the room at Hatfield House went from nice and warm down to just above freezing, and then somebody squeaked 'Hello Harvey,' more of a warning to let everyone know we were in the Presence, rather than an informal greeting. Just like the Queen he had a few quiet words with a nervous looking actress and then left, and everyone relaxed and the temperature went back up again.

The success of Shakespeare in Love was impressive. It cost just $25m to make and took nearly $300m. A couple of years later Weinstein put another movie together, Captain Corelli's Mandolin. I didn't work on this one but a lot of extras I knew did, and they came back from Cephalonia saying they weren't sure about it. The film bombed, only just recovering the $57m it cost to make. Perhaps Weinstein had agreed to do Nicholas Cage and Penelope Cruz a favour. They certainly didn't do any favours for the audience, who had to endure watching them for two hours as they delivered a poorly written script – badly.

Disregarding the quality of the film we always got paid – well nearly always. Down from the heady stratosphere of Shakespeare in Love, which paid well, the only job where I never got paid was a very small one for a TV soap, called Hollyoaks, being made in Chester. Some agent I'd never heard of rang me and said they were casting for a road sweeper – a morning's work. I turned up at a pub in the city centre early morning before it opened. A man with large pink rimmed spectacles and far too many teeth, looking more like a stressed out geography teacher from an inner city school, was sitting alone in a back room with a clipboard.

'And you are?'

'Simon Dewhurst.'

'Ah yes, well we're auditioning for a road sweeper. Have you ever driven a road sweeper's truck?'

'No.' He wrote something on his clipboard.

'Right. Could you go and get that fire extinguisher in the corner over there and bring it back to me.'

'Certainly.' I went to the corner, picked it up and brought it back to him. It was quite heavy.

'Well done. Impressive. You've got the job. The pay is £32 for the morning. I'll be in touch.'

That was that for the time being. I went home wondering about the fire extinguisher. Later, the production company rang up and a rather breathless girl at the other end told me where to report and what time and 'please wear something scruffy as you're a road sweeper.' That wasn't difficult. I turned up to the shoot wearing an old sweater with holes in it, covered in paint splodges, and a pair of ripped track suit bottoms with more paint splodges and some muddy boots. I didn't shave either. There was a lot of bustling, many clipboards, and flustered girls with big blonde hair, rushing around in pink gilets outside the town hall. A harassed looking middle aged woman of some weight emerged from this mêlée. She also had a clip board and seemed relieved to see me.

'Simon?'

'Yes, that's me.' She looked me up and down.

'Darling, you look absolutely wonderful. Just wait here and the driver'll be here shortly with his truck.' At that moment we saw the small green and white vehicle with circular brushes whizzing round on either side of the front wheels coming slowly up the street. It parked next to us and a very dapper little man wearing a smart green tweed suit and a matching flat cap climbed out. He had a small Hitler moustache and was wearing shiny brown shoes.

'You must be Charlie,' says harassed middle aged lady.

'That's right,' replies Charlie somewhat stiffly.

'Well this is Simon and he'll be driving the truck.'

'No he won't. I'm not having him driving my truck,' with the emphasis firmly on 'him' as he looked me up and down.

Charlie obviously thought he was going to drive the truck himself and was wearing his Sunday best. Harassed lady stood there with her mouth opening and closing like a stranded fish and her bosom heaved a few times, and then, with a melodramatic sigh she said, 'Right. Simon, you'll have to go in the truck with him,' and strode off.

Charlie wasn't even happy with me getting in the truck with him, but for the next hour we cruised up and down while the camera crew filmed us from every angle. After a sticky minute or two in the cab, Charlie turned out to be an amiable fellow and he told me a lot about road sweeping that I didn't know before.

A week later I sent my bill to the agent, who replied telling me that as I hadn't driven the truck and as I'd finished by ten o'clock, I hadn't fulfilled the contract. Short of finding him and wringing his neck there was not much I could do. It certainly wasn't worth suing him for £32.

I've no idea why they needed a road sweeper, and in most of the films I have worked on, I've never asked that sort of question. Extras are the bottom of the pile when it comes to the hierarchy on a film set. You learn very quickly not to ask questions, to keep a low profile and keep quiet. The mantra for extras is 'hurry up and wait.' You sit there all day watching, talking quietly or reading a book, and then suddenly you are shouted at to take part in some frantic activity for ten minutes. The third assistant directors, who are normally in charge of herding you to the right place at the right time, are next up the ladder, and they can be easily riled and pick on you if they are being stressed by those above them.

The politics and relationships are wondrous to behold. Typically, a crew and cast of perhaps a hundred people can be thrown together on a three month shoot, sometimes in a studio and sometimes on location in some godforsaken spot in awful weather. We just come in for a few days to do our bit and are not really a part of this melting pot, but we can watch and learn. A lot of nothing much at all seems to happen on a film set, but underneath it can be a seething cauldron of politics, emotion and hanky panky which I guess helps to fill the vacuum of tedium.

Making films is a slow, repetitious and laborious process, and there is not a lot of glamour or excitement in the mechanics. If a director can get two minutes of film in the can each day, he's doing well. When an actor or director is interviewed by a breathless journo for the publicity of a forthcoming movie, I smile at the responses, more often than not saying how wonderful it was to work with so and so, what an inspiration he is bla bla. For an actor, someone who has spent his life on the stage projecting his amplified emotions via speech to the upper circle, it can be daunting in front of a camera, where the aim is to do as little as possible, even less than in real life. Sometimes actors are little more than wind up dolls, just part of a portrait that the director as an artist is trying to paint, to be tinkered with in small brush strokes, as he wants. When an actor says 'It was wonderful to work with so and so', what he often means is 'I did what so and so told me.' Believe me, few actors like making films. They may like the end results, and most of them certainly like the money, but sitting doing very little, and then doing quite a lot of the same thing over and over again, is immensely tedious, and in no way does it compare with the buzz they can get from a live audience in a theatre.

I worked for a few days on a television film of Nicholas Nickleby in the old Ealing Studios in West London, and had a walk-on part as a landlord, but I was still classed as an extra. All I had to say to Mr Squiers, the evil headmaster of Dotheboys Hall was 'Mister Squiers, there's a gentleman to see you, a Mister Squawley.' Mr Squiers was being played by Gregor Fisher, who achieved some fame with his alter ego, Rab C Nesbitt. Poor fellow had to wear a plastic prosthetic blind eye for five days and people avoided him in the canteen because he looked so ugly. The director, Stephen Whittaker, took me into a corner and asked for a rendering, which I did. 'Can you do a little less Cockney and a bit posher?' and I did. 'Just a fraction more Cockney,' which I did. 'A teeny bit posher,' which I did. 'Perfect.' It was as though he was tuning a dial on a radio. When I did it for real he didn't complain, but I've no idea if the footage was used. I was happy – I'd earned the extra £25 for 'a few words of dialogue' fee.

Sometime in the early nineties before all this began, I had a call from a lady called Tilly who ran the Pony Club somewhere in West Wales. This is the call that started off my new part time career as an extra. She had known my mother from a young age when my mother was an Obergruppenführer in the Cheshire Pony Club. Tilly was quite formidable and wanted me to find twenty people and their horses for a film in Trawsfynydd[83] in Snowdonia. We were to be part of a hundred strong

---

[83] 'Trouse-finith'

army of mounted Arthurian cavalry in a Hollywood blockbuster called First Knight starring Richard Gere and Sean Connery. She was quite dogmatic and forceful. 'Shooting is starting in ten days time and you'd better hurry up and find the people, and yes it's well paid but you'll have to find your own places to stay, and yes it rains a lot in September in Trawsfynydd, and no you won't die of radiation poisoning', and after a few more instructions she put the telephone down.

Ten days later after going through some fairly chaotic logistical hiccups, an assortment of horse boxes and trailers from all over Cheshire arrived at the First Knight unit base in Trawsfynydd. Most of us were friends or friends of friends and generally we got on well, but there were one or two divas, who moaned a lot, as did most of the mainly English film crew, which came from London and probably found the vagaries of Welsh weather off the scale. The unit base was a large watery field full of tents and stabling, where eighty horses and riders and crew were already squelching around in the mud. It was raining and the wind was blowing. We were due on the set the next day at the edge of a lake that for thirty years had cooled a nuclear power station, housed in a huge concrete edifice at one end.

Hollywood studios love challenges and spending vast amounts of money, and this was no exception. In front of the power station was a two hundred foot long re-creation of the walls of King Arthur's castle at Camelot. It was a great improvement as it hid this brutal eyesore and fitted well with its surroundings. Even Hollywood was willing to concede that King Arthur didn't have a nuclear power station at his disposal.

After we had stabled and fed the horses in the lines of temporary stabling, we went for our costumes which were made of wool and very heavy, with another layer of fake wool armour on top and then metal breastplates. We got hot just standing there while the dressers fussed around us. After picking up our shields and lances, it was time for tea. The food was good and afterwards we drove off to our digs in the village. It was still raining.

It rained for four days and we were either sodden and cold or sodden and hot, depending on whether we were standing with our horses or riding them up and down. On the fifth day it stopped raining and a hundred of us rode in a long and dejected column up into the hills on the way prepare for battle or something with our new friends Richard and Sean at the front. We passed a cottage where there was a little old lady standing by her front door. For some reason now hidden in the mist of time, Connery got off his horse and went and had a cup of tea with her. This took an hour and a half and everyone, including the crew, who wanted to film before it started raining again, got very annoyed. We had heard that the daily budget for this horsey week was $250,000 a day so this was a very expensive cup of tea. The film, in passing, cost $55m and took $127m so it was a success.

On the seventh day it was still raining when we went home. For most of my lot it was the first and last time they ever did extra work. No one caught pneumonia and two weeks later Tilley sent me a cheque for £20,000. I remember walking out of the bank with over £18,000 stuffed into my pockets as the others all wanted paying in cash, and thinking this extra work isn't all bad and I signed up with a few agents, and whenever the coffers have got low I've done it ever since.

# 21 – MOUNTAIN COCAINE

To me that's snow – real snow – the stuff that floats from the sky late at night until it lies three feet deep on the ground, covering everything and muffling sound until all you can hear is phup phup as fat snowflakes land on your upturned face. It's the white rolling carpet that sparkles in the sunshine as you look down from the top of a high, breathless mountain peak the next morning. It is the stuff that falls past the red check curtained windows of a log Stüble half way up an Austrian alp, and persuades you with little protest to fall into the warm heady embrace of gluhwein, wood smoke and laughter for the rest of the day and possibly the night and what does it matter maybe even for ever.

Without a doubt it was this cold, fluffy, sparkly stuff that finally suffocated whatever trace of responsibility I had for myself or anybody else. It was the stuff of dreams, tempting and seducing, this overwhelming desire for sliding on snow.

It was a cold night, perhaps minus twenty five Celsius, and I was standing outside a tiny cabin in the mountains of central Norway. The snow squeaked underfoot and the hairs up my nose were starting to freeze. In the silence I could hear my heart beating and my breath was clouding in the sharp, crystalline air. What a great day, what an amazing thing this skiing game is, heavens above just look at the stars, hell it's cold, am I going round and round or is it the mountains or is it the stars, who knows, who cares, what a great day, what about tomorrow, what about some more aquavit …

Most of us had only been skiing for a week. One had given up, but the rest of us were well and truly hooked. Despite the battering and the bruises, the crashes, the ribald laughter, the snow clogging every orifice, the thumping headaches the next day from aquavit and beer, we still went back to the ski school every morning for more punishment from a gnarled and weather beaten Norwegian farmer called Arne Geilo[84].

Thus began the addiction that has held me for the past fifty years. Back at Eton I'd listened to the stories John Robson and Charlie Mann told about their skiing holidays in a place called Zermatt, and now I was on a ski holiday, and couldn't believe why I'd waited so long. It was these two weeks in 1968 that must have activated some dormant gene from the last ice age. Every year, when the first leaves began to fall from the trees at home, a little voice in the back of my head got louder and louder – it's time to go, it's time for the snow. I didn't argue. It was a soft sell – the thrill of speed, the high from thin mountain air, the friendships born of like minded souls, and the challenge of the mountains that could never be taken for granted.

Fifty years ago Geilo was a one horse ski resort with six lifts. Although it boasted downhill skiing, it was mainly a

---

[84] Pronounced 'yay-lo'

place where the more well off Norwegians from Oslo and Bergen came for the cross country skiing. It lies midway on the railway line between the two cities, two thousand feet up, but there are no towering mountains – just scrubby birches struggling to survive on the low hills at the top edge of the tree line. There is one mountain, Hallingskarvet, but it's six miles away from the village, and although we longed to ski on it, there were no lifts – the weather higher up the valley, where Hallingskarvet lay on the Hardangervidda plateau is notoriously vicious, and used to stop the trains until a tunnel was built. The Hardangervidda was only fit for cross country skiing in good weather – and sometimes in the foulest conditions for British soldiers on exercise.

We landed up in a campsite outside the village sometime in February 1968. There were about eight of us, girls and boys, and I can't remember any of their names. They had asked my brother, Jonothon, if he knew anyone who wanted to go skiing for a fortnight and I signed up. Two of them were parents and had driven out from England towing a caravan – hence the campsite. They were brave. The temperature at night would drop to minus 20 Celsius and once or twice it hit minus 30[85]. Theirs was the only caravan on the site at that time and no wonder. The rest of us lived in two cosy wooden huts that had electric radiators and showers and bunk beds.

Each evening after a crazy day skiing we would pile into the caravan and start on the beers. Later it would be aquavit. I can't remember how or what or where we ate. It certainly wasn't in one of the four hotels in the village, which were very expensive, although we would visit one or more of them for a drink, and looking for some action, find none. Towards the end of the fortnight there

---

[85] In Fahrenheit – 53 degrees of frost

was one hotel left to visit a mile away on the edge of the village. We'd left it till last because we had to walk everywhere and it was very cold and the parents, who were quite happy in their caravan, didn't want to drive us around.

I got talking to the owner of the Bardøla Hotel in his bar over a very expensive glass of beer. He was a go-ahead sort of chap who had moved into Geilo from somewhere else and was perpetually tearing his hair out and trying to overcome the stodgy locals, who were really averse to outsiders of practically any kind, yet still tried to run hotels. I say 'tried' because they were so bad at it. The food was bad, the service was awful and the prices were sky high. Nevertheless they liked us Brits and hated the Germans.

The oldest watering hole in Geilo was the all wooden Holms Hotel. It had been built by Dr Holm in about 1900 as a place for Norwegians to stay who had respiratory afflictions, and wanted to breathe some clean mountain air. In the Second War the Germans used it mainly for rest and recuperation for U-boat crews. Shockingly, it was also used as a breeding centre and maternity hospital for Himmler's lebensborn programme. The Nazis thought it would be a great idea to improve the racial purity of the Aryan race by interbreeding their handsome SS officers with the local Norwegian girls. It was not a good idea at all; in reality it was an appalling project that left a dreadful legacy for decades afterwards.

Now Dr Holm had an old parrot which was very well respected and held court from inside a large cage hanging in the reception area. Someone had obviously taught him, but whenever he saw an SS uniform he would squawk 'Tysk dritsekk! Tysk dritsekk![86]' For a long time the Germans had no idea what he was saying, but a man eventually came to sit there who did. After listening to one more 'Tysk dritsekk!' than he could handle, he pulled out his Luger, aimed carefully and shot the parrot stone dead. Dr Holm was bereft, and the people of Geilo never forgave the Germans whom they obviously didn't like in the first place, what with the breeding programme, and for just being there.

They locals were charming and likeable and a lot of fun, but they were somehow pathologically averse to running a business efficiently and giving punters what they wanted. Egil Walhovd was different. Together with his wife Elsa, they had virtually rebuilt the Bardøla Hotel ten years before and turned it into something verging on five stars. It had a swimming pool, saunas and the most amazing food. One element was missing – a functioning night club – and he took me down into the basement where he had built one, complete with state of the art bar, dance floor and disco equipment, but he couldn't find anyone he could trust to run it. He had already christened it Walhall[87], a play on his own name and Valhalla, the hall of the slain where all the warriors go to after being killed in battle. Of course I said straightaway without a thought that I knew somebody who could run it. He went back upstairs and as I stood in that dark and silent tomb of a place with its wood carvings of trolls and Norse Gods looking down at me from the walls, I had no idea what adventures would start from Walhall during the next four winters.

Back home Twiggy was cool when I said I was going

---

[86] 'teeska-dreet-sek' – 'German shitbag!'
[87] Pronounced 'Val-hal'

to be a DJ in Norway, and would need to take all the records back with me next winter. We could still take summer bookings when most of the parties took place, and he would send me the latest releases from the UK every two weeks as Norway was not quite up to the mark in 1969, and singles were very expensive. By now I had another job working in a drycleaners close to the flat. Yet again there was no compulsion to find a proper job, especially as next winter was all fixed up.

The flat in Lennox Gardens had become the centre of our existence. There were four of us permanently installed there but there were many who drifted in and out over the next three years. Apart from myself there was Vaughan Rees, who always said he was the son of a coal miner from Penarth, but I never fully believed him. He was small and very dapper and highly intelligent and was high up in the Ministry of Pensions or somesuch. We got on well, sometimes a little too well I felt, and he introduced me to the finer things in life such as his tailor, his hairdresser and his favourite restaurant. He never married and on weekends he would disappear to his uncle's flat somewhere behind the King's Road. Then there was Treve Rosoman, now very involved with rare antiquities, who luckily liked cooking and cleaning and generally kept the place in good shape and made us keep it neat and tidy. He had to keep the dust down as he had bad asthma so we were continually hoovering. It must have been the cleanest flat in Knightsbridge. Last of all was Geoffrey Edwards, who is still a good friend although I haven't seen the other two for fifty years. He had been at the LSE and was doing an arcane thesis about foreign policy running to thousands of pages, which he never seemed to finish; the eventual book probably needed two trees to make the paper when it was eventually printed. He is now a Fellow of Pembroke

College Cambridge, and lives there with Toria his wife. While I was working in the dry cleaners I met Toria working in the posh ski chalet agency on the other side of the road called Supertravel. She came back to the flat, met Geoffrey and I notched up another job on my cv – as a matchmaker.

My humdrum job was a lot more fun than it sounds; for a start there were the girls across the road, and then there were a lot of makers and shakers, who would come in with their dirty hand made shirts and well cut suits to be cleaned; the middle aged ladies in the back of the shop who bustled around doing stuff, would get very excited and tell me to disappear while they leant against the counter vampishly, adjusting their hair and discussing the latest film, book, or record that the said customers had made or written or recorded.

We did a lot of dances with the discotheque that summer too, including one at Cholmondeley Castle up the road from Barmere, where my old dancing class partners, Margot and Zanie had their coming-out dance. We set up the gear down in the cellars and during a break I remember dancing with one Angelica Huston[88], who was a lot taller than me but I was used to that. She was pretty and eighteen and still had an Irish lilt to her voice. We discussed each others noses, which were remarkably similar, and to her credit hers has remained so ever since.

That summer whizzed by in a haze of dry cleaning fluid, parties, tobacco and marijuana smoke. I find it hard to imagine now but we all smoked cigarettes like chimneys too, everywhere, and no one really thought twice about it. We were all addicted to nicotine, this physically corrupting stuff and as I've mentioned

---

[88] Irish actor

elsewhere, we were dying in our hundreds of thousands, but no one even cared. Late in 1969 there was a music festival in Woodstock, upstate New York where 400,000 descended on Max Yasgur's farm and listened for four days to the great bands that defined the hippie counter culture of the sixties. Alternative social drugs defined this culture too; some of course were potentially more dangerous than the legal ones like alcohol and tobacco – LSD for example – but marijuana seemed to me to be pretty cool and gave me the chance to cockily stick a finger up to the hand that was feeding me. At the same time I grew my hair long and for a time had a droopy moustache, which occasionally reminded me what I'd had to eat the previous meal.

One warm summer's evening just after sunset I was riding a bicycle back from a girl friend's flat near Sloane Street. She had given me quite a large lump of cannabis resin which I had in my pocket. All of a sudden a car screeched to a halt in front of me and four bulky looking men in jeans and trainers jumped out and surrounded me. They all had long hair and moustaches too.

'Where do you think you're going?' said one.

I used to have a real problem with people saying annoying things especially if they were aggressive with it. I was apt to wind people up even more than they wound me up. Who the hell were they? Why pick on me? Why are they surrounding me like this? Shit! They want the cannabis! They work for drug barons! This time I was getting nervous as well as shirty. Even as my bowels liquefied I still managed:

'Home – where d'you think I'm going?'

'Without lights? Don't you know it's an offence to ride a bike without lights after sunset?' says their leader. I twigged then – plain clothes plod!

'Cheeky sod this one,' says another 'I think we

should arrest him.' The lump of cannabis was now digging into my leg and I could smell it too.

'I only just b-borrowed this bike – it belongs to my s-sister. I can put lights on it,' and this time I backtracked.

It went on a bit longer and the tension relaxed, and after a bit more bullying they let me go. I've no idea if they'd just had a bad hair day and were looking for someone to nail, or if they'd staked out my friend's house, hoping for bigger stuff. They looked like heads themselves.

The summer quickly turned to autumn and I bought some state of the art skis and boots. I would keep taking them out of the cupboard and clean the invisible dust off them. The skis were 210cms long in those days and the boots were made of leather and had shiny metal clips. The bindings that fixed the boots on to the skis were shiny too and a recent innovation in ski safety, which up till this time had been non-existent. Until safety bindings, boots would be clamped solid on to the skis and a fall directly forwards could mean a broken tibia just above the boot, unless the ski broke first, which it often didn't.

Just before Christmas I piled all the ski kit and boxes of records into the car, which was now a sleek blue Vauxhall Viva. Unfortunately the van we used to carry all the gear in had been severely dented on the M1 as we were heading back to London one Sunday night after a week end bash. My good friend Jude volunteered to drive because Twiggy and I were only half conscious. This was a bad idea as the last time she had driven was during her driving test five years before. She had trouble steering and with her foot hard down in first gear the van was careering from one side of the motorway to the other, until it gave up the struggle and turned upside down in the middle lane. The back doors flew open and the records rolled out on to the motorway. It seems extraordinary now that we climbed out and picked all the kit up and stuffed it back in without being killed. Other drivers even stopped and helped us and we eventually carried on towards London.

I took the overnight ferry from Newcastle across to Bergen and then began the long day's drive up to Geilo. The road across the Hardangervidda was closed in winter, which meant a long detour north to a fjord and a short ferry that chugged between impossibly high dark cliffs that came down to the water. I then drove up into the mountains through walls of snow that had been cut by the plough to keep the road open. I hardly saw another vehicle and once out on the plateau the car threw up a thick cloud of spindrift as it cruised at sixty along straight hard packed roads. For about four hours the sun came above the horizon and reflected off the bleak white landscape. It was nice and warm in the car, but climbing out to stretch made my eyes water. It was very cold.

Most of the people who came up to Geilo were Scandinavian and young. The news that there was now a disco up there spread far and wide and Walhall became a money making machine for Egil Walhovd and at the same time a nightmare. We opened just before Christmas and the first few nights were chaotic. Luckily there was a separate entrance away from the smart front door of the hotel, and apart from solid chairs and tables, very little that could be destroyed. It would be minus 20°C outside and there would be people clamouring for ages to get in and pay their ten kroner wearing practically nothing. The first night there were two hundred crammed in, but it was such a scrum, it was impossible to move, and from then on we dropped it to a hundred or thereabouts depending on how drunk they were at the door.

It was a steep learning curve for all of us. There was

a lower age limit of sixteen but it didn't really seem to make any difference what age they were. They'd never been in a place like this before, where they could drink and dance and let everything down. The bar served mainly beer, and John Elliott ran it. Considering what he had to put up with, he coped well in the mad house. One night around ten o'clock he pushed through the crowd on the dance floor, and told me to cut the music and order everyone to go home. I followed him out into the reception through ankle deep water to the toilets, and found a large Norwegian lying on the floor unconscious with his arms embracing the lavatory which he had broken in half and pulled off the wall. We eventually found the stop tap and hauled him upstairs. It was a good decision. The crowd couldn't carry on dancing and splashing around like penguins.

The other main man was Benny Eriksson and you didn't mess with him. He was only about five ten but weighed 195lbs. Barrel chested and built like a gorilla, he was in charge of the door and security. He didn't need anyone to help him, and although he was good at turning away the drunks, he couldn't do much about the ones who were sober when they arrived and then hit it hard. He had a very good memory though, and he didn't let them in again. He was Icelandic, and had spent the past five years teaching skiing in California and we became good friends. He could be even more infuriating than I was, mainly because he always beat me at chess, which we played a lot of in the café we went to every evening after skiing. He would sit and read Aftenposten[89] and play two or three of us all at the same time. He was a very keen skier but the year before had broken his leg. It wasn't a bad break but he was in plaster up to his knee.

---

[89] Highest selling newspaper in Norway

About three weeks later he decided he was fit enough to go skiing again, quite happily on just one ski, and he fell and broke the other leg, this time quite badly. I met him a year later while he was still trying to get fit again and he had become quite a legend in Geilo.

It was a great time. After a good dinner in the hotel restaurant we worked until midnight, had a good night's sleep, or not, and then skied all day. After the fortnight's holiday I had something basic to work on but I went crazy and was always skiing over my limit, rather than gently pushing it like most sane people would do. In those days we'd strap the skis to our ankles so they wouldn't run away down the hill and kill somebody, but there was still a danger they might flap around if you fell and slice through some vital bit of your own body. Towards the end of that first winter I landed up in the four bed Geilo hospital with a long gash on my leg. In fact I got to know Dr Hval quite well and he wasn't someone to mess with either. 'Hval' means 'whale' in English; he was huge, about six three and quite gruff with large spade like hands. I suppose at some time they must have been pectoral fins; he was no seamstress and I've still got a livid blue scar running down my right leg. It got infected, hence the hospital, and his big blonde nurse would inject me in the backside with half a gallon of penicillin every twenty minutes. In fact Dr Hval already knew me quite well and had injected me before with the stuff, as a result of one or two social encounters with girls in the night-club. He was a good man but even as a broad-minded doctor, who had lived through the war in Geilo with the Germans, he must have found the onset of the swinging sixties one occupation too much.

Over the next four winters we skied, and skied and skied, and at night we partied. By the second winter I was ready to take my instructor's exam, which included tests over three days in both downhill and cross country skiing. The head of the ski school was a chap called Arne Palme. Fiftyish, with blonde wavy hair and a brown face that had the texture of a heavily crevassed glacier, he was a cool good looking dude and a wow with the ladies, and they flocked from all over Scandinavia and even America to have individual lessons with him. He tested a few of us for our instructors' exam and the others passed, but I failed the cross country and spent weeks and weeks following Benny round a thirty kilometer track up on the Hardangervidda until I got the hang of the kick and glide. There was no written exam or stuff to learn like the invented piffle ski associations demand today from potential ski instructors. Anyway, second time around at the end of the season, Arne Palme made me ski in a circle round him for a few minutes and then gave me a certificate and a cup of hot chocolate in the ski school hut. Apart from getting my GCE O levels, that's the only official qualification I've ever had.

The locals, all instructors, were a great bunch and very good skiers. Learning with somebody better and trying to get as good as them was the best training I could have asked for. Skiing is all about mileage. It's not about intense discussions on technique. I've taught skiing for forty five years and the most effective instruction I've given anybody is to shout over my shoulder 'Follow me!' and when they start breathing down my neck, I go a bit faster. I like to think I've been a ski nanny for forty five years.

To be honest, teaching people to ski in those early days was just a nuisance. All we wanted to do was ski. The upside was the kudos of wearing the ski school jacket and a bit of extra cash, but we found that the more we taught the worse we skied. Occasionally taking a group of children was a lot of fun as they had no interest in the technical stuff and it really was 'follow me' skiing, right from the start. The first thing I taught beginners was to stop, either by learning to fall over well, or a basic braking movement while moving without running into somebody. Everything in between they learnt to do with mileage and basically hammering it.

Many times I was lumbered with older beginners, who didn't want to do it. On the whole women did not hide their fear but men did their best to conceal it. One day, years after Norway, I was working for the ski school in Cervinia, Italy, and was told by the director to go to a certain hotel to meet a potential client. There were four people at the bar. Three of them were Mr and Mrs Rothberg and their sturdy good looking blonde daughter Rebecca. With them was a chap called Ira, about twenty, tall thin and white faced with black side curls and wearing a yarmulke over his shaved head. On first glance he seemed distinctly miserable and not at all inclined towards skiing. He looked as though he would be far happier with his pale white nose deep in the pages of the Talmud. Mr Rothberg explained that Rebecca was engaged to be married to Ira and because she was an expert skier, it was decided that Ira should have some lessons. I had been recommended as an expert beginner's teacher by the lying toad of a ski school director, and it was vitally important that by the end of the week, Ira should be as competent as Rebecca. It was of the utmost importance, and I hope you understand this, Simon, to the success of the betrothal – on your life. I agreed to take him for two hours a day for the next four days, but swivelling a sidelong glance at Ira, I privately doubted Mr Rothberg's optimism.

The next morning I took him up the mountain in the

cable car to a quiet beginners' run just outside the top station. This was a mistake. Small beads of sweat were breaking out all over his chalk white face. Towering above him was the vast mass of the Matterhorn, and five thousand feet below him was a vertigo inducing view of Cervinia. He wore black from head to foot – black woolly hat pulled down, minus the yarmulke, black gloves, and a black one piece shiny ski suit with elasticated bottoms over black ski boots. Our conversation was limited; it was like talking to someone who was about to die when you are both aware of the inevitable but try to skirt round it. Neither of us wanted to be there. It was a gloomy day too – just grey and white and a lowering sky promising rain. I spent a lot of time trying to get his skis on. He was monosyllabic and I was gabbling far too much, attempting to fill the empty spaces, but he wasn't listening. I eventually got him to walk round in circles on the flat snow and then sidestepping up a little gradient and sliding down. There was a tow of sorts on this beginner's slope – a button lift where you get hold of a metal pole with a plastic plate on the end, which you ram up between your legs and behind your bum. The other end of the pole is attached to a cable which pulls you gently up the slope, and you let go at the top. My second mistake was attempting the button lift, but there was the pressure of Mr Rothberg's ultimatum. After falling down a few times as the pole jerked him off at the start, he managed to reach the top, where he failed to let go and was plainly not going to let go. The cable pulled him through some upright plastic poles and then into a six foot high mound of snow. By now he was on the floor and still refusing to let go. Then the lift stopped as the dozy operator sitting in his hut at the bottom of the slope had seen him and pressed the stop button. Ira was not gibbering. He was in shock and strangely silent and his eyes had a glazed look. There was worse to come. We were at the top and somehow had to get to the bottom, and that's when I noticed a rather unpleasant smell. Now the Italians were quite lax in those days about getting rid of their sewage in Cervinia, but this was altogether – how can I put it – fresher, and it appeared to be emanating from Ira, who now had a very strange expression on his face.

Thank goodness for the elasticated bottoms on his trousers. At least I now had the excuse and without any protest Ira miserably agreed that skiing wasn't for him. He took his skis off and we walked forlornly back to the cable car station, accompanied by a somewhat embarrassing slopping sound. I suggested he could do some temporary repair work in the toilet. We got back to his hotel without the others knowing, but I remember being summoned again that evening to an audience with Rebecca and Mr and Mrs Rothberg, and given a stern talking to by Mr Rothberg. Ira was not there and I never saw him again, but I did get paid and Ira, if you are reading this now, I hope you are happy with your wife Sarah.

# 22 – VALHALLA MADNESS

In the Walhall night club the music is throbbing, and the hot, sweating crowd is stamping the floor to Jumpin' Jack Flash. This is the third winter I've been doing the job and I'm able to multi task – putting on the next record and dreaming at the same time about tomorrow's skiing. John Elliott, behind the bar, has turned the air conditioning off so that after twenty minutes of foot thumping and arm waving, everyone gets hot and thirsty. I then play something slow for those who want to cling together for a little while – 'Je T'aime' is a hot one – and he turns up the air con, while the boys and girls buy more beer. This is a finely balanced operation between making as much money for the hotel as possible, and having to close the night club when a riot breaks out.

Three girls are standing in front of me. The one in the middle is being held up by the other two and looks quite wasted. Her eyes are half closed and she has a mane of long dark brown hair falling straight around her shoulders with an uplifted cowlick to the left of her central parting. She wears no makeup and is the most beautiful girl I have ever seen. Something passes between us as our eyes connect for a split second. I'm overcome. It feels like I've been hit on the head with a soft rubber mallet and a bag of marshmallows is exploding behind my ribcage. Smaller than the others but with broad shoulders, she has high prominent cheek bones, a strong nose and eyebrows, and the hint of a smile on a wide mouth with lips to die for. She opens her eyes again, tries to focus on me, gives up and closes them. She could be sixteen, maybe seventeen. One of the girls says something and I have to lean forward to hear. 'Hei Simon, this is Helle. Please, she wants you to look after her.' I can't speak. They climb up on to the little stage with the stumbling Helle between them and stand beside me.

The girl says 'She can go down in there,' pointing to the space under the desk of equipment where my legs go, 'and afterwards she wants you to take her home.' My heart misses a beat, I move my legs out of the way, Helle crawls in, curls up in the tiny space and goes straight to sleep.

At twelve I stop the music and clear up. I lean down and gently shake her. She comes round and I help her upstairs and we put her coat on which seems to be random goatskins sown together with a hood and worn with the fur on the inside and we crunch out with others on to the hard packed snow. I avoid saying goodnight to John and Benny.

The night is so cold it takes our breath away and each exhalation swirls round us in silver clouds that turn to glitter in the moonlight. The full moon reflects off the snow, which squeaks with every footstep. It is like being in a fully lit black and white movie and I'm suddenly Trevor Howard and I can hear Rachmaninov somewhere playing from the trees, and I can't help glancing down at Helle. You stupid boy. This vision of loveliness is no different from all the others – just another attractive Norwegian girl. The cold has woken her up, but she says nothing and unsteadily leans on my shoulder, and smiles that half smile again. As soon as we are in my cabin, she falls on to the bed. I take her coat off and then her boots, and jeans and socks, but leave on her high necked woolly jersey and white panties. I pull the duvet from under her and lay it carefully back down. She moans, turns her head towards the wall and begins to snore gently. The white mound of the duvet rises and falls like a cloud. I take off my ski jacket, sit in the arm chair next to the bed, and try to sleep.

Just before dawn I'm drifting off and must be sleeping. I'm woken by the touch of her fingers on my arm. When I look down at her this time her eyes are very open. They are blue with a tinge of violet. In the morning light her skin is like alabaster against the pillow, translucent as though lit from the inside. Something is melting inside me again and I'm feeling dizzy and floating and everything is turning to jelly.

'Hei – I'm Helle – you must come into bed with me,' and she throws back the duvet. She has taken off her jersey and her panties and lies there naked. As I slowly undress I can't take my eyes away from her.

The next two days the next two days … there was no skiing for the next two days … oh the sweet anarchy of love.

On the Sunday night with the swollen white snowflakes falling silently around us she climbed back on the train to Oslo and I wrapped my arms around the smelly goatskin coat and the perfectly smelling Helle who was wrapped inside it with just her face showing and this time it really was Brief Encounter and Rachmaninov all over and we said goodbye and then we said goodbye again and once more for the last time wetly and for the first time I didn't join the other ski instructors in the café as they waited for the Bergen train and the next intake of gorgeous Viking girls. At any moment I expected to see them standing further down the platform playing imaginary violins but they had seen I was too far gone for that. Bereft I padded home through the soft deep snow and wrote a letter and Helle wrote back and I drove down to Oslo two weeks later and stayed in a friend's flat and we were together again. Towards the end of that winter in Geilo, she came to stay once more. I sometimes imagine that perhaps I touched her perfect body with my mind[90]. But it had to end. We met like embers rising from a campfire, two sparks fanned by the breeze briefly touching, coming together, and then rising up into the night and veering off on our own separate journeys. I wonder now fifty years later where she might be, how her life turned out, whom did she meet and marry and what has become of her children and perhaps even now her grandchildren.

Many other adventures must have started in Walhall. There were only three million people living in Norway in 1970 – today there are more than seven million. Even now when I meet unknown Norwegians of my own age skiing, I ask them about the night club in the Bardøla Hotel. Invariably they have a tale to tell. It was an epic place, notorious too, where the only drugs were the alcohol, mainly pils on draught, and the dancing. It was a heady mix for these young Scandinavians who were not used to all the action and the partying and the alcohol. Neither were we; it was a steep learning curve and sometimes we just had to wing it.

One night the laconic John Elliott pushed through the

---

[90] Leonard Cohen lyrics 'Suzanne' 1966

throng. John was square and laid back at the same time. He didn't ski and was only there to make money, having a half share in the bar profits. He was ten years older than us, and wore a blue blazer, white shirt and some regimental tie. He seldom took the tie off but was known to hang up his blazer, and roll up his sleeves when the going got hot. He was tall with a head of wavy black hair and thick tortoiseshell glasses. He was serious and grown-up but sometimes he laughed – mainly at other people's misfortune. This time he didn't laugh but there was a smirk on his face.

'Simon, I think you'd better go upstairs. Benny seems to be in some kind of trouble.'

I changed the tempo and put on 'The House of the Rising Sun', which would give me four minutes, and went upstairs. No Benny. I looked outside. God was it cold. There on the ground just a few feet from the front door was a dimly lit body. Even lying flat on the hard packed snow it was enormous. Then I heard Benny's voice, a high pitched plaintive squeak.

'I s-say Simon, do you think you c-could get this f-fucking arsehole off me. I c-can't move and I'm getting fucking cold.' He was well accustomed to the English vernacular having lived as a ski instructor for many years in Colorado.

Now Benny, I've already said was built like a gorilla. This fellow had passed out with both his arms locked around Benny's neck in a lover's embrace, and was lying with his full weight on top of him. I began with some vain attempts to roll him off, but he was just too heavy. I managed to prise an arm out from behind Benny's neck and then the other and then I was able to roll him, first the top, and finally his legs. Benny lay there for a few seconds like a flattened cartoon cat, shook his head, then slowly got up mumbling obscenities in Norwegian, Icelandic and English all at once while he tried to finger snow out of one ear. He was wearing a suit and the snow had frozen in lumps to the back of it. We shouted at the Norwegian and then kicked him in the backside to try and wake him. I could hear 'The House of the Rising Sun' finishing and another song starting so someone had taken over. After five minutes of slapping, kicking and shouting, the hulk partially regained consciousness, and stood up. He was at least six foot eight and heavily built and wearing a suit too. He looked like a blonde version of Frankenstein's monster and was very unhappy. But he was still far too drunk to start breaking heads. A shaken Benny went inside to fetch this giant oaf's friends, and they came upstairs to deal with him. At least he hadn't caused any damage – only to Benny's ego and possibly his suit.

# 23 – A MAGICAL SUMMER

In the late Spring of '71 at the end of the winter, a group of us travelled north to Balestrand on the Sognefjord[91], where the sea snakes inland for more than a hundred and twenty miles. Smaller fjords, like lizards' fingers, branch off right and left all the way along this artery, sometimes only a few hundred yards wide. The branching fjords near Bergen and the west coast have benign gentle slopes with grassy fields bordering their shores, but closer to the inland end, the cul de sac, towering ebony cliffs rise nearly four thousand feet directly out of the water. Trolls with long bristly tails and bad teeth lurk here in the dark cracks and gullies, and goodness knows what lies far below the limped black water, which goes down nearly as deep as the cliffs are high.

We came down to the Kvikne Hotel to sow more wild oats during a warm sub-arctic summer with little to care about apart from the next beer, the next joint and the next party. We changed spots hardly at all and

---

[91] 'Bala-strand' and 'Son-yer-fiord'

became chambermaids, baggage boys, tennis court repairers and receptionists.

Among our group from Geilo was Randi, an attractive freckle faced red head from Oslo, who was the ski school secretary, who sometimes clipped the punters' ski lift tickets for hours on end from a little hut at the bottom of the nursery slope. She spoke better English than all of us. Then there was Norman the Pessimist, older than us, a thin Scottish ski instructor, who had spent a lot of time castigating us on the perils of avalanches and modern venereal diseases. These two now worked in the hotel reception. Then there was an American girl from Indianapolis, who was half Finnish. She had been a waitress at the Bardøla and was a waitress again, and we had been together for a short time until Helle arrived, but she was a good friend and bossed me around and tried to get me interested in modern American poetry. In our little band there were a dozen others – a few Norwegians as well as Americans, Canadians, and Dutch.

The rest of the Norwegians worked all over the hotel too but the Norwegian cooks had to be kept from the guests; they smoked foul smelling roll ups, were mostly drunk or hung over, and swore a lot. Per Kvikne, a great lumbering man who wouldn't have hurt a fly, ran the place without any concern for the operation whatsoever. He hovered around with a benign smile on his face until a problem arose, which was every waking hour, and then disappeared. So we ran the show with the kind of anarchic irresponsibility more befitting a Friday night rave in Magalouf.

My new job was easy to grasp – carrying bags from busses to bedrooms and back again. I became a baggage boy with two other baggage boys. One was a farmer's son from way up the Sognefjord. He was tough, rough and bulky, a much larger version of the bags we were carrying. He swore in Norwegian and spoke the dialect of the Sogne but his English was good. He spat a lot and he was always hungry and he drank all of us into the ground, but he was an amiable fellow and laughed at our jokes. At week ends he would go home to his farm and for Sunday lunch would rip a sheep apart with his bare hands and cook it outside in a bucket of boiling water over a log fire. He was quite gruff with the guests and he was not the sort of chap to argue with when drunk. The other guy was a charming hippie from Oslo – a tall and lanky gentle man with black hair below his shoulders. He played the guitar well and we spent time smoking grass and making up songs. I wrote the bad lyrics and he would put them to music.

Generally, the busses would arrive in the evenings and we would carry the bags up to the bedrooms. Sometimes there were three or four busses and two hundred people and it would be chaos. We'd invariably deliver bags to the wrong rooms; half the time the guests didn't seem to mind. All the bags looked the same depending on the nationality of the owners. As most of them were only staying a night, I guess they just pulled out a toothbrush from someone else's bag or perhaps they were swingers or cross dressers and enjoyed putting on each other's clothes. Some actually tried to find their own bags and this would lead to more chaos in the corridors. Most of the guests were very fat Americans in identical shell suits; they were doing Europe in seventeen days and didn't really know which country they were in. They lived in the busses all day and only got out to take pictures, smoke, fart, eat or sleep. Taking little or no exercise most of them had to be helped off the busses, where they panted and waddled and puffed their way into the reception area; we would escort them to the lifts and then down the long passages to their rooms. All the exercise they took during their overnight stay was a further trip to the dining room for dinner, then to bed, and the next morning down to breakfast and back to the bus. I guess they may have taken other kinds of exercise in their rooms, but I tried not to think about that too much. There was an old carpenter called Knut, who worked from a little hut round the back, and he was forever repairing the beds and grumbling mild Norwegian obscenities.

The main building of the hotel was a beautiful wooden construction from the nineteenth century, fifty metres long and feather boarded with ornately carved barge boards and fascias. The second floor was fronted by a spectacular colonnaded balcony running the length of the building and divided between the rooms. The hotel was painted a light cream and stood proudly on a jutting headland looking out over the Sognefjord. Approaching it from either left or right by boat, it resembled a fairy palace and was, without doubt, one of the most magnificent buildings in Norway. In its own way it was alive, creaking, groaning and bending like a rheumaticky old mountain farmer with every change in the weather. Unfortunately, in order to maximise its earning potential, the Kvikne family, who had built it, decided in their stupidity to extend this gem by building a brutal concrete blockhouse on the back, reshaping the whole into a T. From way out in the fjord from the front you could hardly see it, but today the fairytale palace has been completely wrecked by the addition of another four storeys on top of the blockhouse.

Back to the guests. I remember little of the other nationalities, who came from all over Europe. There were some Japanese too but very few Scandinavians. The Americans rarely ventured outside to breathe in the wonderful salt laden mountain air. The hotel was surrounded by an almost natural garden. Out front there was an unfenced terraced path down to the fjord. One of the few guests who did venture outside after dinner for a crepuscular constitutional was a rare sprightly ninety year old American. Slightly the worse for wear, he toppled off the top of the path and fell twenty feet. Luckily he survived but the next morning the bus left without him. There was no braking the giant wheel of commerce and I remember him limping forlornly round the hotel with his wounded face covered in scabs and his arm in a sling from a broken collar bone. He disappeared after a few days; I hope he didn't crawl into a dark nook somewhere to be discovered in 2065, a skeleton wearing dusty clothes with an arm in a sling.

All the Americans really came for was the food – to refuel after a heavy day on the bus. And there was actually one person in that hotel who did have some responsibility. He may have been a first prize quality arsehole, but he was a bloody good cook. I suspected he learnt his trade in some black hole of a top Paris restaurant and came out intact but mildly insane. He had the arrogance of many a top celebrity chef, and treated his Norwegian staff rather like a sadistic sugar plantation owner – minus the bull whip. I hated him and my heart sang on occasional evenings when I saw him watching the lard arses descending on his perfectly orchestrated sideboard groaning with intricately designed salads and puddings and pies, as well as whole fish, huge slabs of roast beef and massive boiled hams, which his slaves carved furiously, sweat pouring off them, driven on by the mass of humanity bearing down on them in front – and the chef's looming presence behind. These people did not understand courses. They entirely missed the point of the different sized plates. Instead they went for the biggest plate available and started raking everything they could on to it. Be it salads, gravy, fish, meet, custard, fruit, potatoes, chocolate mousse, mayonnaise, they were all shovelled on together. If bits started to drop off, they would put their plate down at the table, waddle back and fill up another plate before settling in. The chef's face was a mixture of dismay, contempt and hate; he was tall and well built with blonde loose hair and a small ginger goatee. He stood silently, arms folded, with his thin mouth firmly shut, glaring at the rabble.

His territory also extended into the staff dining room where he had contempt for us too, but here he had little authority, and all he could do was to get his slaves to cook us the worst meals possible like fish balls and thin meagre soups with the odd lump of rotting troll floating in them. Although we were very badly paid most of us had private means or other forms of support; I and the other baggage boys relied on the tips we twisted out of the Americans so we could supplement our diets from stuff bought at the local shop, but eventually things came to a head. I was appointed trade union leader and one lunch time I stood up and in very bad Norwegian started to berate the head chef on the quality of our food. He stood there implacably with a smirk on his face – arms folded as usual. At the end of my unintelligible Norwegian rant I made a fatal mistake. I said to the assembled diners 'If you don't like the food, stand up!' Nobody moved and I sat down, which only piled embarrassment on top of defeat. What I should have said was 'If you like the food, stand up!' The head chef smiled the smile of a hangman about to pull the leaver on a condemned man, turned on his heel and walked out. I was summoned to Per Kvikne who hummed and hawed and vacillated in his usual way, said I did my job well but couldn't I stop being quite so rebellious, and sent me on my way. The food, however, did improve and instead of the aforementioned we were now given whale and penguin and albatross and the occasional roast leg of fresh troll and even the odd apple and banana, stuff which most normal Norwegians eat every day. From then on the head chef and I were deadly enemies as he'd hoped I'd be sacked, and I avoided him like the plague.

For many reasons that summer was a magical one. A finger of the Gulf Stream permanently caresses the southwest coast of Norway so even the rain is nice rain, but mostly we were in the sun and it was warm. The sun shone for eighteen hours a day and even when it dipped below the horizon it never went dark. I remember being out in the fjord with Cathy drifting in a small boat and reading a book at midnight. Bedtime was any time and then only for a few hours with or without someone else. We partied, made music and love, smoked dope and drank beer, often chased with spirits – the only bad memory I have is drinking too much slivovitz from goodness knows where and the smell of it even now makes me feel sick. But it was a small price to pay for such a wonderful summer of anarchy.

Our official bedrooms were dotted in garrets and broom cupboards all over the hotel. Mine was at the back with no view but a lot of light streaming in. There were no curtains and there was only space for a bed and a doorless cupboard up against it; the cupboard hid behind the bedroom door. It was the smallest room in the hotel and the only floor space was where the door opened. If I invited anyone in they had to get on to the bed before I closed the door so foreplay was cut to a bare minimum. It was a womblike sort of room – all white and pure – and being gnome like myself I liked it. Girls liked it too and my line was I have the smallest bedroom in Norway or maybe even Europe or possibly even the whole world and would you like to come and take a look at it?

We would quite casually invite friends and relations to stay from all over and then arrange with reception to put them up in the guest bedrooms for free. Subsequently, there were many times when a bedroom, which should have been allotted to a guest, was taken by one of our mates. The receptionists, like Randi and Norman were all in on the game, and would say to punters, who arrived on the off chance of a vacancy, that there was no room in the whole hotel – awfully sorry. Several times friends of ours who had been camping in the best rooms in the hotel overlooking the fjord with their own colonnaded balcony where they had quietly set up barbecue and washing line facilities for six weeks at no charge, would be kindly asked if perhaps it was at all possible they could move out into a lesser room in the attic for one night if it wasn't an inconvenience as the King of Siam and his wife were down in the reception and they really wanted the best room which they had booked over a year ago... I'm really sorry about this but hey, please don't look like that, you can still eat in the dining room!

There would be regular kafuffles, and once there was a pitched battle with hand luggage in the reception area, because rooms had been double and sometimes treble booked. The worst occurrence was when a bus load of Israelis arrived just in front of a bus load of Germans. The Norwegians in reception, who as we already know were not terribly keen on the Germans, told them that the Israelis got to the hotel first so the rooms were theirs at which point Fritz went for Yitzak; Norwegian Special Forces were called in and World War 3 was declared. Luckily it didn't last long and rooms that we had hoped to keep for friends were temporarily allotted to the Germans.

Another time a lot of people from Walt Disney arrived to make a huge blockbuster film about Vikings and damsels in distress and found that some of their rooms were full. As they were coming for six weeks of filming and Walt Disney himself had sent Per Kvikne an advance of $20 million in a suitcase to cover things, there was naturally a certain amount of resentment, but it was somehow all sorted out and the storm passed – while out of sight the next storm lurked.

Honestly, we couldn't care less and I don't think Per Kvikne could either. The money continued to roll in by virtue of the hotel's architecture and its position. It was a beautiful building in a beautiful setting and it sold itself no matter how incompetently it was run. In fact, because the staff and the owner appeared to be so completely useless, it made the hotel unique.

Obsequiousness and good manners were definitely not on the menu at Kvikne's Hotel Balestrand. We were there to have fun, cheaply, at someone else's expense and it was all good.

# 24 – CYPRUS TO CANADA

Back in England during 1970 I'd taken up bricklaying – all the local ski instructors in Geilo turned into builders during the summer, so I gave it a try. The first attempts weren't promising but people were prepared to pay me and over the next few years I added plastering, landscaping, roofing, joinery, electrics and finally plumbing to the list. I'm still doing it and many of those first attempts are still standing – garden walls, house extensions and even a whole farmhouse. We've been building houses for so long that the basic principles are pretty straightforward, and as long as you are good with your hands and obey the basic rule of measuring twice and cutting once, you can't go wrong …

So as well as travelling round the country during the summers with Twiggy and the disco at weekends, I was getting mucky with mortar, concrete and bricks during the week. The previous year my brother, Jonothon, had also bought two small trucks and was dabbling in the transport business. He had got a contract with a nationwide dairy distributor to carry butter and milk and cheese all over the country and we went into partnership working from Barmere. We called ourselves Wheels Express. The two trucks were open flat bed wrecks that had seen better days, but were just serviceable, except when they weren't. Once, after I'd loaded five tons of butter on the back at the depot in Crewe and thrown a tarpaulin over the top, I drove down to Somerset on a hot summer's day. Somewhere on a busy road in Gloucestershire, the truck started snorting on a very steep hill, farting belligerently with much smoke, and refused to go any further. I left it by the side of the road for a few hours, while I went for help. By the time the mechanic had got it going again quite a lot of butter had melted and dribbled out of the bottom in the July heat, but nobody at the other end seemed to mind.

Eventually we got a more or less permanent contract with a firm called Hunters Seeds in Chester, run by a good friend Peter Hunter. By this time no one else was going to give us a job and, realistically, no sensible person would have taken the job on either. We would drive to Chester for eight o'clock in the morning, load up five tons of grass seed in hundredweight[92] sacks and drive all over the UK, dropping the bags off at impossible to find farms. We'd have to unload these bags ourselves and would get home at two in the morning after eighteen hours on the road, completely knackered.

The end of this venture came quite suddenly. After arriving about six hours later than expected at a farm in the Yorkshire dales, I was confronted by a grumpy old farmer, who had no intention of helping me. I'd been on the road for nearly fifteen hours, humping and dumping and this was the last stop, and as it turned out aptly, the last straw. Unfortunately two of the ten sacks were one

---

[92] 50 kilos

and a half hundredweight bags, and as I pulled the first bag off the truck I knew I was in trouble. I fell whumph flat on my face with the bag on top of me. The farmer had to help, because I couldn't get out from underneath, and because there were nine more sacks that he still wanted unloading.

Jonothon agreed with me and the Wheels Express fleet was towed to the scrap heap round the back of Lou Coffin's garage. A month later he did a runner to Israel, escaping among other things from an emotional bust up with his long term girlfriend, Primrose. Israel suited him well, and he went to work on a kibbutz picking oranges, but six weeks in he fell off a step ladder reaching for that last elusive jaffa, and broke his shoulder. When he left school he'd managed to do what I hadn't and had gone into the army for three years and joined the Scots Greys, the regiment with the eagle cap badge. He was no longer with them but all his old mates were serving in Cyprus, so he caught a boat from Haifa to join them and convalesce. This was two years before the Turks invaded and they were all based on the north of the island in Kyrenia, which was then a friendly little village where both Turks and Greeks lived happily side by side. He made up with Primrose and they rented a house by the harbour, and he taught water skiing.

In the summer of '72 I hitch hiked to join him with my sister Gemma. It took us about five days down to Trieste on the Italian Yugoslav border, where we caught the Orient Express to Athens. This train was far removed from what you would imagine the Orient Express to be. It was smelly, overcrowded and quite filthy. It was the only time I've ever dozed off standing up. The smell was so bad I stood for a time next to a window in the passage. At the Yugoslavian border an armed guard tried to get in through the door but it wouldn't open so he climbed in through the window with a rifle on his back and somehow slid between me and the guy next to me and asked to see our passports.

We didn't recognize Jonothon for a few seconds. After eight months in the sun he was almost black. He'd only come back to England once for a short week end to be best man at a friend's wedding. The night he flew back he'd been partying with his army mates, and they'd put him on the plane at midnight with just his passport. This was the middle of February and when my father went to pick him up at Manchester Airport where the temperature was way below freezing, he saw him come down the plane steps, tripping carefully through the snow on the way to the terminal building, wearing just a pair of flip flops, Bermuda shorts, and a vest.

It was hot in Cyprus, between ninety and a hundred during the day and not much less at night but we soon got used to it. A friend in the regiment, Arthur Blair, lent me his motorbike, a BSA 350, as he was going back to England. Could I ride a bike? Of course I could. I'd ridden my mother's scooter. With Gemma on the back we headed to Six Mile Beach; sensitive to the locals' cultural heritage the army had named each beach along the northern coast with flair and creativity. I remember the first corner we came to. This bike was bigger than the scooter and it was missing the petrol cap so I had jammed a plastic bag into the tank's filler hole. There was a lot of grit on the road and the bike went over. Gemma, a good rider on a horse, baled out, but I hung on as the bike toppled and the petrol spewed out all down my front. We were well suited up for biking – T-shirts, shorts and flip flops, and I can say this with conviction. If you are thinking of ways to self harm and if you are thus endowed, don't pour petrol on your knackers. Yowling like a scalded cat I made a quick decision – run like hell for the sea which was straight ahead on One Mile Beach. Gemma, when she caught up with me, was laughing fit to bust, but for some reason wouldn't come on the bike again.

I became good friends with that bike after finding a filler cap, and we went everywhere together. I also made friends with the police in Kyrenia as it wasn't licensed and neither was I. They knew the bike well and Arthur too, and I was arrested and taken to the police station, and after a lot of waffle and excuses, I was made to buy a licence, and for the next six weeks I'd go up there every morning and have a full English in the police canteen – after a week or two I knew them all well and was getting a good discount.

One day a group of us in different vehicles made our way eighty miles up the island to the end of the Panhandle, which points towards Turkey and the Lebanon. It was freedom man, chugging along through the oranges groves, where the men would wave from the shade under the trees, while the women bustled and slaved around their houses and in the fields. Further east, on the brown desert scrub of the Panhandle with a handkerchief tied round my head and wearing my Aviators, I was in yet another movie  following Dennis Hopper and Peter Fonda as they toked their way across the desert on the road to Nowhere[93].

Unfortunately at some stage late in the afternoon, after the long mainly liquid picnic lunch, I climbed back on the bike and drove it headlong into the sea. It went well for a while but when the water was up to my chest the engine stopped and I still have a picture of it lying on its side in the clear blue water. We hoisted it up and pushed it on to dry land with water dribbling out of all the holes. We thought about dumping it, but after a

---

[93] Easy Rider – 1969

couple of hours of intense discussion I kicked the starter and it fired. O sweet music. I arrived home well into the night, spattered with dead insects that had come out after dark, but relieved that I hadn't completely destroyed Arthur's bike.

It seemed such a relaxed and easy life in Cyprus and especially Kyrenia where we never noticed any hostility or conflict between Greek and Turk. Before the Turkish invasion Cyprus was demographically Greek with many Turkish enclaves dotted all over the island. But similar to the Balkans there was a suppressed undercurrent of hostility and hate among a minority, that had festered over many years, primarily against English occupation, and had been held in check till then by the Greek Archbishop Makarios. When the military junta in Greece decided to declare Cyprus a Greek republic and kick out Makarios, the Turks had their excuse. Within five days they arrived in Kyrenia and after lobbing a few shells into the village, they used it as their beach head. Within a year there was a new frontier from east to west dividing the island in half. The Greeks in the north were all driven southwards and the smaller indigenous Turkish population was reinforced by immigration from the mainland, primarily into Kyrenia, which they proceeded to wreck, and which is now forty years later, a huge sprawling half built eyesore of a city. The aftermath of the Greek coup and the Turkish invasion caused even more conflict and hostility. When will we ever learn?

All good things come to an end until the next thing starts. In early December Gemma and I piled into Jonothon's Mini, and the three of us headed for the UK. I had to be back in Norway by Christmas and the others had commitments too. We took a ferry to Mersin in southern Turkey and drove across the cold wind swept plains of central Turkey and then into Bulgaria and Yugoslavia. These two countries were tricky as all the signposts were in Cyrillic script. The first city we had to find was Сфоия and the next one Београд.[94] The people were not very friendly either and in Zagreb, when they learnt we had just come through Serbia, they were sullen, bordering on murderous. This was the quickest journey across Europe I'd ever made in a car as Jonothon was never keen to prolong any travelling. He drove as though someone was chasing him, with constant references to the map. 'Do you think we could get there quicker by going through Sarajevo?' or 'We'll have to miss lunch – we've only done 450 miles since breakfast!'

We reached Obertauern high up in the Austrian Alps in what must have been record time for three people in a Mini from Mersin. It was also a miracle that we hadn't been murdered or murdered each other. I can hardly remember a thing about that journey, not even how long it took, but thankfully Jonothon realised that we needed a break and we stayed for a couple of nights. I persuaded him to put some skis on and he nailed it first time with no help from me. He wouldn't have listened to me anyway.

I was back in Walhall two weeks later and a final adventure that took me to the west coast of Canada. Just after the New Year, when the Christmas holiday was over and the ski slopes empty, the night club would be empty too, and not even John Elliott would turn up to open the bar. This night it was just Benny and me who walked down there at about ten past eight. The lights were on and some awful musak on the hotel system was dripping from the wall speakers. Sitting at the bar were

---

[94]Sofia and Belgrade

two girls, both dark haired, and both attractive. Janet was tall and Maria was small. They were gagging for a drink so with no John we went upstairs to the hotel bar and got talking. They were both Canadian and working as waitresses at another hotel up the road and this was their night off and it was dead in their own hotel and practically dead here too. Maria went for Benny in a big way and Janet and I got along pretty well, and when we skied together, that was it. She was very good. Most of the time we were skiing on ice and she'd been brought up on it in eastern Ontario, and she was very competitive too. We were similar in many ways. She called a spade a bloody shovel, laughed like a drain and swore like the squaddies at Catterick. She was better looking though – long dark hair, blue eyes, a ski jump for a nose and a perfect set of snow white teeth. It wasn't love at first like it had been with Helle, but it crept up slowly. We took a few weeks to topple over the edge of the cliff, and fall somersaulting down into that crazy little place called love.

She went back to Toronto at the end of the season and I returned to England, and then she came to England and worked as an au pair and we had a hot, heady summer. At the end of the summer she went back again to Toronto and this time I followed her. But she had changed. Back on her home turf she became responsible and grown up, attitudes that I still found quite disturbing. Back in May we had called on her sister, Cathie, who had a flat in London on the King's Road. Cathie was there of course and her mother and father too. Cathie was a model who had worked in Paris and had been in Casino Royale with David Niven and she was a stunner. She had a few words to say in the film that was written by Wolf Mankowitz, the man my old girlfriend Jude had worked for at the time, thus completing a circle of sorts.

When we walked in her father was lying flat on his back on the lounge floor in a white towelled dressing gown clutching a glass of champagne. Janet was more than embarrassed but I took to him straightaway.

'Hi Simon. Frank Shirriff. I make marmalade. Sorry I can't get up. I'm very drunk.'

Later he told me that he sometimes needed some escape from his four daughters, a wife and a spaniel bitch, but he was a good man and I liked him and his wife Barbara a lot.

I flew to Toronto and found a grubby apartment near their family house and got a job in a ski shop downtown running the cross country ski department. It was a mad house. Most of the others who worked there were addicted to skiing too, and they seemed more intent on filching ski equipment from the shop than serving the customers. It was bitterly cold in Toronto. The freezing wind howled down from Lake Ontario through the high canyons and with the temperatures well below zero it was a grim place to be in winter.

Added to this there were also thunder clouds – emotional thunder clouds. I had decided earlier to buy a car and go west to the Rockies with Janet, possibly the following Spring, but Janet had other ideas. Matters went from grim to unbearable as Janet realised that however hard she tried she was never going to turn me into something I could never be, and the emotional bust up came a little earlier than I'd expected, between Christmas and New Year, not a good time for a break up and especially three thousand miles from home. On New Year's Day I packed my bag and threw it in the back of the car I'd bought, and all cut up, headed out west.

Somewhere between Sudbury and Saux Ste Marie in a place called Blind River, I stopped in the driving snow as darkness fell and bought a half bottle of bourbon, pulled into a cheap motel and necked most of it, while the needle sharp snow pattered against the window and the wind howled round the building. I thought the whisky would take the pain away. It did – until the next morning.

It took four days to get to Calgary – roughly 1700 miles from Toronto – passing through the forests and lakes and then across the Prairies after Winnipeg. I drove round or through towns and cities, with names like Moose Jaw, Swift Current and Medicine Hat, and got quite attached to the few cars and trucks along the way. We'd drive at 55 miles an hour with half a mile between us and sometimes stop at the same motel or diner. One evening I pulled into a gas station which was a shop, a motel and a restaurant, run by a Chinese fellow. There was no one else there and he cooked up the best Chinese I've ever eaten. That night the temperature outside dropped to minus 24°F (-31°C), which was pretty chilly and the first thing I did after stopping the car was to plug the block heater into the mains before the engine froze.

It had stopped snowing soon after Winnipeg but then the temperature had dropped rapidly. On the fifth afternoon approaching Calgary, the wind began to blow down from the north, and I could feel it buffeting the side of the car. I was cruising along yet another ten mile straight bit of road, when I saw a large truck approaching. The car was sucked into the vortex as it passed, and then caught the full blast of the wind. I held on to the wheel as it had happened before but this time there was a crack and the bonnet[95] flew up, was ripped off its hinges, and flew away to the side, taking a windscreen wiper with it. By the time I'd suited up in

---

[95] The hood

gloves, hat and ski jacket, it was already a hundred yards away being blown like a large blue leaf across the snow towards the US border. I caught up with it after about three hundred yards – it had blown up against some barbed wire – and I somehow got it back to the car and tied it over the engine with the tow rope.

I drove slowly for the rest of the day straight past Calgary as my destination was Banff. At some point after Calgary I must have passed the turning north to Bears Paw, a mile off the highway, where my Uncle Peter had landed up fifty years before on his brother-in-law's ranch, but I was in no mood for detours. I started to climb up into the Rockies, and by dusk had arrived in Banff.

The next few months were all about skiing in the Rockies. In Banff I got a job working the ski lifts at Lake Louise, a half hour journey every morning. The ski area there was run for the workers by a group of very rich money men, who were all skiers themselves. Each job had two people doing it so half the day we could ski. It was very cold up there most of the time and there was another reason for working in twos – we needed to check each other often for the white skin signs of frost bite. Everything was paid for and we were paid some wages too. At mealtimes in the restaurant we even had our own queue with priority over the 'turkeys', which was the rude name for all the holiday skiers. We slept in a large cabin in Banff and were bussed up to the resort in a haze of marijuana smoke every morning. I used to be woken up by the bison as they munched their breakfast hay outside my bedroom window, and snorted clouds of exhaled breath into the crisp cold air.

At some point during that winter I must have got bored of helping people on to ski lifts and climbed back into the car and headed further west across the Rockies to Vancouver, aiming for Whistler Mountain, which by the seventies was just becoming the Mecca for all ski bums. My head was still full of shit but I'd stopped drinking the whisky straight from the bottle. Somewhere on the way, running out of money, I stopped at a two bit ski resort next to the road, and asked if they had any jobs. They didn't, but between the car park and the ski lift office I dropped and lost my last $100 bill, which left me with only $5 to get to Whistler. 'Had anyone handed in a $100 bill?' Well of course they hadn't but I came back to the office at the end of the day in desperation and asked again. Somebody had found it! It was another skier, a guy the same age as me who was hard up too, so I bought yet another bottle of whisky and we drank most of it.

A day later I was standing in the rain in a muddy car park in Whistler looking up at the ski runs which disappeared into the lowering grey cloud. The ski school then was just a mobile home on breeze blocks. It wasn't a place for sitting in, but the man who managed it gave me a job. He was Guy Baeverts, an alcoholic from Quebec, who didn't say much but threw a ski school jacket at me and told me to report to the Round House at the top of the mountain at ten the next morning. I kind of sympathized with him as I felt sometimes I was going the same way too.

It was still raining the next day in the car park but up at the meeting place it had turned to wet snow. There were about ten of us up there, mostly ski bums like myself, and we'd sit for days waiting for a lesson. I only remember taking one lesson for the three months I was there – the rest of the time we spent skiing when the weather improved. These guys were really good, especially off piste in fresh snow, and I was a beginner again and had to learn from scratch. There was plenty of fresh snow, nearly every day. The snow depth mid season was thirty five feet at the top ski lift. That's ten feet higher than the ridge on an average sized house! When the weather got better later on towards May, we would take punters helicopter skiing in the back bowls where it was nearly always waist deep.

The director at Whistler was Jim McConkey, who was already a legend. To most of us, at nearly fifty he was an old geezer. We seldom saw him but each week he would turn out for the weekly instructors' slalom race and he would beat all of us. At the time of writing he has just hit ninety. The good weather would bring all the hippy skiers out too. They were on every recreational drug known to man and would attempt some pretty insane stuff. One morning I went up in a bubble lift with a small curly haired fellow with finger nails that had been bitten to the quick. He was going to attempt four back somersaults which had never been done on skis before. He managed three and a half.

At the end of May, when the lifts closed, there was a freestyle skiing competition, which included acrobatics and a long jump on ordinary downhill skis. A bulldozer built some kicker jumps and a huge mound of snow, which we hurtled down at forty miles an hour. All we could see was the other side of the valley until we took off. The take off was ten feet above a flat section till it started to drop to a steep landing. It was a real rush – not so much before – but definitely afterwards. On my last practice jump before the competition I went forty metres but landed in a tangle of skis and poles and other bits of kit, and twisted my ankle, but it was a reasonably good ending to the skiing that year.

A few weeks later I was in Vancouver and staying with a close friend, Ricky Bates, who had moved to Canada some years before and married a Canadian,

Diana. He was a big man, whose favourite occupations were drinking vintage port and blowing things up with dynamite. His family had lived for generations in a large grey castle up in the hills of North Wales just above Prestatyn. We'd gone there as small children to parties and then later in our teens on wild week-ends. One night while his father was away and we were all eating and drinking in the kitchen, he disappeared for a few minutes and came back with a revolver which he fired into the ceiling. It made the hell of a bang and the next second water started cascading down. The bullet had gone clean through the mains. We had to leave the next morning before his father came back.

His father was a bit of a card too. Sir Geoffrey Votelin Bates, 5th Baronet, had won a Military Cross in the war and must have understood his wayward son well. He drove tanks in the Western Desert and while waiting to attack the Germans one night, being bored and a bit of a fidget, had turned on his headlights by mistake. He then couldn't find the switch to turn them off, so he climbed out and shot them out with his revolver, before the Germans zeroed in on him. It was probably the same revolver Ricky used later on. During a grown-up lunch at his castle in deepest Wales I was sitting next to one of Sir Geoffrey's past girlfriends, a very well preserved seventy year old with a lot of white makeup, big hair and highly glossed thin red lips. I didn't know her very well and she turned to me and in a languid and well cut voice asked, 'Now tell me Simon, who's fucking who in Cheshire these days?'

Ricky was well known in Vancouver as he ran a demolition business and was apt to destroy things while the client was still thinking about whether to employ him or not. Once or twice he would blow trees and rocks up when he was annoyed with somebody or they hadn't paid, and he was always in trouble with the Mounties as he called them. He bought a small island out in Vancouver Sound, about fifty yards long and thirty wide, where he built a large shack and erected a flag pole, which flew the Union Jack every day the family was in residence. He also had a house in Vancouver, from where his two children went to school and where Diana was based. I would do building jobs for him and we would flit from island to city in his motor boat, which went fast and was very noisy and seemed to be held together with string.

Vancouver was a cosmopolitan city where there were a lot more laughs than there had been in the rest of Canada, but it was now a year since I'd been away and time to get back home again. One day late in the summer with some difficulty I got through to Barmere and spoke to my father, and said I was catching a plane, and I'd call him from London with the time of the train to Crewe Station. 'Could you come to Whitchurch instead? It's nine miles less in the car and I'll probably be going there to do the shopping.' And so I did.

# 25 – AFRICAN SAFARI

The pineapples had been planted two years before, a few feet away from the side of the red earth road. It was a good place to plant pineapples because the old man could keep an eye on them from his hut at the forest edge. They got plenty of sunlight and the ground drained well. There was very little motor traffic, and everyone who walked past knew about his pineapples, and would comment on how well they looked. In a few days he would harvest them and get his friend who knew someone with a pick-up to come and take them to market in Bossembélé. He would keep the suckers from the mature plants for the next crop-but-one in two years time.

Now one of these pineapples was growing on its own some way from the main plantation. We'd been on the road for a couple of hours and Jonothon had said it was time to change drivers, and as I got out of the passenger side there it was – all alone as though it was growing wild and I could almost hear it asking to be picked. I got the machete and chopped it off from the stalk and climbed into the driving seat. As I drove off, I heard a shout from the forest and in the rear view mirror saw a little old man chasing after us. I still feel guilty about stealing his pineapple, but we all agreed that it was the best we'd ever eaten.

I had met Nick a few years earlier and we'd got on well and were good mates. He's become responsible now, but at the time he had an anarchic and madcap attitude that I really appreciated. If you wanted to liven up a party, you asked Nick. At a certain point in the evening, quite often on demand and with the right music, he would go into burlesque mode and rip all his clothes off. He thought about his performance a lot. Sometimes he would fire up at a black tie do, and at other times just kicking around with friends. Occasionally he would arrive in fancy dress and rip everything off. Once a girl friend he quite fancied asked him to a dinner party and told him that everyone was to wear something pink, so we trawled around for a pink tutu for him, and then tights, pumps, a wig and a wand with some pink glitter on it and off he went. He walked into this smart drawing room full of her crusty friends and relations all wearing black ties and long dresses and not a sign of pink anywhere. That particular time he kept his tutu on.

Mary was an old friend from when we were a lot younger but she was much more placid than the rest of us, and more sensible. Thank goodness she agreed to come too. When things got a little heated she was always the one to cool things down.

We bought a long wheel base Land Rover and started to convert it for the desert and jungle. On the side went some blurb for Hunters Seeds of Chester, as Peter Hunter from our Wheels Express days was keen for exposure in Nigeria and Kenya. In return he sponsored us the gas fridge and a few litres of gin. We got lots of vodka from a local brewery. It took a month or two to get all the kit together including an ex army trailer, lots of dried food and tools and spare bits, and the various visas. None of us were mechanics but luckily we took along a Land Rover manual for night time reading.

A few days before we were due to leave Cheshire, I had a hissy fit with Primrose and stamped my tiny foot and said I wasn't going, but Mary stepped in and calmed things down. Two nights before we left, Nick had a goodbye bash for all our friends. It was a good thing we left a day to recover as the party was a wild one, but on the Monday we set off from Barmere on our four month safari.

We got about three miles south of Whitchurch when all five plastic jerry cans fell off the roof. In the hurry to get going we'd forgotten to rope them on. At the first petrol station just before we got on the Dover hovercraft, someone opened the back door and the two litres of vodka fell out and smashed. I can't remember what the third thing was.

Driving down through France and Spain we alternatively sulked, argued, and then sort of made up after we'd had a beer or three. We stayed in campsites, cooking one of the three main course selections of dried food – goulash, chicken supreme or stroganoff. They were good to start with but after a month or two, we would have to buy locally or splash out in the odd restaurant. We could sometimes get through a whole day without having a fight but one of us was nearly always ratty with someone else. If there was ever a problem, like an oil leak or a half shaft snapping, then we would all come together and mend it.

We went quite slowly taking detours down as far as southern Morocco. We swam in the sea off Torremolinos one hot afternoon, but only for a few minutes because Primrose was confronted by a large turd floating past her. In Tangier we were approached by a boy who offered us a joint which we duly smoked. While we were off our heads, he came back with a slab of hash with the tiny bit we'd smoked cut out. We paid him half what he asked for and felt quite smug about that, but when we unwrapped it later we discovered it was compressed dung from some animal – probably a donkey. I guess it was their sense of humour. In return we began selling the small boys who pestered us stuff that we no longer wanted for what we thought were exorbitant prices. I had a box of a hundred Hamlet cigars and sold about thirty of them for a rip off price. The little boys hoovered them out of the box, no doubt planning to sell them later.

Dropping down the eastern side of the Atlas Mountains I remember driving and having an argument with Jonothon over something paltry, slamming on the brakes, getting out of the car and shouting 'That's it! I've had it up to here! I'm walking back to England!' And off I stalked, petulantly, back up the mountain.

We took the third road from the left through the Sahara. This avoided Mali to the west, which was short of petrol, so we missed out on Timbuktu. The surface was tarmac at the start, but with the sand sometimes hiding it, and the constant traffic forming corrugations either side, we often veered well off on to the hard packed, flat, pebble strewn hamada. We had to watch out that we didn't wander too far from the road which was marked by stone filled oil drums and the occasional burnt out wrecks of similar Land Rovers. This was always a little disconcerting.

It was very hot during the day, but with the low relative humidity we somehow managed to live with it. One afternoon with the shade temperature at 47°C

(117°F), we had to sit and wait at a gas station until the evening, because the petrol would have evaporated before it got to the tank.

The desert was quite beautiful, especially at sunrise and sunset. The landscape varied between flat expanses of hamada, sand, and ochre rocky outcrops, and right in the middle were the Alhaggar Mountains, which went up to 10,000ft. On an afternoon's detour it snowed briefly while we were up there. Lying awake at night on our camp beds in the deafening silence and the coolness of the night, and watching the vast expanse of the Milky Way in the black velvet sky is a memory that will stay with me for ever. The joint we usually smoked after yet more chicken supreme may have had something to do with the memory too.

We saw no animals apart from camels and donkeys, and the occasional small, slightly transparent desert scorpion, which was very dangerous. We quickly learnt to shake sleeping bags and boots before getting into them. There were a few other travellers doing the same as us and quite a few trucks, and apart from one or two instances, everyone helped everyone else and was very friendly, even though it was the middle of Ramadan when we started, which made the locals quite grumpy. The 1300 miles took us just over two weeks, when we arrived at Agadez in southern Algeria.

There would be furious arguments over where to stop each evening. They were worst when there were no landmarks. It was always best to camp near to rocks as we were quite shy about performing our toilet in front of every Tom, Dick and Ahmed, and we'd often have to veer off the road to find some and then try and remember where the road was the next morning. Once we veered off too far and realized we were lost, and then someone discovered an old beer can, half buried in the sand next to a rocky outcrop, so we camped there and the next morning waited till we saw another vehicle in the distance and went after it.

This happened once again but for different reasons. In Tamanrasset we had to buy enough petrol and water to last four days before the next town of In Guezzam. We'd worked it out very carefully, but late in the afternoon heat of the third day, we came across a truck. The men standing around it waved us down and told us they had run out of petrol. It was all my fault and after a lot of objections from the others we poured a couple of gallons into their tank. We camped that evening about thirty miles north of In Guezzam, and of course after ten miles driving the next day there was a sputtering from the engine and we ran out. I was not the most popular guy that morning. We set up some shade on the side of the Land Rover and we waited. And we waited. After three hours away to the west we saw a cloud of dust. The road in that part was a bit random. We waved a pair of Y-fronts on the end of a stick and the vehicle veered towards us. It was a battered old Peugeot taxi. The driver didn't exactly say 'Where to Guv', but he seemed quite relaxed and unsurprised, and took me with an empty jerry can into town, where I filled up and then he drove me back. Quite a few notes changed hands and off he breezed. We got to the petrol station that evening and there was the same truck from the day before filling up too. Only it wasn't filling up. From the truck's tank there was a pipe going into the ground. They were emptying the petrol from the tank I'd filled the night before. We then bought our own petrol a second time! Of course trucks run on diesel and there was a diesel tank on the other side. I guess they had a good business going. The garage was short of petrol to sell to the travellers, the taxi driver was short of rides, the punters were wadded, tired, gullible and short of petrol too, so why not?

After Agadez and the Niger border the landscape began to change. There was sparse vegetation and more people living by the side of the road in mud huts. There were goats and sometimes cattle but this was a devastated region. We were invited into one and offered a bowl of water to drink. It was white and cloudy and we politely refused. The desert was literally moving south and the rains, plentiful in the past, had failed for many years. At one time the Sahara had been covered in forest and we had come across fossilized trees further north. The people in the desert proper had acclimatized to their lot, but here the people and their animals were finding life hard to sustain and living on the edge of starvation.

Nick and I had also found life hard to sustain. At various points we all got ill with stomach bugs, but this was kind of different. Back in the southern Sahara we became listless and quite feeble, and by the time we got to the border into Niger we were losing the will to live. We sat by the border waiting to cross, still listless and feeble, when along came a very smart Land Rover and out got an immaculately dressed couple. They were called David and Ann and they did the trip every year. David was a doctor in Uganda. He wore a smart safari suit and Ann a flowery skirt and a frilly white blouse. We looked them up and down and they looked at us and we looked at each other in our grubby clothes and couldn't believe it. It was lucky David was a doctor, because he knew what was wrong and gave us some salt pills, and they arranged to meet us later. We caught them up at sunset. They were sitting at a table, drinking tea and eating Dundee cake. They'd even changed for dinner. We sat with them and swopped some Dundee cake for gin and tonics – the fridge was still working and we could make ice and kept the tonic in there and would bring it out on special occasions.

We were heading for Kano in northern Nigeria, where we stayed with some friends of friends. At the Nigerian border the landscape had changed yet again, and we were driving on bad roads through fertile grasslands, where the laughing children would come running out from the villages and chase after us. Every so often spontaneous fires would erupt either side of us which encouraged the grasses to regenerate. To start with we found this quite alarming and thought maybe we'd lit them by mistake.

In the evening after we had set up camp and the sun set, and the children gathered round, the locals would start on the drums and their home made guitars, mostly one stringed and made of gourds, and the rhythms accompanied by the cicadas and the singing, would be captivating. At one point we had met Ginger Baker[96] in a desert garage, grumbling that his Range Rover was a pile of shite. He was always looking for new rhythms and spent a few months a year travelling round those parts.

After a week end in Kano, we headed east through Cameroon, which was a beautiful lush green landscape dotted with ancient volcano cores that towered above us like giant green fingers. The roads were getting steadily worse as we followed the rains, and once or twice we had to dig the Land Rover out of the ditch when we slid off the road. Time slowed down and even Jonothon conceded that we just had to live in the moment and take things as they came. Towards the end of October we crossed into the Central African Republic which borders the Republic of Congo to the south, and at the border post a spare tyre exchanged hands in return for tourist

---

[96] Drummer – Cream founder member with Eric Clapton

visas. Every other town began with a B – Baboua, Bouar, Bossembélé, Bangui – even the President was called Bokassa. I can't remember why we risked the RCA after hearing that Bokassa used to reward his subjects by occasionally having them for breakfast – literally. Every now and again we would see men wearing the Bournemouth football strip, in red and black vertical stripes. There couldn't be that many Bournemouth soccer supporters in darkest Africa. Once, driving rather more quickly than we were used to, more out of fear then anything else, we glimpsed one of these supporters held in the air by all four limbs, being beaten by a small crowd with sticks. It turned out he didn't support Bournemouth FC at all. He was an ex-con, forced to wear the strip for two years after being released from prison.

There was only one road through the RCA, which joined up all the towns. In the capital, Bangui, we stayed at the Protestant mission, little more than a camp site. Large men wearing pale suits and a menacing air, wandered around in reflective Aviators. We were now 5000 miles from home and the safety of a soft cool bed, and we didn't make any jokes or laugh a lot on that humid damp night. We cooked up yet another magnificent supper of chicken supreme, but while we were eating it, I dropped some on to the red earth, scraped it up and put it back on my plate. Around midnight I woke up sweating and in a paranoid fever. I was already in prison and we were all going to die. I started shouting and the others were around me wondering what the hell was going on. And then everything exploded both ends. By morning as I got worse there was a mention of doctors, but it was only a mention and after another night my temperature went down and we high tailed out of that hostile town. I never eat anything I drop on the floor now.

As we drove east towards the Sudanese border, the road got worse. We were travelling with a splendid Swiss couple, Iris and Kurt, who had converted an old bread van, and were going to Kenya too. Iris baked cakes in a gas oven in the back of the van and Kurt was a bit of a mechanic. We all looked after each other when we got stuck and would pull each other out from holes and ditches. One morning after breakfast Kurt walked into the bush with a shovel – for a crap. A minute later there was a howl of pain and he came staggering back with his shorts barely up, whimpering and holding one side of his face. While he was squatting he'd been stung on the lip by an irate hornet. Within an hour he was shaking with fever and his face and neck had swollen badly. We didn't say so at the time but we all thought he might die. By the next day he was feeling a bit better and the day after that he could eat again. On the fourth day, being Swiss and a man with a strict routine, he walked into the bush with a shovel – for a crap… This time the howl was even louder and accompanied by swearing in German. The hornet, which probably came from Switzerland too, also had a routine and stung him once more, this time on his bum. We decided to move out. Even Kurt, now immune to any dangerous reaction, thought it was quite funny, but spent the next few days frantically scratching his arse.

The mosquitoes were bad and although we took pills to prevent malaria, we were always being bitten and slept every night under nets. We had eaten well on one particular night a bit further along the trail. An old man had approached us cradling a bedraggled live cockerel in his arms. It was obviously not very well and its head flopped over every time he tried to hold it up. We spoke mostly French through Africa, but this exchange was all sign language. He wanted us to buy the chicken. We'd no idea what it was dying of but we bought it and an hour later he'd brought it back, grey and plucked, without its head. We chopped the claws off, took the guts out and boiled it with some vegetables. It was quite the worst chicken stew I've ever eaten, but it was a change from chicken supreme.

We slept well that night even though we were full of stringy cockerel, but about five in the morning I woke to see Primrose's naked bottom, very red, up against the mosquito net. A few moments later there was another scream and Primrose spent the next few days scratching her arse as well.

Two weeks into November and somewhat relieved, we left the tropical forests of the RCA and skirted across the bottom of the Southern Sudan. There was no war at the time and the locals were more friendly. Rather perversely we tried to get into Uganda. This was the time when Idi Amin was the President, and we were already quite aware that he made President Bokassa look like a beginner. But we had heard that Uganda was a beautiful country and worth visiting, and it would be a short cut to Nairobi. Luckily, after waiting for four days at the border, they wouldn't let us in, and we headed for northern Kenya.

Sitting at an open fronted bar overlooking Lake Turkana, we necked the first beers for nearly six weeks since leaving Cameroon. We'd made it to Kenya and we were still alive. We discussed going for a swim in the lake and the bar man pointed behind him. There, pinned to the wall was a large black and white photograph of an elegant lower leg, toes up in a plastic bucket. The toes were painted and had obviously belonged to a woman. He pulled a few more grisly pictures out from under the bar and told us they had been taken a few days before. Some

Germans had arrived like us a week ago and decided to camp down by the lake. This was all that was left of one. The crocodiles had eaten her. We decided not to swim in the lake.

Five days later we arrived at Nick's cousins, in the Highlands at Limuru, west of the Rift Valley. Six thousand feet up the climate was like a summer's day in England, and we could understand why all those characters from White Mischief had moved from Cheshire back in the twenties. For a while we wallowed in the simplest comforts – a hot bath, a beer at sun set, home cooked food, cool white sheets. After twelve weeks on the road and nearly ten thousand miles, after a journey fraught with irritability and often bloody mindedness, we became friends again. We relaxed with a return to the simple pleasures of life, and to be honest I've appreciated them ever since.

During the second week in December we flew back to England after selling our battered Land Rover in Nairobi for £1000 more than we'd bought it for. Christmas once again was calling and the safari came to an end in a brothel in downtown Nairobi where we got very drunk, and toasted togetherness and non violence and compatibility without wondering for a moment about the strange and sometimes contradictory nature of the human species.

18 January 1978. It's just more than two years later and I've left London, not returned to Norway, and am living back at Barmere. I'm nearly thirty one. Jonothon and Primrose have bought a run down cottage close to home and I'm re-building it for them. It's a cold sunny day at lunchtime. My mother and father left the house at the same time as me to visit our grandmother down south. It's her ninetieth birthday.

I'm sitting on some bags of cement in a bare room, taking a break from building a breeze block wall. I'm halfway through my lunch and am polishing off a cheese and tomato sandwich.

I can hear a car arriving and seconds later Leslie Shorto, still a fixture at Barmere, is standing in the doorway. He's looking very distressed and his eyes are red rimmed.

'Simon – I've some very bad news to tell you. Your mother and father have been killed in a road accident.'

What? What? What did he just say? I stop eating the sandwich. I stop breathing. For a second there is a pause in the cosmos, a split second when the universe freezes, and in that millisecond a door slams shut in my head. New synapses fizz into life and fire up a billion untouched neurons lying in some hitherto unexplored recess of my brain.

In that instant I grew up. It was some sort of an end, but at the same time it was also a beginning.